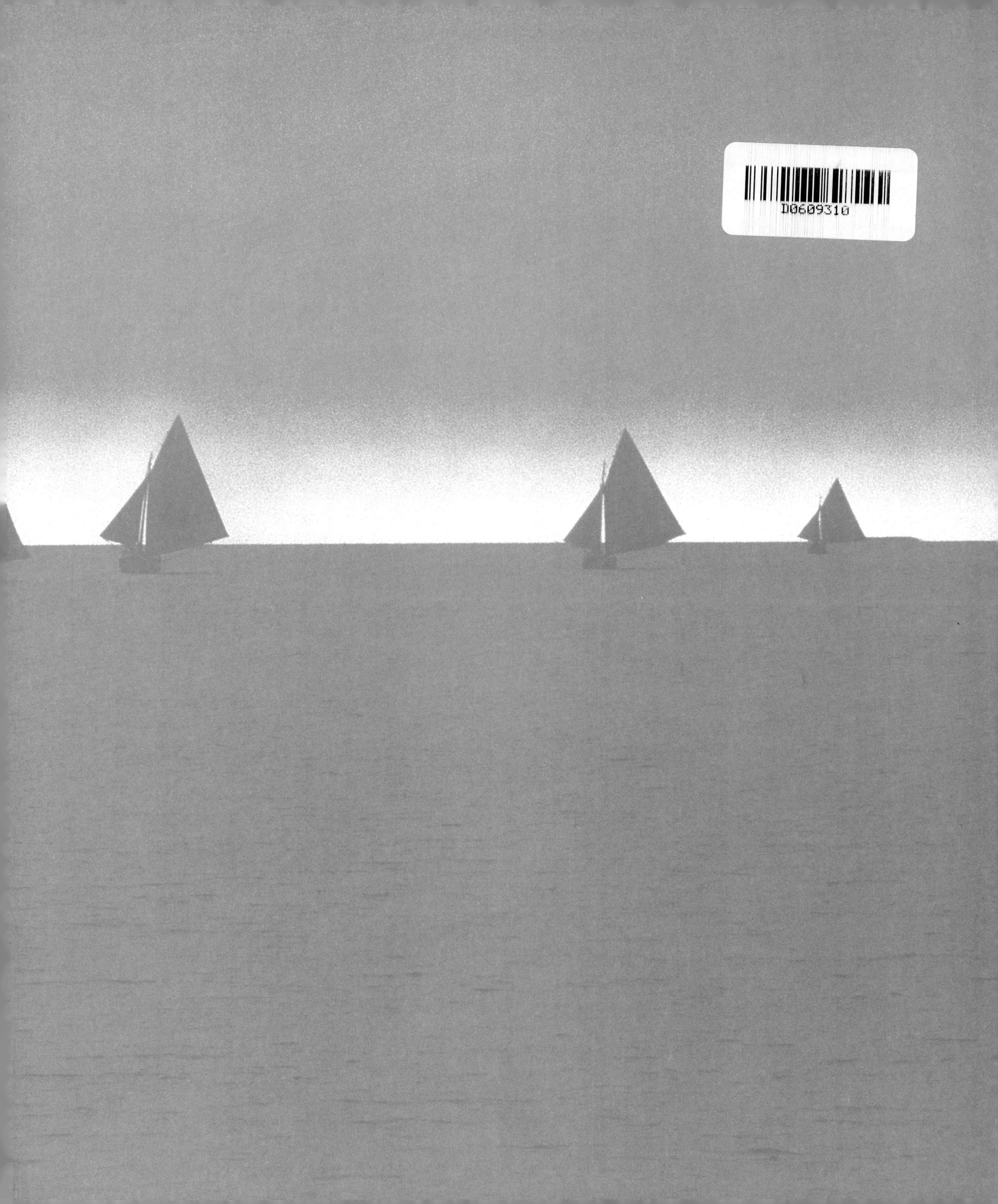

THE IRISH TODAY

A CELEBRATION OF IRELAND
AND THE IRISH DIASPORA

Dedicated to Rose Kelly

Cadogan Publications Ireland Limited
1-3 Dungar Terrace, Dun Laoghaire, Dublin
Tel: ++353 1 2300322   Fax: ++353 1 2300629

THE IRISH TODAY

Publisher: Kevin Kelly
Group Editorial Director: Sonya Perkins
Art Director: Heidi Gross Kelley
Researcher: Anne Healy

Colour origination by Typeform Repro, Dublin
Printed and bound in Italy by Mondadori Printing S.p.A ñ Verona

British Library Cataloguing in Publication Data
A catalogue record for this book is available from The British Library
ISBN 0-9534276-4-1

THE IRISH TODAY

A CELEBRATION OF IRELAND
AND THE IRISH DIASPORA

edited by Sonya Perkins

CADOGAN
PUBLICATIONS LIMITED

So long for the air to brighten,
Time to be dazzled and the heart to lighten

SEAMUS HEANEY, 'FOSTERLING'

✣

As the title indicates, *The Irish Today* is a celebration of Ireland and the Irish Diaspora at the beginning of the third millennium. Some years ago, John Simpson, the distinguished *Spectator* journalist and BBC broadcaster, marvelled at the influence of Ireland and the Irish people around the world. At that time, Simpson cited Bill Clinton (President of the USA), Paul Keating (Prime Minister of Australia), Brian Mulroney (Prime Minister of Canada), and James Bolger (Prime Minister of New Zealand), and suggested that no other small country could claim so many people in so many positions of power and influence.

Over the last decade of the last millennium, the Irish economy and the lifestyle of the Irish people have been transformed beyond all recognition. Ireland has been the most successful economy in Europe for some years now, and experts suggest this will continue for the foreseeable future. Indeed, the International Monetary Fund, an organisation not generally given to hyperbole, declared the performance of the Irish economy over the last decade to be spectacular. Ireland today is a confident and entrepreneurial country, our young people are the best educated in Europe, and we have no colonial baggage to weigh us down. To be Irish, the glossy magazines tell us, is to be chic and fashionable and not without good reason are our musicians, entrepreneurs, singers, dancers and sports people renowned around the world. However, in our headlong rush towards prosperity, many of our traditions have fallen by the wayside. Materialism has largely replaced Catholicism. The flight from the land continues. Our major cities are choked by traffic congestion. Drug abuse, crime, and, to our shame, resistance to the refugees who seek, as we Irish have always done, a better life in a new country are all problems that we need to address. But none is insurmountable. The balance sheet is in our favour, and an affluent and confident Ireland will be better equipped to find solutions to our social ills.

The Irish Today brings together Ireland's leading journalists to write of subjects dear to Irish hearts and profiles 220 individuals from among the exotic tribe of 70 million people around the world who claim or could claim Irish descent. It is an eclectic list. You will agree with some of our choices, disagree with others, you will criticise our omissions, and marvel at the less well-known individuals we have tracked down around the world.

There is cause for celebration. *The Irish Today* is our celebration. We hope you enjoy it.

KEVIN KELLY

Publisher

ACKNOWLEDGEMENTS

Many traditional book publishers, when they heard of our plans to produce this book, were astounded that we had the ambition to complete such a project in such a short time. That we have succeeded is due primarily to the talent and commitment of all those involved with this exciting labour of love. To Sonya Perkins our Editor, my thanks and admiration. Her vision for the book and her writing skills are evident throughout. Sonya encouraged and managed our writers, photographers and all involved with quiet charm and supreme efficiency, and her management of this complex project reflects the immense talent of young contemporary Irish women. To Heidi Gross Kelley, our art director, for her stunning designs. To Anne Healy for her indefatigable people chasing and picture research. To our contributing writers, Michelle Adam, Thomas E. Mackin and Thomas J. O'Gorman, thanks as always. To Colette O'Brien in our Dublin office, Lynda Weatherhead in our London office, and Michael Slimmer and Lili Beneda in our New York office, my thanks for all their efforts. To Des Fry at Typeform Repro in Dublin, appreciation for a job well done. To the writers, Eileen Battersby, John Bradley, Dermot Gilleece, Tom Humphries, John Kelly, Robert O'Byrne, Frances Power and David Walsh and the many photographers whose work graces our pages—in particular, to my good friend Nutan whose stunning photography reflects his deep love of Ireland—my appreciation and thanks.

KEVIN KELLY
Publisher

A Modern Economy

BY JOHN BRADLEY

In a remarkable comment on the state of the Irish economy today, Intel president Craig Barrett recently reflected on why his firm had come to Ireland. Speaking to Thomas Friedman, author of *The Lexus and the Olive Tree*, Barrett said: 'We are there because Ireland is very pro-business, they have a very strong educational infrastructure, it is incredibly easy to move things in and out of the country, and it is incredibly easy to work with the government. I would invest in Ireland before Germany or France.'

Thus, the leader of one of the world's most successful and innovative firms tells us that Ireland is among the best possible business locations. Following Intel, Microsoft, Apple, Dell, Gateway 2000, Xerox and others, like invitees to a desirable and prestigious social function, firms now come to Ireland because other world-class firms are already here.

Success feeds success. It was not always like this. Anyone born in the immediate aftermath of World War II has seen the country undergo an extraordinary transformation. Once upon a time we were an inward-looking, inefficient, economic basket case, haemorrhaging our population through emigration. Today, we attract the admiration and envy of the nations and businesses of the developed and developing world. How did this come about, when as recently as 1988 *The Economist* magazine portrayed us as a beggar nation seeking alms? The Celtic Tiger explanation industry is in full swing, each commentator having his or her own story to sell. But nobody can deny the most sobering aspect of our recent success—that we largely failed to predict it. Indeed, we never believed that it would happen, even though, with the benefit of 20/20 hindsight, we can now look back and see that we did indeed plan for it, albeit in ways that were ill-understood at the time. Rather, we seem to have behaved more like stumbling, groping sleepwalkers than confident agents of our own future. Success surprised nobody more than ourselves. Nevertheless, it is sweet!

The early Industrial Revolutions of the 18th and late 19th centuries bypassed most of the island of Ireland, with the exception of the Belfast region of what is now Northern Ireland. Our modern economic age dawned only in the late 1950s. The successes and challenges that we face today are an extraordinary reversal of the failures and problems faced by policy makers at that time. In the words of Dr Ken Whitaker, writing in the late 1950s, we had 'plumbed the depths of hopelessness'; today, we bask in the world's

admiration of our success. Then, we began to take
our first tentative steps out from behind stultifying
barriers of tariff protection and economic and
political isolation; today, we have embraced
the global economy to an extent that few other
countries have managed, and we are cosmopolitan
citizens of the world. Then, we were predominantly an agricultural economy; now, while agriculture
remains important, we are a major supplier
of Europe's pharmaceuticals, computers, and software and our concerns are with maintaining
a leading position at the cutting edge of new tech-
nology-based manufacturing and quality services.

The 1960s represented a watershed for the
Irish economy. Policy changes made from the
late 1950s and early 1960s onwards launched
the economy on a development path that differed
radically from that pursued before and after
independence. The central policy dilemma was
not whether the Irish economy should be open to
trade and investment flows with the wider world
economy, since Ireland already had a relatively
open economy when compared to the other small
European countries in the late 1950s. Rather,
the issue was the nature of this involvement
and whether there was to be a break with an
almost total dependence on the UK market as the
destination for exports of a very restricted variety
of mainly agricultural products. The opening of
the economy and the removal of tariff barriers
were necessary policy changes if we were to be

The Irish Financial Services Centre in Dublin—a booming business complex for a booming modern economy

Ireland has earned an enviable reputation as a centre for cutting edge pharmaceutical research

kick-started from stagnation. Free trade with the U.K.—our main trading partner—was an initiative of Taoiseach Seán Lemass, and gave us our first opportunity to 'test the water' of outward orientation. Free trade with Europe came later when we joined the EEC (as it was known then) in 1973. The strategic orientation of Irish economic policy-making over the past three decades has emphasised the need to face the consequences of the extreme openness of the economy, to encourage export orientation towards fast-growing markets and products, and to align the economy with European initiatives. We joined the European Monetary System in 1979, breaking a long link

with sterling and escaping from economic and psychological dependency on the U.K. We embraced the Single Market of 1992 and most recently, Economic and Monetary Union from January 1999. Perhaps this is the main legacy bequeathed to us by the prescient policy-makers of the time of Seán Lemass. Their enthusiastic embrace of an open economy provided the enduring strategic backbone of our economic planning.

But Ireland was not a very attractive investment location in the early 1960s. It was remote, unknown, had little by way of natural resources, and no industrial heritage. To offset these handicaps, the main inducement offered to inward

investors was initially a zero rate of corporation tax on exports of manufactured goods. Under pressure from the EU, this was later replaced by a low ten percent tax rate on all manufacturing profits. This tax policy, combined with aggressive and sophisticated marketing initiatives designed by the IDA to attract and aid inward investors, provided the main driving force behind the modernisation of the economy through export-led growth. However, the attractive tax rate and the absence of tariffs were only a start, and would not in themselves have made Ireland a major destination for high-quality foreign direct investment. Other factors came together to reinforce Ireland's

New era, new battles—the Treasury Building is located on the site of Boland's Mills, DeValera's headquarters during the 1916 Rising

Ambassadors for the modern Irish economy clockwise from left: Denis O'Brien Alastair McGuckian, Dermot Desmond, Margaret Heffernan, Michael Smurfit, Dr. A. J. F. O'Reilly

success and interacted to create a virtuous circle of superior performance that replaced the previous vicious circle of decades of under performance. Educational standards in the Irish workforce had lagged behind the world. Policies were urgently needed to bring about a steady build-up of the quality, quantity and relevance of education and training, and this had been initiated by far-seeing educational reforms starting in the 1960s. These reforms were extended by the emphasis given to scientific and technical skills through the use of generous EU Structural Funds from the late 1980s. Although issues of social inequality are still of concern, the general level of educational

attainment in Ireland rivals that of other wealthier European countries. Low taxes, bright people, but bad roads and unreliable phones are incomplete and unsatisfactory recipes for success. Here, Ireland was remarkably lucky that it was granted Objective 1 status for EU regional policy aid. Because of a generally low standard of living in the late 1980s (less than two-thirds of the EU average), as well as a peripheral location far from the rich European markets, generous aid was made available to improve infrastructure, train young people and stimulate the business sector.

Few would claim that everything is perfect today, and, indeed, growth itself has brought

congestion in its wake. But dramatic improvements have taken place in the quality of roads, airports and telecommunications. A recent U.S. consultancy report included Ireland among the highly desirable 'broadband four' (USA, Canada, U.K. and Ireland), these being countries best prepared by infrastructure and deregulation to meet the challenges of the new age of e-commerce. These were the building blocks of the new Irish economy, and they brought success through their interaction and combination. The far-sighted targeting by the Irish Industrial Development Authority of inward investment in clusters of industries in pharmaceuticals, computer equipment, and software, was pursued with a degree of diligence and professionalism that became the envy of all aspirant developing countries. Such firms needed highly skilled workers, and these were available in ever-increasing numbers from the universities as well as from the new, assertive and bustling Regional Technical Colleges. Business and knowledge spillovers from the initial clusters encouraged further growth in the high technology areas, and provided the basis for additional benefits, often in the older more traditional areas (such as food processing and clothing) that needed injections of new strategies

The Irish Financial Services Centre has rejuvenated a previously neglected area of Dublin

and technologies—for example, a recent television programme on the Irish fashion industry showed computer-controlled knitting machines being used by native Irish speakers on Inis Meáin to produce high-quality customised Aran sweaters for export to fashion-conscious customers in the USA and Japan!

The dominance of the Irish manufacturing sector by foreign multinationals was unexpected and quite unique by OECD experience. With falling transportation and telecommunication costs, national economies were destined to become increasingly interdependent, and in the words of President Clinton's former Labour Secretary Robert Reich: 'the real economic challenge ... [of a country] ... is to increase the potential value of what its citizens can add to the global economy, by enhancing their skills and capacities and by improving their means of linking those skills and capacities to the world market.' Global competition is organised today mainly by multinational firms and not by governments. Production tends to be modularised, with individual modules spread across the globe so as to exploit the comparative advantages of different regions. Hence, individual small countries like Ireland have less power to influence their destinies than in earlier eras. Today, they must focus their economic policies on location factors, especially those that are relatively immobile between countries: skills, infrastructure, efficient functioning of labour markets and superior economic and social governance. Dramatic economic changes invariably have serious social consequences. Young people, with their superior education, are easily absorbed by burgeoning high technology sunrise sectors and the spin-off professional and other services. Older people, however,

are locked into traditional skills in sunset industries, and tend to lose out. During the 1980s the Irish unemployment rate soared to 20 per cent, threatening to tear apart the social fabric of the nation. Prompted by the terrible recession of the 1980s, employers, trade unions and government came together in the mid-1980s to design a consensual process of social partnership. They understood the urgent need to ensure that there would be as few losers as possible in the economic dislocation that accompanied modernisation. Unlike the UK, which had been wracked by violent class conflict during the 1980s, in Ireland the social democratic institutions of Sweden, Germany and the Netherlands were emulated and

adapted to local conditions. In this way, Ireland became a remarkable and slightly exotic blend of American business efficiency and European social equity. The path chosen by Ireland for its economic development is not without risks. The most dynamic part of our manufacturing is almost completely foreign owned and is concentrated in a narrow range of technologies that are fast moving towards maturity—for example, Ireland excels in making personal computers, but who knows what new devices will be used to surf the Internet five years from now, and will they be made in Ireland? The policy initiatives that ensured Ireland had an advantageous head start in the early 1960s may not be sufficient to facilitate the

Well-educated young people are easily absorbed by the burgeoning high-technology industries

inevitable switches to newer technologies since other countries have been learning by watching Ireland doing! Until recently, we could rely on an abundant supply of highly trained Irish workers, but birth rates fell dramatically in the 1980s, and if economic growth is to continue, we may have to rely on inward migration to supply the labour. We have long had a manufacturing sector dominated by multinational firms. But how easily and gracefully will we make the transformation to a multinational society? Nevertheless, today Ireland enjoys the many economic advantages that come with membership of the European Union. Policy makers are able to plan in a more stable environment, with the co-operation as well as with the active financial support of other member states through the European Commission. The managers of the Irish public finances have Brussels bureaucrats checking their sums. Since we belong to the euro zone, monetary policy, as well as the responsibilities for defending the euro against speculative attack, are decided in Frankfurt by the European Central Bank. Our task in Ireland is to embrace with enthusiasm whatever the outcome happens to be, and the outcome so far has been remarkably favourable.

Meanwhile, Irish businesses compete in a global economy and only the most innovative and efficient will survive and prosper. College students no longer aspire to pensionable jobs in the public sector, but are more likely to be planning business ventures and dreaming of how stock market floatations will make their fortune. This is the very best time to be Irish, when our rapid economic progress has catapulted us from the role of poor laggard to successful Tiger. Our society is at once traditional and modern, and the tension between these forces serves to animate our thought and artistic expression. The Irish economy may be small in size, but its experiences during the 20th century provide a rich source of information and guidance for other small countries that seek to develop and prosper.

The far-sighted targeting by the Irish Industrial Development Authority of the emerging high-technology industries has become the envy of all aspirant developing countries

The Irish Financial Services Centre at the heart of the modern Irish economy

The Sport of the Irish

BY DAVID WALSH

People claim they remember exactly where they were when powerful figures were assassinated, countries invaded and wars declared. Maybe. It is more likely they recall events closer to their lives. The great Monaghan poet Patrick Kavanagh wrote about his neighbours, the Duffys and the McCabes, and their argument over an area of rocky ground. He called his poem *Epic*. At first he chastised himself for making so much of something so local, then Kavanagh remembered Homer had made **The Iliad** from such a row.

It was fashionable once to tell where you were when J. F. Kennedy was killed, but I have a clearer picture of where I stood when Dawn Run raced with the bravery of a lion up the hill in the 1986 Cheltenham Gold Cup.

I recall, too, from an earlier life the dreadful melancholy that fell on the nation during the weeks of Arkle's injury. Then came the solemn announcement—the horse would not run again. Life, of course, went on but it was a lesser life. You can say I was one of the smitten, but horses were like children—easy stock to get into. Temptation was everywhere.

In our little south Kilkenny village, there were no racehorse trainers or jockeys or owners. But there was Betty, the woman who ran (and still runs) the local shop. She has views on most subjects—politics, hurling, young people, the weather. But racing is her passion.

Back when I was a boy, Betty would leave her shop around midday, walk the 40 yards down to the village's public telephone and ring her bookmaker with the daily bet. No one thought it odd or even unusual that this God-fearing and upright member of the village community should gamble on horses six times a week. There was no Sunday racing then.

If Betty knew you were interested in horses, buying the *Irish Independent* could take half an hour. On Thursdays her brother Sean would pull up in his red Triumph car and wait across the road. Betty would soon be ready. So, too, would I and by early afternoon we were on our way to Gowran or Clonmel or Wexford or our local track at Tramore. For all the fun of reading about horses and watching them on television, nothing touched the real thing.

Imagine the thrill for a young boy of being swept aside as grown men surged to get the fast disappearing 5/2 on bookmakers' boards. Some days you caught momentary fear in the their eyes, but mostly they stood there without flinching. Imagine, too, the jolt to a boy's senses caused by the sound of horse and birch colliding; the thud of the fall, the sprawling hooves, the poor jockey and the panic as others tried to avoid him. At the second last fence in Clonmel, they fell regularly and it cost nothing to wander down there and wait for the accident to happen.

Not everyone in the village was as devoted as we, but few were indifferent. Sport was a part of village life in a way that more refined cultural pursuits could never be.

But it was more than that—the kinship with horses related to how things were at that time. Ireland had a talent for breeding good racehorses

Previous page, Blue Lotus, ridden by Michael Kinane;
this page, View over the Down Royal Racecourse

Above, The thrill of Cheltenham; opposite page (top), Dawn Run in training; (bottom), pounding the sands at the Laytown Races

and for producing men who knew how to get the best out of them. Our geography books said it was to do with the suitability of the soil, that horses thrived on our calcium-rich earth. But Vincent O'Brien didn't eat grass and he trained horses better than any man in the world. By reaching the summit of a very demanding profession, O'Brien told us something about being Irish. It need not necessarily mean being second best. That was important in the 1950s and 1960s, when national self-confidence wasn't what it is now. Then the economy limped along, people emigrated in droves and Ireland had a name for being one of the poorest countries in Europe.

O'Brien trained the winners of the Champion Hurdle, Cheltenham Gold Cup and Grand National in the late 1940s and early 1950s before taking his genius to the quicker and even more temperamental thoroughbreds of flat racing. Within no time he mastered that, too. He won the Epsom Derby when it was the race to win and then returned to win it again and again.

The Minstrel was one of his Derby winners, a brave and excitable horse. Fearing what the noise of Epsom would do to his horse, O'Brien pressed cotton wool into The Minstrel's ears to dull the sounds of Derby Day. The Minstrel won by a short head.

And then there was Arkle. The paragon of all steeplechasers. Like O'Brien's greatest horses, the Tom Dreaper-trained Arkle achieved his greatest victories on English soil and without wanting to be too nationalistic, that was an important part of the story. History had decreed that any plundering of English prizes would be cherished.

If you were around on the afternoon of 7 March 1964, it didn't matter whether horse-racing interested you or not. Arkle and Mill House competed for more than the Cheltenham Gold Cup. It was, in fact, Ireland against England—Arkle for us, Mill House for them. Tom 'the Builder' Walsh came to our house to watch the race on television. The Builder was a good neighbour, decent on our first communion day, always there for funerals, a welcome visitor on Christmas morning and otherwise a very infrequent caller. He came that Saturday afternoon because, like the rest of us, he had a personal stake in the result.

Johnny Lumley, the stable lad who looked after Arkle, tells a story about the scene in the stable lads' canteen on the evening before the 1964 Gold Cup. The lads were arguing the toss—Arkle or Mill House? As might be expected on the eve of battle, opinions on the outcome were nothing more than expressions of patriotism. The English could not see Mill House losing, the Irish were even more fervent about Arkle.

Arkle, they said, had more speed, he was still improving and he was the greatest horse ever to come out of Ireland. The English lads told them to stop fooling themselves—Mill House had beaten Arkle comfortably the previous time they met, and he would slaughter him this time. It was then that Tipperary's Joe Carey spoke up for his country. 'He will not beat Arkle,' he said. Joe was then in his mid-fifties and had driven Aubrey Brabazon's horse box to Cheltenham. His build was that of the lorry driver, not that tall but portly and weighing maybe 15 stones. 'You know,' said one of the English lads pointing at Joe's midriff, 'Mill House would win tomorrow's race with you on his back.'

The English were wrong. Very, very wrong. For three miles Arkle raced just behind his great rival and even though Mill House set a furious pace, Arkle never seemed to find it that fast. At the second last fence, he crept closer to Mill House and going to the last Arkle's superiority was obvious. Peter O'Sullevan was the BBC commentator and at the defining moment, his

words carried the authority of a judge delivering a death sentence: 'It's going to be Arkle if he jumps it,' said O'Sullevan. He did, and then he surged up the hill all the way to the line, his rival battling gamely but vainly. Mill House was never the same horse afterwards.

I can still see The Builder leaving our sitting room as soon as the race ended: 'That Arkle,' he said, with a hint of a smile, 'He's a good one.' The smile spread right across the country. We grew up with it. It forged a bond between ordinary people and the Sport of Kings. Because of Arkle and

Vincent O'Brien and the other greats of Irish racing, we moved with a little more confidence into the 1970s.

The thirty intervening years have changed almost everything. Money now grows on Irish trees—where once you couldn't sell a house, now you cannot buy one. There are more jobs than applicants, more diners than restaurants, and Dublin moves at the pace of a Barcelona or an Amsterdam. Houses are bigger, roads wider, cars more powerful. There will be a national sports stadium to compare with the finest and when you go to the Leopardstown races, a rolling escalator takes you to the top of the popular stand where you can sit and watch your money disappear down the drain.

Yet, not everything has changed. The bond with horses remains as integral to Irish life as it has always been. We might argue about the greatest horse race in the world—the Kentucky Derby, the Melbourne Cup, the Epsom Derby, or the Aintree Grand National? Well, in Europe, the Grand National is the race. For the last two years it has been won by horses bred and trained in Ireland. On each occasion the trainer's son rode the winner.

An extraordinary coincidence you might think—the trainer having a son good enough to ride and win on his star horse in Europe's biggest race! But it goes with the territory of Irish racing and isn't the chance happening it might first seem.

The genes that are passed on in Irish racing wear silks and carry whips. Not just the genes in the families of most recent heroes Ted and Ruby Walsh and their predecessors at Aintree, Tommy and Paul Carberry, because it is the same with the Mullins from Kilkenny, the Kinanes from Tipperary, the Edderys from Kildare and countless other Irish families.

Tommy Kinane rode Monksfield to win the Champion Hurdle at Cheltenham in 1978 and had a family of four boys and three girls. From the time they could walk, the children worked with horses. Thomas Junior has a vivid recollection:

'There were always horses where we lived and before cycling to catch the bus to Ballingarry Convent they would be fed, hayed and mucked out. When we got home from school, we had to ride out.'

Michael Kinane, the second eldest boy in the family, has become the greatest Irish flat race jockey of his generation—his victories include the Epsom Derby, the Prix de l'Arc de Triomphe, the Belmont Stakes and the Melbourne Cup. In other countries, it doesn't happen like that. Trainers' sons become lawyers and accountants, bloodstock agents and estate agents, anything that means they don't rise at 5.30am to feed a yard of horses.

In Ireland, folk have this curious belief that it is a privilege to work with horses. As a young man Paddy Mullins helped his father Willie to turn out winners in the 1940s from their farm near

Charlie Swan on Fox's Den Cloughjordan

Left, Horses galloping in County Meath; above, The Heineken Gold Cup at the Punchestown Races

Goresbridge in County Kilkenny. Sixty years later, the venerable Paddy is still doing it. Eighty-one years of age now, at a point in his life where the candles cost more than the cake, and still one of Ireland's best trainers. Paddy's own son, Willie, is now a champion trainer.

Once I asked Paddy how he kept going. At the time he was in his seventies and he talked about how he relaxed in the evenings:

'I might pour myself a drop of whiskey and sit in front of the television. I find something good, I'm just getting into it and then I fall asleep. When I wake up it's time to check the horses.'

He liked it to be the last thing he did every day of his life. Add that devotion to the intuitive understanding of a great horseman and you end up with a special racehorse trainer.

'When you rode for Paddy Mullins,' said his one-time stable jockey Ferdy Murphy, 'you quickly realised he could tell you more about the horse from watching it race than you could tell from having ridden it. What he has is genius, no other word for it.'

Willie, Paddy's son, is cutting his own trail through the same jungle, and Willie himself has a very young son, also called Patrick, who will end up being called Paddy and the future probably won't surprise us. Though many of Ireland's racing fraternity were conceived in a stable and delivered in a horse-box, others drove out from towns or cycled from nearby villages. A vague yearning to be with horses being their only link with racing.

Kieran Fallon has been the champion flat race jockey in Britain for the last three years, riding over 200 winners each season. His father, Buddy, was a plasterer and Kieran didn't ride a thoroughbred until he was 18 years of age.

'I watched racing on television and I liked it, but what encouraged me to be a jockey was my size and the fact that I wasn't very good at school.'

Hitching a ride from his home near Crusheen in County Clare to the secondary school in nearby

Sycamore Boy ridden by G. Cotter at the Laytown Races; opposite, Charlie Swan and Istabraq, the heroes of Cheltenham 2000

Gort, Fallon remembers the conversation with the Good Samaritan who picked him up:

'What's your name?'

'Kieran Fallon.'

'Where you from?'

'Just back there.'

'Where you goin'?'

'Gort.'

'What are you going to do when you leave school then?'

'Goin' to be a jockey.'

'Well, at least you have the size for it.'

That wasn't all Fallon had. He joined Kevin Prendergast's stable yard on the Curragh when he was 18, moved to England a few years later and at the age of 30 he became the champion flat race jockey in Britain. That was three years ago. He has been champion ever since. How highly should we rate Fallon? He is not as stylish as Frankie Dettori and he does make his share of mistakes. But when the figures are added up at the end of the season, he rides more winners than everyone else and he performs outstandingly in the biggest races.

What Fallon has is a natural empathy with the thoroughbred and he is particularly effective on sensitive and highly strung fillies. He came late to the sport, but not unarmed. He intuitively understood them. It may seem far-fetched to propose that this is something that goes with the gift of Irishness, but I believe it does.

How else can one explain that at the end of the 1999/2000 jump racing season in Britain, eleven of the top fifteen jockeys were Irish? The table appeared in Britain's daily racing newspaper every day: 'Top Jump Jockeys For The Season'. And there they were—Richard Johnson, Joe Tizzard and Andrew Thornton from England, Welshman Carl Llewellyn and eleven Irishmen. There is no rational explanation for this domination, this penchant for excelling in one sphere of human endeavour. 'I think it comes to the place of racing in Ireland,' says one of the eleven, Mick

Fitzgerald. 'Charlie Swan [a highly successful Irish-based jump jockey] walks into a pub in Ireland and there are sure to be people who will recognise him. It is not like that in England. A. P. McCoy [the Irishman now perennially champion in Britain] could walk into most pubs over there and not be recognised. In every Irish village somebody knows somebody who is a great man for the horses. It is the culture.'

Fitzgerald is right, in as far as he goes. But any explanation that doesn't take account of Irish people's natural flair for horses doesn't go far enough. Fitzgerald himself had to work hard to get to the top, but when he arrived it was clear that he was a gifted horseman. Not a gifted jockey, a gifted horseman.

I remember, too, the March day in 1991 that Adrian Maguire arrived at the Cheltenham Festival for the first time. Maguire was 19 years old, from Kilmessan in County Meath and it was his first time at Cheltenham.

'Know how to get to the weighing room?' Maguire asked a friend.

'That way,' pointed the friend.

Maguire was there to ride a horse called Omerta in a race for amateurs. His talent had first been noticed in pony racing and then nurtured on the point-to-point field. Not knowing his way to the weighing room didn't hinder Maguire when the tape went up and he had to find his way around the track. Maguire and Omerta flew home well ahead of their rivals—an old horse rejuvenated by a dashing young jockey.

A year later Maguire returned to the Festival and had his first ride in the Gold Cup. The year was 1992, Cool Ground was a 25/1 shot and Maguire rode the race of his life. They won by a short head. This was a 20-year-old kid in his first season as a professional—where had he come from, how could he be so good? As he was leaving the weighing room that evening Maguire asked about Fakenham, where he was due to ride the following day.

'Where's Fakenham?' he asked.

'In Norfolk,' came the answer.

'Where's Norfolk?' Maguire asked.

The tradition of Irish success in racing goes back to the 1940s and even before. But it was the success that came immediately after the Second World War that impinged upon the consciousness of a nation.

Young trainers like Tom Dreaper and Vincent O'Brien sent their best horses to take on England's best and the people were behind them. Dreaper's Prince Regent won the first Cheltenham Gold Cup after the war and then O'Brien won it three years in a row from 1948 with Cottage Rake. They wrote

The St. James Gate Q. R. Handicap at the Laytown Races

Limestone Lad ridden by Shane McGovern

a song about Cottage Rake and his rider, Aubrey Brabazon from Kildare:

'Aubrey's up, the money's down

The frightened bookies quake

Come on me lads and give a cheer

Begod 'tis Cottage Rake'.

One generation begot the next; in some cases literally, but mostly metaphorically. After great Irish jockeys like Brabazon and Martin and Tim Molony, came Arkle's great rider Pat Taaffe and his great friend and rival Willie Robinson and in the next generation Tommy Carberry and Frank Berry. And so on until we arrive at today's class which may be better than any. A. P. McCoy and

Norman Williamson, Paul Carberry and Adrian Maguire, Mick Fitzgerald and Ruby Walsh—men you would trust with your best horse.

The young trainers are there, too. Aidan O'Brien has taken the reins at Ballydoyle, the training complex made famous by the achievements of Vincent O'Brien. Young Aidan is unrelated to his namesake, but they do have much in common, not least the driving ambition to be the best. Only a foolish man or one with deep self-belief would have agreed to follow in Vincent O'Brien's footsteps. No one has ever accused Aidan O'Brien of being a fool. And because our racing men have gone on being successful,

they have brought us with them. And in greater numbers than ever. Although still keen to go to our local tracks, we now have the means to travel further. The Cheltenham Festival is eminent in European horseracing because thousands of Irish make the pilgrimage. Pilgrimage is the correct description because there is a religious fervour to the trip to the Cotswolds in the middle of March each year.

There is a story told of an Irishman who, feeling unwell, went to his doctor in early January. Christmas excesses had aggravated the man's already chronic heart condition. The doctor did a battery of tests and was shocked by the results.

'This is not looking good,' said the doctor.

'Give it to me straight, Doc. I can take it.'

'You don't have long to live, not long at all.'

'Exactly how long, Doc?'

'Three days,' said the doctor, 'I can give you three days.'

'Could you make them 15, 16 and 17 March ?' asked the man.

We know how he felt. Yet when it comes to defining the attraction, to explain why we remain so devoted to Irish racing, it cannot end with Cheltenham because it did not begin there. This is something that goes back in time, the roots stretch into small farms and deep into the national psyche.

Let us try to illustrate this a little more plainly.

A woman friend, visiting from England, went to a point-to-point meeting in County Cork. The day was cold when not downright freezing, but she found the experience enthralling. She raved about the informality, the banter and the esteemed place of the horse in this part of the racing world. Invigorated but cold, she decided to run back to her car. It was a long, slightly uphill run but my friend had always been a runner and even though out of training and in her early thirties, she still moved sharply up that hill.

As she did, two elderly Cork farmers noticed her speed.

'By God, see that?' one said to the other.

'I tell ya what, Johnny,' replied his friend, 'I'd have backed her to win the Mare's Race.'

The lords of Leopardstown

Into the West

BY NUTAN

Snail, The Burren

Left, Islánder on Inis Meain; Above, The Shannon in Castle Connell; Below, Lakebed, Coole Park

I was born in Belgium and knew nothing of Ireland until 1966, when I decided to study photography in the Saint-Luc Institute of Fine Arts in Liege, thirty miles from my home town of Verviers. I remember standing in awe before the stunning photographs of Ireland taken on an old Rolleyflex by a Belgian photographer named Yellow. He had visited Dublin, Connemara, and the Aran Islands and brought back black-and-white masterpieces filled with soft light, rugged landscapes and faces carved from granite.

I was so impressed that my first ever 'international' photographic venture was to spend the summer of 1968 following in the footsteps of my friend. However, my landscapes were mainly restricted to the faces of pint drinkers and traditional music players in O'Donoghue's of Merrion Row, the Cellar Bar in Galway and Flaherty's of Dingle. I had fallen under the influence of Galway man Joe Dolan (of Sweeney's Men fame) who introduced me to the pleasures of the high stool. Leica in hand, I would spend days exploring Dublin with my Belgian girlfriend Miou, meeting great people in the Liberties, around St. James' Gate Brewery or down along the docks. My nights were spent with Joe and Betty in O'Donoghue's. I remember a famous homecoming party for Joe Heany—we stayed up for two days and two nights adrift on a endless tide of songs, pints, rashers, fried eggs, more pints and more songs. Connemara men with blue eyes, jet-black hair and gravelly voices hypnotised me with sean nós singing. And when Joe Heany sang, the eyes of these tough men grew soft with tears.

Left, Bowan Tree, County Galway; above, Sunset, County Galway

To a young man such as myself, this was a vibrant and crazy life, striking the same chords as the Belgian surrealist and dadaist world when I was a student. Too much porter, however, does not great pictures make, so Betty, Joe, Miou and I headed for the clear skies of the West. Our head-quarters was a two-man tent pitched behind Flaherty's pub in Dingle. The town was shrouded in mist and hundreds of Kerry men and women, hired as extras for *Ryan's Daughter*, drifted in cos-tume in and out of pubs and transport trucks. Robert Mitchum, perched on a high stool drank whiskey like it was mother's milk. This was heav-en. Joe and I decided to shoot a cowboy film on an old 8mm camera in the streets of Dingle and the hills of Dunquin. We chased each other in and out of foggy alleyways, firing toy guns as bewildered film extras looked on. I was twenty years of age, and Ireland was under my skin.

On my return to Belgium, I finished my degree. My photographs won one or two prizes, and I worked for a while on film sets in Amsterdam.

But it was not long before I returned and settled in a camper van in Leitrim. I divided my time between Drumshanbo, Sligo and Donegal and fished for a few years in and around Killybegs while photographing features on the fishing industry. I taught photography at Sligo Art College and then in Dublin at the National College of Art and Design. Gradually I worked my way up as a photojournalist, first in Ireland than everywhere work took me, and eventually joined the French photo agency Rapho in 1989. But I always based myself in Ireland.

One day, I found myself on the back of a motorbike hurtling down the Champs Elysees in Paris, on the last stage of the Tour de France, when my driver had a moment of madness and drove into the crowd. It was a miracle nobody was killed. As he lay screaming on the side of the road, he removed his leather jacket to show me where I had been beating him black and blue for the last three weeks—I was so tense as a photographer on the Tour that I had been passing it all on to him,

Hookers in County Galway

demanding that he take me to the best places for pictures. He declared that he wouldn't work with me again, that I had stopped using my cameras as toys and was using them (and him) as tools. Well, he may have been a bad driver but he was right about me. The next day, I packed my gear and came back to Ireland.

Except for a few years chasing spirituality in India, I stayed here and was naturalised as Irish in 1980. I now live in The Burren, a frustrating place to photograph, because the light and the colour and the mood changes continuously—it is like working on a boat. All that grey stone makes it very repetitive, so you continuously have to re-invent yourself. I spent a year photographing the four seasons in The Burren using a panoramic camera, then I photographed the flowers using macrophotography and all kinds of improvised gimmicks to shelter from the ever-persistent wind. It is wild out here, and you can still find places where the silence is omnipotent and you can hear yourself hum in tune with the place.

For the last few years, I have grown more and more frustrated with the technical perfections one can achieve in photography. I am also quite unimpressed with the current trend for getting results at the click of a few buttons. Everything seems to be about shortcuts, saving time, being more efficient—the mystery is gone out of it.

A friend, Garda Frank Daly, Cootehill, County Roscommon

Walking horses in Faroe, County Clare

So, I am taking a break from editorial photography. For the past two years, I have taught part-time in the Art College in Galway and I have started painting again, with a vengeance. I traded my brushes for cameras thirty years ago and now I seem to have reversed the process—it is as though I want to express with paint all the images I have accumulated over thirty years of looking through lenses and taking pictures quickly. I am also trawling through my photographic archives to select a few hundred pictures taken between 1968 and 1998 for a book about my work on Ireland. I am planning a book on The Burren with John O'Donoghue, the poet, and a photographic study of Ireland 1966–69 with my Belgian photographer friend Yellow. And I am working on a top secret project with a designer friend of mine that will hopefully make us both very rich!

What attracted me to Ireland initially was the music, the light and one or two close friends, but what appealed to me most is unhappily fast becoming rare. People are too busy making money to allow themselves time to enjoy the country around them. Beautiful old stone walls are being replaced with concrete fencing, rivers are being polluted, and dozens of new houses are being built to the size of mansions, most of them totally out of proportion with the surroundings. The Celtic Tiger is very greedy on space and little grassy boreens,

Left, Bringing in the hay; above, Young traveller at Ballinasloe Horse Fair

Above, sea pinks, Faroe, County Clare; below, Bluebells in Lough Key Forest Park

where once one had time to see the world pass by, are slowly being transformed into kamikaze roads along which new inhabitants commute at a mad speed to Galway or further afield to Limerick, Shannon or Dublin. Nothing is ever static and change is unavoidable.

A Buddhist friend of mine says we should be thankful for having known the place as it once was, wild and undisturbed. I am. On the other hand, no one seems to be bothered whether I get out of bed, wear a tea cosy on my head or pay my bills on time.

I know of a man who lives somewhere between Castlebaldwin and Colooney on the Sligo road, and for the last twenty years or so he has worn a female nurse's uniform. I see him working in the fields or in the bog, wearing this blue dress and wellington boots. I gave him a lift in my car once and he sang all the way to Colooney. He had a wonderful voice. When I enquired about him at the local post office, the woman behind the counter told me, 'Ah, sure isn't he a gas ticket?' If that happened elsewhere, I am sure he would be locked up.

There is more creativity, madness and innocence in a square mile of Ireland than in a hundred square miles of continental suburbia. It is wonderful, although when you need your plumbing fixed in a hurry, it can be infuriating.

A Roscommon farmer once used the spring of a biro to 'fix' a problem with my VW camper. It did the trick for two years or so, until the engine exploded one day on a dual carriageway. Well, he had told me to get it repaired properly. The attitude rubs off on you—if it is working, leave it alone.

The madness also attracts tourists looking for a bit cf grit and chaos—my Buddhist friend says we should be thankful for the bad weather over the past few months because it keeps most of them away. The problem comes when they fall in love with the place and decide to stay, but they want to fence off their patch to keep it smooth and keep the chaos out.

A few years ago, I went to photograph otters near Ballyvaughan on the coast. I photographed them there every year, but that year the new owner had fenced all around the area with barbed wire. It was impossible to get through. A local council man was sitting close by, enjoying his tea break.

Pointing to the barbed wire embedded in concrete that was crowning the wall, I said to him, outraged: 'What do you think of that, Mattie?' 'Ah', he said, puffing on his pipe, 'it'll rust.'

The Celtic Voice

By Eileen Battersby

Few nations appear more confident of their literary tradition than Ireland. Judging by the amount of new Irish prose being published by eager British publishers as well as the number of Irish playwrights impressing West End and Broadway audiences, it has become the most natural thing in the world to say, 'I'm Irish, therefore I write'.

This explosion of writing has been accompanied by a new confidence, exuding brashness and bordering on defiance, with many of the emerging new prose writers firmly rooted in the urban experience. Alongside the prose and drama is the astonishing continuing achievement of Irish poetry, most obviously the contribution of the poets of Northern Ireland—Seamus Heaney, Derek Mahon, Michael Longley, Paul Muldoon and Ciaran Carson and in the South, the magisterial presence of Thomas Kinsella, the most

TEMPTATION
Dermot Bolger
'A master storyteller' *Irish Times*

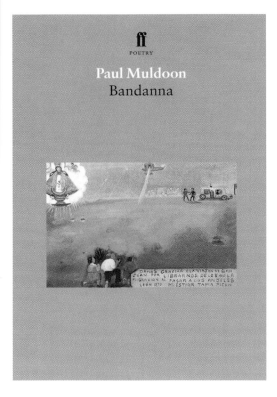

obvious heir to Yeats. But to look to the prose first. Nostalgia and romance, even of the bitter-sweet variety, have been abandoned. The countryside and in particular, the small country town, has retained its hold on the best of Irish theatre, whether from an established voice such as Tom Murphy, or through the young Marina Carr who is introducing the previously invisible Irish Midlands to a national as well as international audience. It is impossible to ignore, however, the fact that many of the younger Irish writers are consciously writing for the readers of today rather

than posterity. Carr, however, is one who will last. Prose and drama have always contained an inevitable yet invaluable element of social documentary, but in the case of some of the new Irish voices what was documentary has become commentary. A glance at the work of most writers under 40 suggests the movement from the field to the street is complete, and this is certainly true of film scripts. Yet if there is a key to Irish writing it is this enduring tension between the rural and the urban. A tension, no longer a battle, which has instead settled into a complex relationship. It is

Edna O'Brien

also worth pointing out that while British and US writers celebrate landscape and nature, just as Yeats had romanticised them, for the contemporary Irish writer with exceptions such as Longley, the countryside is more of backdrop, a geographical location, a state of mind.

In *The Country Funeral*, John McGahern's finest short story, three brothers are told by their ageing mother to attend the burial of her brother, their Uncle Peter, who bullied them as children. As she says:

'If nobody went to poor Peter's funeral, God rest him, we'd be the talk of the countryside for years. If I know nothing else in the world, I know what they're like down there.'

It is a remarkable story. McGahern explores the pain and resentments of the men recalling the school holidays of years past when their mother took them back to her home on the bog, away from Dublin where she had settled with a disappointing husband. He also presents an Ireland divided between the rural and the urban. Irish literature and life has held on to this struggle longer than most, which partly explains why the urbanisation of the Irish landscape has only now begun to shock a population that remained oblivious to planners and development until it was almost too late. The notion of escape from the farm to the big city preoccupied Patrick Kavanagh and his generation, but McGahern is more concerned with defining the subtle differences between romantic flight, desperate survival and weary acceptance. The three brothers in *A Country Funeral* were once country boys in Dublin, but were regarded as townies back on the family farm. Now, as men, their lives have taken different directions. John, the brightest and least confrontational has settled into being a teacher and subdued husband passively seeking an easy life. Philly spends long stints working in the oil fields of Saudi Arabia, (and it is significant that it is Saudi not Birmingham) while the third had his

decisions made for him. Trapped in his wheelchair, bitter, angry Fonsie has gone nowhere. Of the three, he is the one who most resents the past and whose fear of Uncle Peter has been most completely supplanted by hatred:

'The big Mercedes grew silent as it gathered speed through Fairview and the North Strand, crossing the Liffey at the Custom House, and turned into the one-way flow of traffic out along the south bank of the river. Not until they got past Leixlip, and fields and trees and hedges started to be scattered between the new raw estates did they talk about the man they were going to bury.'

John McGahern is the bridge between the Irish writers who helped establish the new literature of an aspiring independent state—writers such as Yeats, Joyce, Austin Clarke and Kavanagh, and the artists who picked up a story that is best divided into two main headings—the North and the changing society of the South. It could well be argued that anyone interested in reaching an

Seamus Heaney

'The big Mercedes grew silent as it gathered speed through Fairview and the North Strand, crossing the Liffey at the Custom House, and turned into the one-way flow of traffic out along the south bank of the river. Not until they got past Leixlip, and fields and trees and hedges started to be scattered between the new raw estates did they begin to talk about the man they were going to bury.'

–THE COUNTRY FUNERAL, BY JOHN McGAHERN

understanding of the heart of Ireland need look no further than McGahern's stories. He has explored the way the dark 1950s endured into the 1970s. Novels such as *The Barracks* (1962), *The Dark* (1965), *The Leavetaking* (1974) and of course, *Amongst Women* (1990), remain central to the Irish literary consciousness for readers and writers. Indeed in his lifetime McGahern, the thoughtful prose lyricist, has become as vital a source as Chekhov to many writers.

It is true that one of McGahern's close contemporaries, Edna O'Brien, remains as yet more celebrated for her early than subsequent work. Her themes and settings have moved on from the rural landscapes of *The Country Girl* trilogy. Yet O'Brien's presentation of aspirations and denials, as well as her courage in directly confronting feelings that were previously more alluded to than explored, has won her a lasting place as 'an Irish Writer' albeit more in an international than national context. O'Brien's early books and stories are suspended in truth, not a time warp. The nostalgia surrounding the reading of her work is certainly well deflected by the sharpness and candour of much of her writing, the best of which is to be found in the short stories.

William Trevor remains one of the enduring giants of international, never mind Irish literature,

Marina Carr

and despite his range of themes and settings and his feel for west London or ex-pats in Italy, he has never lost his sense of native place. Take Trevor's early classic, *The Ballroom of Romance* (1972), in which Bridie reflects upon her life and the years spent tending her widower father:

'The youths who'd danced with her then in their Saturday-night blue suits had later disappeared into the town, or to Dublin or Britain, leaving behind them those who became the middle aged bachelors of the hills.'

In *The Piano Tuner's Wives*, Belle finally gets her man, his first wife Violet having died:

'There was a little more to it than that, because in choosing Violet to be his wife the piano tuner had rejected Belle, which was something everyone remembered when the second wedding was announced. "Well, she got the ruins of him anyway", a farmer of the neighbourhood remarked, speaking without vindictiveness, stating a fact as he saw it.'

Of the several major Irish international writers Trevor, who began his career writing about London with the wonderful debut *The Old Boys* (1963), is the most often overlooked, just as he is the one who most often surprises by his quiet, relentless perceptions and versatility. *Reading Turgenev* (1991) could well be his masterpiece while *Felicia's Journey* (1994) and *Death in Summer* (1998) testify to his not having lost his feel for the pain of small lives nor for the dark and sinister.

From the mid 1980s onwards and throughout the 1990s, critics and commentators decided an urban literary revolution had been begun, spearheaded by Dermot Bolger and Roddy Doyle. Both won large followings with Doyle going on to win the 1995 Booker Prize, an honour that has to date eluded McGahern, Trevor and John Banville, all of whom have been at least short-listed. But it was less a revolution and more a return to the territory favoured by the social realism of James Stephens' sinister parable *The Charwoman's Daughter* (1912) and of O'Casey's theatre, as well as Joyce who made the streets of Dublin his landscape.

The now famous film-maker Neil Jordan suggested as early as his first collection of fiction,

'There was a little more to it than that, because in choosing Violet to be his wife the piano tuner had rejected Belle, which was something everyone remembered when the second wedding was announced. "Well, she got the ruins of him anyway", a farmer of the neighbourhood remarked, speaking without vindictiveness, stating a fact as he saw it.'

–THE PIANO TUNER'S WIVES, BY WILLIAM TREVOR

Night in Tunisia (1976), that he was poised between several versions of Irish life. His Kafkaesque *The Dream of a Beast* (1983) is about as physical an evocation of the suburbs and city as could be imagined. An extraordinarily subtle writer, Jordan draws the city as a place of sensations. Doyle's surburban Dublin is about character as created through the use of strongly vernacular speech. Acknowledged as the writer who single-handedly gave a voice to working class

northside suburban Dublin, it should be pointed out that the backdrop to Doyle's evocative Booker-winning account of one boy's childhood, *Paddy Clarke Ha Ha*, is actually the breakdown of the narrator's parents' marriage. Social class is irrelevant in this, the most untypical of his books.

Another novel meriting examination for the wealth it offers about modern Ireland is Bolger's sprawling but passionate *Father's Music* (1997), which juxtaposes the realities of crime with

Dermot Bolger

cultural realities such as traditional music and a de-romanticised, abruptly urbanised sense of Irishness. Playwright Paul Mercier has, like Bolger written of the city while conveying a sense of taking the odd glance back at the countryside. Another Dubliner Conor McPherson brilliantly used the simple setting of a country pub for *The Weir* (1997) in which a Dublin woman upstages the locals with a ghost story of her own.

Social class has always had a part in the work of Jennifer Johnston, a gifted miniaturist who, though lacking the range of Trevor, has written elegant, well-observed studies of the Southern Irish Protestant experience. Through novels such as *How Many Miles to Babylon?* (1974) to *The Invisible Worm* (1991) and *Two Moons* (1998), she could well emerge as the Irish writer who brought the Big House novel to its logical conclusion, by transferring it from the countryside to the more compact comforts of Dun Laoghaire and Dalkey.

An Irish writer who first asserted himself with an hilarious variation of The Big House novel is John Banville, born in County Wexford in 1945. *Birchwood*, a grotesquely comic picaresque

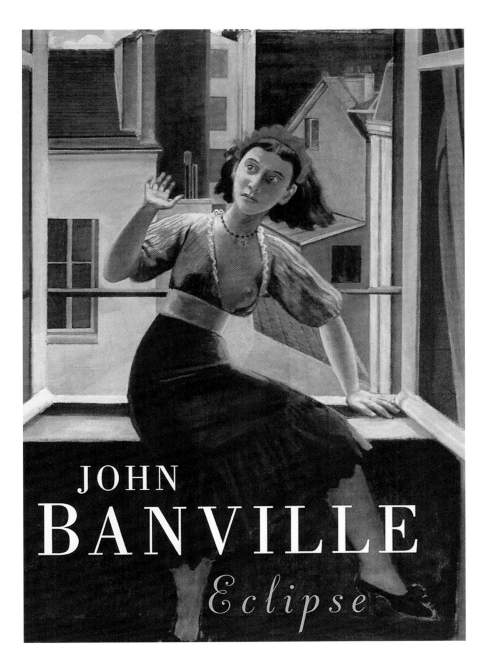

JOHN BANVILLE *Eclipse*

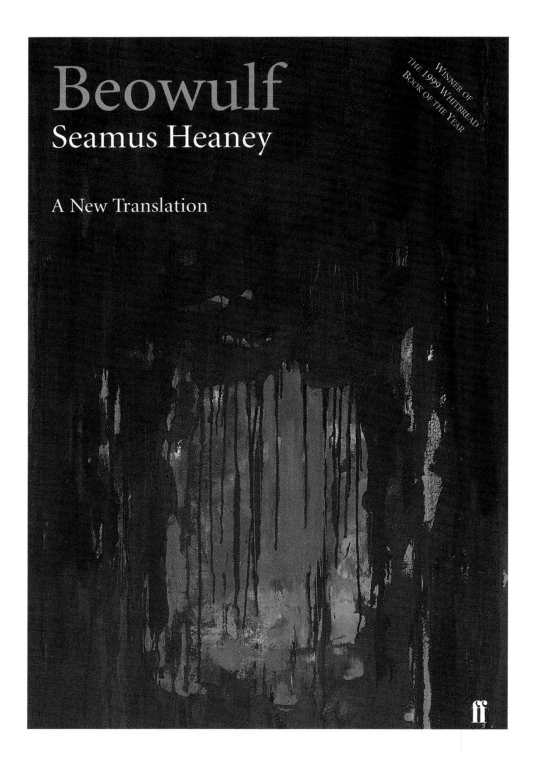

WINNER OF
THE 1999 WHITBREAD
BOOK OF THE YEAR

Beowulf
Seamus Heaney

A New Translation

ff

published in 1973, was his second novel and followed *Nightspawn* (1971), a brittle work belonging to the Angry Young Men school of fiction. Of far more interest than that debut is his early collection of short stories *Long Lankin* (1970). Banville appeared to walk away from the traditional Irish novel with his outstanding science novels, drawing on the chaotic lives of two famous scientists in *Doctor Copernicus* (1976) and *Kepler* (1980) and placing them in a medieval, foreign world. Laconic black comedy is his natural tone, while his style is elegant, almost mannered. The intensely cerebral fiction of this most European of Irish novelists has remained preoccupied with themes such as truth and art, yet the voice retains a distinct Irishness. When the writing-blocked narrator of *The Newton Letter* (1982) arrives at a faded Big House to complete his beleaguered biography of Newton, the action unexpectedly develops into an account of tormented love by proxy. All is not what it seems. Again, appearances for Banville are everything and nothing. One of the most interesting and enigmatic of Irish writers his work is sustained by an intriguing ambivalence—is it cold and mannered literature doggedly aspiring towards high art? Or is it funny and heartbreakingly human. It is all of these things. While the dazzling *Mefisto* (1986) with its theme of duality remains his finest, most daringly imagined work, he won his widest audience with his Booker runner-up *The Book of Evidence* (1989), the stylish and funny confession of Freddie Montgomery. *Ghosts* (1993) and *Athena* (1995) followed, both again reflecting Banville's preoccupation with art and truth. *The Untouchable* (1997) is an astonishing feat of storytelling in which Banville achieves his most concentrated plotting and sharpest characterisation in a story drawing on 50 years of British history. His art historian narrator Victor Maskell is the complete Englishman, and utterly self-invented, an Irish outsider who becomes involved in the Cambridge spy circle. For all its apparent cold flair, moments of genius, hilarious comedy and the faultless Banvillean narrative voice, *The Untouchable* is ultimately a moving love story. *Eclipse* (2000), which has just been published, is far more narrow. Alexander Cleave is an actor in flight from his world, having faltered on the stage. An intense, relentlessly argued near-monologue, laconic yet riven by personal pain, *Eclipse* is Banville at his least intellectual though it never achieves the pathos of *The Newton Letter*. Cleave returns to his smalltown boyhood home to re-assess a life dominated by Banville familiars such as the narrator's abiding self-hatred, ghosts, guilt and a flare for grotesque comic observation. Random and exact, a sophisticated anger simmers throughout, while the novel and the reader, are mesmerised, at times overwhelmed, by the virtuoso use of language.

Banville's influence is to be seen in the work of Mary Morrissy (born 1957) whose cool, confident voice was apparent from her first collection *A Lazy Eye* (1993). Within three years her debut novel *Mother of Pearl* reiterated her unusually mature and individual voice. Set in an unspecified cityscape it is the story of two mothers and a stolen baby. The novel's genius lies in its rigorous unsentimentality and its relentless emotional power, which leaves the reader in tears. Few books are the real thing. This is one of them.

Colum McCann (born 1965) stepped outside the Irish, if not the emigrant experience, for his second novel *This Side of Brightness* (1998), about the doomed heroes who built the New York subway. It has echoes of Sri Lankan Michael Ondaatje's *In The Skin of the Lion* (1987) and is also heavy with symbol, not least the Christ-like central character Clarence Nathan Walker, the black man from the lush South who walks to the grim North for work. Still it is an exciting work of imagination and vision and is, above all, daring because McCann is writing outside the tradition. Even so, it is fascinating to realise exactly how persuasive the rooted Irish tradition remains. We tend to think of the best of Irish writers such as Heaney, McGahern, Trevor, Friel, Murphy and Longley in terms of their oeuvres. Some individual works stand alone such as Eugene McCabe's unforgettable gothic pastoral *Death and Nightingales* with its Shakespearean sense of unease reflected by upheaval in nature. Published

Many new Irish writers are firmly rooted in the urban experience

Paula Meehan

voice, this is a rich, atmospheric performance. Many recent Irish novels have been over-praised, none have been as seriously underrated as this beautiful subtle account of a life that is also a vivid portrait of a rural world that is disappearing. Nolan's social history is less complex than the political dimension Neil Jordan—to return to him for a moment—brings to his recreation of 1920s

Ireland in his fine first novel *The Past* (1980), another of Irish fiction's underrated master works.

The past, particularly his family's past, has proved a treasure trove for Sebastian Barry, poet, playwright and storyteller. *From The Engine of Owl-Light* (1986) a novel daringly woven of six narratives, to *The Whereabouts of Eneas McNulty* (1998), a gentle picaresque chronicling the

in 1992 and overlooked by all shortlists and prizes, it has nevertheless emerged as the most admired of Irish novels. McCabe is a gifted writer of short stories but nothing he had previously done prepares the reader for the psychological force of what is a 19th century Hardyesque dramatic narrative rooted in history and concerned with the betrayal of love and trust. At heart one women's odyssey towards hurt and retribution, it is also a terrifyingly lucid metaphor for the tragedy in Northern Ireland.

Christopher Nolan's engaging and profound novel *The Banyan Tree* (1999) is the story of one woman's life. Set in Westmeath, it spans the century and manages to be as fresh as it is familiar. Minnie O'Brien's destiny is settled when she sells a mousetrap to a kindly man who walks into her father's shop. The language is earthy and inventive. There are several wonderful set pieces, particularly the opening sequence in which she performs 'a miracle' with a butter churn. From young mother to ancient widow patrolling the farm neither of her sons are interested in, likeable Minnie, though overwhelmed by the passage of time, survives. Told through a dreamy third person

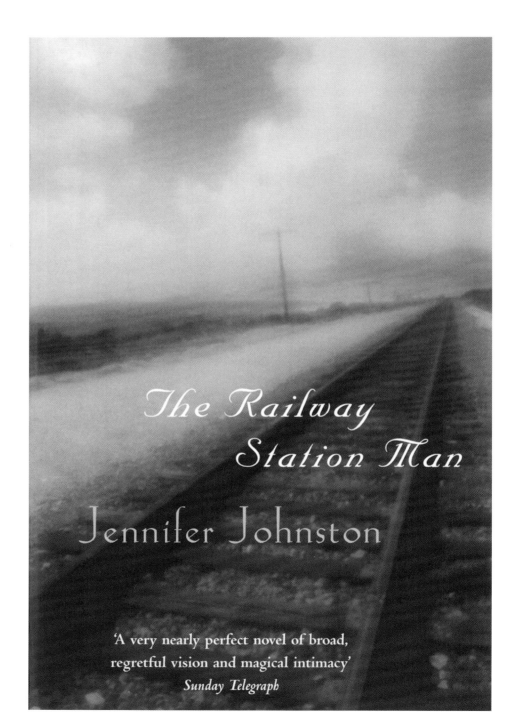

The Railway Station Man

Jennifer Johnston

'A very nearly perfect novel of broad, regretful vision and magical intimacy'
Sunday Telegraph

innocent central character's life odyssey, Barry has always been drawn to story and a dreamer's vision of the past. At his best in plays such as *Boss Grady's Boys* and *Prayers of Sherkin*—though he is internationally best known for *The Steward of Christendom*—Barry has an uncanny feel for phrase and image. In ways he defies genre, as does poet Seamus Deane's haunting memoir-as-novel, *Reading in the Dark* (1996) which explores the fears and fantasies of childhood against the burden of history and tribal war. Deane's achievement highlights the way Irish playwrights and poets have addressed issues ignored to a surprising extent by the fiction writers.

His fellow Derryman Brian Friel took on the role of artist as spokesman. His range is as ambitious as it is diverse and while his achievement is obvious from works such as *Philadelphia, Here I Come!* (1964), *Translations* (1980), his masterpiece *Faith Healer* (1979), and the heavily nostalgic yet mythic *Dancing At Lughnasa* (1990), *Making History* (1988) underlines his sense of the artist's responsibility as witness.

Tom Murphy's career has run in tandem with Friel's but with a significant difference, social

'I am neither internee nor informer;
An inner émigré, a grown long-haired
And thoughtful; a wood-kerne
Escaped from the massacre,
Taking protective colouring
From bole and bark, feeling
Every wind that blows.'

–EXPOSURE, BY SEAMUS HEANEY

history rather than the political and cultural has preoccupied him. The dynamics of family and the tensions of small town life are his central themes. From his explosive debut *A Whistle in the Dark* (1961) to *Conversations on a Homecoming* (1985), *The Wake* (1998) and his new work, *The House*, Murphy, the author of *The Gigli Concert* (1983) has served Irish theatre very well.

Also poised to enhance the tradition is Marina Carr whose dark, surefooted genius is obvious from *The Mai*, *Portia Coughlan*, *By the Bog of Cats* and her latest, *On Raftery's Hill*. Frank McGuinness is most at home in the theatre of ideas. His Ireland may be on the battlefield in France, in Booterstown or in 1940s Buncrana, but it is ultimately concerned with human vulnerability and the personal. Seamus Heaney is the most widely read, living English language poet in the world; he is also one of the finest, a natural lyricist who combines the personal, an intense feel for the physical landscape as well as a subtle anger directed at the situation in his country. While Heaney seems to have merged as a fully developed poet, the genesis of Michael Longley another lyric artist is fascinating. On one hand an accomplished love poet, on the other a supreme landscape poet. Longley is also increasingly drawn to classical sources with resulting analogies such as *The Butchers*. *Gorse Fires* (1991) and *The Weather in Japan* (00) are among the finest collections published anywhere since World War II. Longley is a poet growing in genius:

'I get down on my knees
and do what must be done
And kiss Achilles' hand,
the killer of my son.'

Paul Durcan

Derek Mahon, at his best in *A Disused Shed in County Wexford* or *Ovid in Tomis*, stands shoulder to shoulder with Louis MacNeice, while the tremendous intellectual energy and inventiveness of Paul Muldoon continues to intrigue.

Such is the diversity of Irish poetry—and this article has limited itself to those working in English—that it embraces the Belfast street songs of Ciaran Carson to the thoughtful, Larkinesque reflections of urban poets Gerald Dawe and Dennis O'Driscoll, to the eloquent rage of Paula Meehan, as in *The Pattern*:

'Little has come down to me of hers,
a sewing machine, a wedding band,
a clutch of photos, the sting of her hand
across my face in one of our wars.'

Assessing modern Irish literature is like photographing a bird in flight. It is alive and vivid, extremely confident—open to the present and the future while remaining powerfully aware if unafraid of the past and a daunting literary legacy.

Dreams of Golf and Greens— The Ultimate Course

by Dermot Gilleece

Portstewart, County Derry—arguably the country's most delightful opening hole

T he assignment, should I choose to accept it, was to produce the ultimate Irish golf course. 'In your dreams,' I protested. 'Precisely,' came the reply. And before there was time for the message to self-destruct, I found myself utterly absorbed in the marvellous possibilities that the concept presented.

Slowly, a routing began to take shape. Starting on Ulster's Atlantic coast, it would whisk the dreamer effortlessly through the other three provinces, over hill and dale, parkland and links, before ending in the pastoral splendour of Adare Manor. In fact, the idea of actually playing such a course in one day is not as far-fetched as it might appear. All that would be required is a helicopter, an enthusiastic pilot and a comprehensive map of Ireland's prime golfing terrain.

As a traditionalist, I went for a par-72 layout with equal halves of 36. And by a sheer fluke, the combined length of the 18 different holes from 18 different courses, happened to work out at 7,060 yards, which is just about right, by modern championship standards. Its four par fives, four par threes and ten par fours are drawn from ten links and eight parkland courses. The only notable exception is the links terrain of Lahinch, which I decided to avoid because current reconstruction will change the sequence of the holes. In the 18 I have chosen, I believe there is not even one hole

that could be described as prosaic—all 18 holes are classics in their own right. Yet it is highly unlikely that the course would meet with the approval of our golfing cognoscenti. From whatever angle, the game is never that simple.

HOLE 1 (425-YARD PAR FOUR)
PORTSTEWART, COUNTY DERRY

Our journey begins at Portstewart, located at the eastern extremity of County Derry's Atlantic coast. This is where Des Giffin, a local schoolteacher with a decidedly useful golf game off four handicap, did a wonderful remodelling job on the links ten years ago. His handiwork had its first serious test in 1992, when Gary Murphy captured the Irish Amateur Close Championship there. And three years later, another international reaped a handsome dividend on what is arguably the country's most delightful opening hole. As it happens, it survives from the original layout, which was used in qualifying for the British Open at nearby Royal Portrush in 1951. From an elevated tee, the left to right dog-leg configuration favours a faded drive between towering dunes, followed by a short-iron approach to a well-protected green. International Mick Morris went down the hole in sudden-death, as Portmarnock challenged for the Irish Senior Cup in 1995. Seeking the decisive point from a tense final, he and his County Sligo

The Old Head, Kinsale, County Cork— a breathtaking creation that had to be carved out of scrub and unyielding slabs of stone

opponent, Tom Ford, were both on the green in regulation. But where Ford missed an eight-foot return putt for a bogey, Morris secured a solid par for the title.

Hole 2 (387-yard par 4)
The Old Head, Kinsale, County Cork
Patrick Merrigan, a member of the design team at The Old Head, described this as 'my favourite par four in the world until I see a better one'.

The breathtaking creation had to be carved out of scrub and unyielding slabs of stone, at considerable cost to men and machines. The problem of the stones was partially solved through the acquisition of a special machine that is used in Switzerland for crushing and planing rock for ski-runs. And to power it, a special tractor had to be imported from Texas. According to Merrigan, this was the most difficult hole he has ever encountered, either from a design or construction

perspective. Negotiating the cliff-edge on the eastern side of the promontory, it dog-legs left at exactly 260 yards, offering a short-iron approach shot, depending on the conditions.

Typical of the challenge to the construction team was that the landing area had to be taken down by three to four yards. Yet it is a measure of the expertise of all concerned that the hole looks entirely natural and very much in keeping with the overall impact of a spectacular site.

HOLE 3 (170-YARD PAR 3)
THE K CLUB, COUNTY KILDARE

They call it the Island Beach, largely because of the way the left side of the green is protected by a menacing bunker, sweeping down to a water hazard. And it used to be the 12th, until its home underwent a major re-routing earlier this year. The original layout of The K Club proved its worth in a run of five Smurfit European Opens from 1995 to 1999. Indeed it was felt that the finish of a treacherous par four, followed by a par three and then a reachable par five, could hardly be bettered. Getting the Ryder Cup for 2005, however, changed things. Owner Michael Smurfit quickly recognised that matchplay imposed different demands from the strokeplay format. And he acknowledged that the existing 16th, ironically called Michael's Favourite, could not accommodate large crowds because of the water down the right, and to the front and back of the green. That was when the routing was changed. So the 10th became the new first; players progressed from the 17th to the old ninth; the old 1st became the new 10th and the finishing holes became the old 7th, 8th and 18th. But through it all, the new 3rd remains a wonderfully challenging par three, whether the pin is to the right or the left of a fiendishly shallow green.

HOLE 4 (419-YARD PAR 4)
KILLARNEY GOLF CLUB, COUNTY KERRY

Tony Jacklin once described Killarney as one of those rare venues where 'great golf and real visual splendour combine to provide an unforgettable experience'. Nowhere in the 54-hole complex is that more evident than on the 4th hole of the Killeen Course. It has been the scene of some splendid exploits—recall the back-to-back Irish

The K Club—called the Island Beach, largely because of the way the left side of the green is protected by a menacing bunker, sweeping down to a water hazard

Killarney Golf Club, County Kerry—where great golf and real visual splendour combine to provide an unforgettable experience

Open triumphs by Nick Faldo in 1991 and 1992. And don't forget June 1996, when Ita Butler led Britain and Ireland to a resounding Curtis Cup win over the USA. On that occasion, the women played the 4th at 323 yards, off the men's forward tee. Even for the shorter hitters, however, one feels the fourth should be played off the back tee, which juts out into Lough Leane and is reached by a narrow, wooden walkway. The clubhouse can be viewed across the lake, with Magillicuddy's Reeks in the background, while facing the fairway water stretches menacingly down the right all the way to

the green. Pat Ward-Thomas, one-time golf correspondent of *The Guardian* in the UK, urged golfers to 'make a pilgrimage to this truly enchanting place, where the beauty of the setting has few peers'. And on Killeen, the 4th is where the fun begins in earnest.

HOLE 5 (174-YARD PAR 3)
BALTRAY, COUNTY LOUTH

On 15 October 1937, Tom Simpson produced a sharply mixed report on the County Louth links at Baltray. While praising it as 'just about as fine a

piece of links land ordained by nature for golf, as we have ever seen', he also made a damning criticism of the par threes. In fact, he slated the one-shot holes as being 'featureless and badly sited'. Simpson also criticised the bunkers as serving 'no useful purpose whatever in governing the play of the hole'. As it happened, the fee for the report proved to be money extremely well spent, when the re-designed links was opened in July 1938. To mark the official opening, Jimmy Bruen played an exhibition with J D McCormack, another leading amateur of the day. And it is interesting to note

Baltray, County Louth — as fine a piece of links land ordained by nature for golf as we have ever seen

that in an outward 35 that contained three birdies, McCormack's only bogey was at the short second, which measured 155 yards at that time. The course was re-shaped once more, in a recent facelift when the old 1st became the new 4th, which meant that the old 2nd became the new 5th. However, the Simpson stamp remains very much intact, most notably in the cavernous bunker that dominates the right front of a treacherous green.

HOLE 6 (605-YARD PAR 5)
PORTMARNOCK, COUNTY DUBLIN

When the Dunlop Masters was staged at Portmarnock in September 1959, the long 6th hole measured 576 yards off the championship tee. Yet it is a measure of the formidable power of Joe Carr that in the final round, he was pin-high right of the green after a five-iron second shot. Gradually, the hole was further lengthened until it slipped past

the 600-yard mark. But in favourable conditions, the green remained reachable in two by such long hitters as Sandy Lyle, who got home with a two-iron second shot during the Irish Open. Such exploits are not without risk, however, as competitors have discovered on pulling a second shot into the pond nestling in the left rough. And for the vast majority who adopt the prudent approach of playing it as a full three-shotter, the short-iron

third can be quite intimidating, especially if the pin is tucked behind the cavernous bunker on the right. Portmarnock is justifiably acknowledged as the premier links in the Republic of Ireland— demanding but eminently fair. And as Bernard Darwin observed, there is the bonus of lovely turf, wildness and solitude and 'the perfect golfing mixture of sandhills and the sea'.

HOLE 7 (421-YARD PAR 4)
THE EUROPEAN CLUB, COUNTY WICKLOW

Designer Pat Ruddy must have had a mischievous glint in his eye when he dedicated this hole to the great Arnold Palmer. For it would require the sort of swashbuckling courage of Palmer in his halcyon days, to go in search of a birdie here. A river borders the hole on the right, all the way from tee to green. And there is precious little comfort to be found down the left side, where a marsh comes very much into play at a distance of 270 yards off the back tee, or 190 yards off the forward men's. According to Ruddy 'there are unseen bail-out areas on the left for both the drive and the second shot, so things aren't quite as bleak as they might seem'. But the fear factor remains a dominant element of the hole. If anything, its menace tends to be heightened by the fact that it lies in a charmingly secluded area of the links. It is an area where the golfer progresses through the heart of an ancient marsh, with flora and fauna in abundance and not a man-made structure in sight. Truly a rare experience.

HOLE 8 (525-YARD PAR 5)
ST MARGARETS, COUNTY DUBLIN

Schoolday memories of *The Rhyme of the Ancient Mariner* by Samuel Taylor Coleridge, spring readily to mind on reaching this menacing par five. For it truly seems as if there is 'water, water everywhere', on a hole where keeping one's ammunition dry can become a daunting challenge. Water is there to the left, off the tee. And it dominates the area between the fairway and the green from a distance of 180 yards. All of which will prompt even the longest of hitters to give due consideration before attempting to go for the green in two. When Pat Ruddy and Tom Craddock collaborated in the design of this fine course, they viewed the 8th as a worthy signature hole. And so it has proved to be. Even with a relatively modest length of 451 yards during the Irish Women's Open, it presented a suitably searching test, even for Laura Davies. Situated on what was relatively flat farmland near Dublin Airport on the northern outskirts of Dublin City, St Margaret's is a fine example of what can be achieved by a combination of imaginative design and modern earth-moving equipment.

Portmarnock, County Dublin— the perfect golfing mixture of sandhills and the sea

The European Club, County Wicklow—not a man-made structure in sight

Hole 9 (425-yard par 4)
Royal County Down, County Down

There can hardly be a more beautiful sight in the world of golf than that which greets the player on this wonderful hole. In the background is majestic Slieve Donard, rising high in the Mournes, while lower down, the town of Newcastle stretches along the coastline. The hole was once a 488-yard par five, which is what the precocious Jimmy Bruen encountered when, as an 18-year-old, he captured the 1938 Irish Amateur Open Championship. A year later, he was back for the Irish Professional Open, setting a course record of 66, which stood unchallenged for 29 years. Members still play the 9th as a par five once a year, but it is now viewed as a testing par four, where the drive is played down into a valley. When Old Tom Morris designed the course for a princely four guineas in 1889, he couldn't have conceived of a more spectacular finish to the outward journey. 'No other course of my acquaintance has any hill so magnificent as Slieve Donard towering above it,' wrote Bernard Darwin in 1930. 'To see from one's window its crest just emerging from a great sea of early mist, is to taste one of the intenser joys of shaving on the morning of a workless day.'

St Margarets, County Dublin—water, water everywhere

Royal County Down—there can hardly be a more beautiful sight in the world of golf

HOLE 10 (549-YARD PAR 5)
MOUNT JULIET, COUNTY KILKENNY

The homeward journey begins at Mount Juliet, which had the distinction of being chosen as the venue for the Irish Open in 1993, only two years after its official opening. At the time, designer Jack Nicklaus saw it as the flagship of his European operations. Offering the option of two routes to the heavily bunkered green, the long 10th features a design concept much favoured by Nicklaus, who saw fit to produce a replica of it in another of his creations in Thailand. And it begins innocently, with a drive down a generously wide fairway. It is only beyond the brow of a gentle rise that the conundrum is revealed. Depending on the position of the drive, the player hoping to reach the green in two can take a shorter line down the right, where a veritable host of bunkers lie in wait for the slightly mishit shot. A more cautious route is offered down the left, ruling out the possibility of putting for an eagle. Instead, the 2nd is essentially a lay-up shot, leaving the player with the challenge of a pitch and putt for birdie. Either way, sound decision-making at this hole can be the key to a productive back nine.

HOLE 11 (443-YARD PAR 4)
BALLYBUNION, COUNTY KERRY

'Farther in the distance, at the end of a tight valley between two rows of sandhills, the eye takes in the minute green of a dazzling cliffside hole.' This is how the American writer Herbert Warren Wind, described the old 6th, on a visit to Ballybunion more than 30 years ago. A re-routing of the course means that the hole is now the 11th. But, interestingly, it reverted to being the 6th for this year's Murphy's Irish Open in order to facilitate crowd control. By any standards, the 11th is a classic, for the way it tumbles downhill along the cliffs to an inviting green. Credit for this wonderful hole goes to the English architect Tom Simpson who undertook a major upgrading of the links in 1937. On arriving at Ballybunion, Simpson enthused: 'The beauty of the terrain surpasses that of any golf course we know, not excepting Pine Valley in America.' More than 60 years on, that beauty is nowhere more evident than in this, one of golf's most admired two-shot holes.

HOLE 12 (206-YARD PAR 3)
WATERVILLE, COUNTY KERRY

When asked whether a certain hole might be a little unfair, Eddie Hackett would look somewhat perplexed before answering: 'It is what was there, you see.' As a wonderfully sympathetic architect, Hackett applied this philosophy to excellent effect at Waterville, which remains his masterpiece. It was especially evident in his approach to the

Ballybunion, County Kerry—a dazzling cliffside hole

Mount Juliet, County Kilkenny—where a veritable host of bunkers lie in wait for the slightly mishit shot

short 12th. 'When I was making that hole,' he once told me, 'local contractors vowed they weren't going to touch the ground because Mass was once celebrated in the hollow. And we never touched it.' Aware of Waterville's exposure to the wind, Hackett also made the unorthodox decision of containing the sand through the use of peat dust from the local bogs instead of soil. But he didn't have this problem at the 12th. 'Its plateau green is so natural that it doesn't need bunkers,' he said. 'That's the best tribute you can pay a hole.'

Known as the 'Mass Hole', it demands anything from a long iron to a driver, depending on the wind. And it characterises the essence of a course described by Hackett as 'a beautiful monster', a monster that he lovingly designed in close collaboration with its Irish-American owner, John A Mulcahy.

Hole 13 (471-yard par four)
Druids Glen, County Wicklow

It's quite simple, really. When defending champion Sam Torrance came to Druids Glen in 1996 to promote the Murphy's Irish Open, he stood on the tee in town shoes, hit a perfectly placed drive down into the valley and went on to land a four-iron approach on the green for a simple, two-putt par. But strange things tend to happen there in competition. Like in the 1999 Irish Open when, after carefully taking a five iron off the tee, John Daly ran up a double-bogey there in the second round. And it cost him a triple-bogey seven as he struggled to a miserable 81 the following day. Those sort of experiences explain why the hole is known locally as 'The Snake'. Though Sergio Garcia birdied it *en route* to the title, it has a penchant for inflicting considerable pain, even when treated with caution. Pat Ruddy, co-designer of the

Waterville, County Kerry— its plateau green is so natural that it doesn't need bunkers

course with the late Tom Craddock, likes to recall how the owner, Hugo Flinn, placed no financial limit on the project. Which gave them *carte blance* to blast the spectacular 13th out of solid rock. Even the professionals would concede, albeit reluctantly, that the effort was well worth the trouble.

Hole 14 (205-yard par three)
Royal Portrush, County Antrim

Though Royal Portrush is generally noted as a great second-shot course, this one-shotter merits special attention. It is called 'Calamity', with good reason. A very precise long-iron or fairway-wood shot must be hit along a ridge, with a sheer drop

Druids Glen, County Wicklow—where the 13th hole is known locally as 'The Snake'

down to the Valley course on the right. It is a hole where several of the leading competitors during the staging of the British Open in 1951 opted to miss the green on the left and then take the chance of a pitch-and-putt par. A slightly pushed or sliced tee-shot could leave the player with an uphill recovery from at least 50 feet below the green. Though Royal Portrush has been in existence since 1888, the famous Dunluce course is largely the creation of the eminent English architect, Harry Colt. After much wrangling over money, it was eventually completed in 1932, and Colt was

so pleased with the outcome that he promptly declared it his masterpiece. His view was endorsed by long-time friend, Bernard Darwin, who, during the 1951 Open, described it as 'truly magnificent' in his piece in *The Times*. Indeed he went so far as to suggest that Colt had built himself 'a monument more enduring than brass'.

HOLE 15 (466-YARD PAR FOUR)
MOUNT WOLSELEY, COUNTY CARLOW

The town of Tullow provides a charming backdrop to the delightful parkland stretch of Mount Wolseley, which represents some of the finest design work by Christy O'Connor Jnr. And for the competitor on the 15th tee, the church spire offers

Mount Wolseley, County Carlow—a delightful parkland stretch

Royal Portrush, County Antrim—architect Harry Colt declared it his masterpiece in 1932

a perfect line for a well-placed drive. Back in 1913, an advertisement in *The Irish Times* claimed that Wolseley cars 'always embody refinement and reliability'.

Now a permanent link has been forged between the Royal and ancient game and one of motoring's most famous marques. In 1994, Carlow businessman Donal Morrissey paid £600,000 for the ancestral home of the aristocratic Wolseley family of Staffordshire, who took up residence there in 1725. And it was where Frederick York Wolseley, founder of the British car manufacturing company that bore his name, first saw the light. Though water is in play on seven holes, sufficient problems are provided on the 15th by its formidable yardage and the trees flanking the fairway on

the right. And one wonders whether these might have been some of the trees that an eccentric older Wolseley, Garnet, arranged by way of replicating the troop formations at the Battle of Waterloo.

HOLE 16 (270-YARD PAR 4)
ROYAL DUBLIN, COUNTY DUBLIN

In the final round of the 1966 Carrolls International at Royal Dublin, Christy O'Connor Snr was 11 under par standing on the 16th tee. It meant he was three strokes adrift of Ryder Cup colleague Eric Brown, who was about to take the clubhouse lead on 14 under. Over his home course, O'Connor's response was electrifying. From 15 feet above the hole with his tee-shot at the 16th, O'Connor sank the treacherous putt for

an eagle two. And in one of the great finishes of tournament golf, he proceeded to birdie the 17th before carding another eagle on the 18th for a two-stroke victory.

The excitement generated by these exploits, served to emphasise the merit of having what could be termed a par-three-and-a-half among the closing holes of a championship course. Royal Dublin's version bears comparison with the best. Depending on the wind, it can be reached with a long iron. Indeed, Seve Ballesteros had the audacity in practice to hit a driver onto the green while on his knees. Its strength, however, lies in the difficulty of a severely undulating green and cavernous bunkers awaiting the shot that's not hit on the button.

Royal Dublin, County Dublin—a severely undulating green and cavernous bunkers await the shot that's not hit on the button

Rosses Point, County Sligo—a classic creation by Harry Colt, who designed the links in 1927

HOLE 17 (455-YARD PAR 4)
ROSSES POINT, COUNTY SLIGO

On a mild July evening in 1989, Tom Watson and his friend Byron Nelson made an unheralded visit to Rosses Point for a friendly round on the famous County Sligo links. As it happened, Watson shot a creditable, one-over-par 72, while his venerable partner was content to savour the splendour of the surroundings. Later, Watson spoke admiringly of 'a magnificent links', making particular mention of the closing stretch of holes, dominated by the majestic 17th. Here, the player is generally thinking par, as a long-iron or fairway-wood second-shot is aimed upwards towards the green cut into the side of a hill. Back in 1979, Shandon Park international David Long sank an eight-foot birdie putt there in an epic final to the West of Ireland Championship. It brought him square with Arthur Pierse and led ultimately to a record eight holes of sudden death, culminating in victory for Long. The hole is a classic creation by Harry Colt, who designed the links in 1927 for a fee of 40 guineas, plus expenses. Interestingly, the club minutes inform us that 'due to difficulties envisaged in the construction of the 17th, it was decided to employ three extra men to augment the greens' staff'.

HOLE 18 (544-YARD PAR 5)
ADARE MANOR HOTEL GOLF CLUB,
COUNTY LIMERICK

Journey's end. And there could hardly be a more exhilarating conclusion than a par-five designed by the venerable American, Robert Trent Jones, master of the risk-and-reward concept in golf course architecture. Those familiar with his splendid work elsewhere in Europe, will see a strong resemblance between this and the long 12th at Las Brisas, which is arguably the best course on Spain's Costa del Sol. Both holes combine the crucial ingredients of water, trees and design expertise. At Adare Manor, the 18th has two isolated trees standing sentinel on the right side of the fairway, 340 yards out from the back tee. Depending on wind direction and the purity of the strike, the green is reachable in two from a long-iron or fairway-wood shot, hit diagonally across the River Maigue to a wide but shallow target. But even if the desired length is achieved, tall evergreens guarding the left side of the green wait to punish the hook. In all, it provides a fitting finale to a development where New Jersey financier Tom Kane invested $15 million in what was formerly the family estate of the Earl of Dunraven.

Adare Manor Hotel Golf Club, County Limerick—combines the crucial ingredients of water, trees and design expertise

A B C D

BYRNE

CLINTON

AHERN

DALEY

K L M N

LE BROCQUY

KELLY

NEESON

S T U V

SULLIVAN

U2

Heaney

Ford

220

PROFILES

Quinn

OF

O'Malley

EXCELLENCE

Walsh

GERRY ADAMS

Some readers may feel rather uncomfortable, if not downright horrified, at the inclusion in this book of Gerry Adams. However, when even that most partisan of all British newspapers, *The Daily Telegraph*, refers to Adams as one of the most outstanding politicians of his generation, the reasons for his inclusion are clear. One of *The Daily Telegraph*'s most influential writers wrote: 'Adams doesn't think like other people. He just doesn't want to win. It's not good enough to get the Brits out and the six counties back and be a nation once again and to see the complete victory of the armed struggle against the occupying Imperialist power. Oh no. By no means. Every other protagonist has got to be crushed and humiliated. Words such as

relentless and ruthless do not begin to suffice. It's not very nice, but it's awesome'. Undoubtedly one of the most controversial figures on the Irish political scene, whatever your politics, Gerry Adams' place at the very epicentre of the ongoing search for enduring peace in the North of Ireland cannot be denied. Nor can it be denied that, under the leadership of this former West Belfast barman, Sinn Féin has been transformed from a hardline republican group, ostracised from mainstream politics—it wasn't long ago that Adams' very voice was considered so insidious that actors reported his words to RTÉ viewers—to a party that shares centre stage with the political leaders of the western world. Like all successful politicians, Adams is a polished performer in front of television cameras and master of the headline-

grabbing sound bite. Born in Belfast in 1948, Adams took the route followed by so many of his generation in Northern Ireland—civil rights campaigning, internment, political education in prison, activism in the nationalist movement—but, unlike so many of his peers, he has apparently forged a new way forward. As he says, 'The test for this generation of republicans is how we modernise our ideology to meet the needs and conditions of our time.' History will judge whether Adams has been successful.

BERTIE AHERN

Bertie Ahern, like the country he leads, has undergone a transformation over the past three years—whether the two are linked, of course, depends on your politics. Born in 1951 to staunch Fianna Fáil supporters, Ahern joined the party at the age of 17, trained as an accountant at night classes, and was first elected to the Dáil at the age of 25. His lack of sophistication and penchant for anoraks endeared him to his Dublin constituents and 'the man of the people' was elected Lord Mayor of Dublin in 1986. Spells as Minister for Labour (twice) and Minister for Finance (three times), earned him the tag of Taoiseach-in-waiting, until he was finally elected Taoiseach (the youngest in Ireland's history) in 1997. Since then, he has presided over a period of unprecedented economic success and has been instrumental in furthering the quest for peace in the North of Ireland. He has also broken new ground in his personal life. Ahern is the first Taoiseach to be legally separated from his wife, and his partner, Celia Larkin, accompanies him on official functions. But it has not been all smooth sailing. His predecessor and mentor Charles J. Haughey throws a long shadow, and allegations of past corruption have dogged Ahern's administrtion and at times almost scuppered his coalition with the Progressive Democrats. Haughey once described Ahern as 'the best, the most skillful, the most devious and the most cunning'—praise indeed from a man who could recognise those traits better then most. Yet Ahern's charisma and warmth continue to inspire affection among many Irish people. The rough edges have been some-

Gerry Adams

Kingsley Aikins

Bertie Ahern and Celia Larkin

what smoothed, but Ahern remains far from the manicured polish of his good friend Tony Blair; the anoraks have been swapped for double-breasted suits, but he still prefers a pint of Bass in his local pub to a black-tie affair at Government Buildings. Ahern may be an enigma, but he is clearly a gifted politician who will survive these turbulent times.

KINGSLEY AIKINS

Kingsley Aikins can proudly claim a positive impact on the Northern Ireland peace process. As executive director of The American Ireland Fund and chief executive of the Worldwide Ireland

Funds, he has been responsible for raising an annual $20 million from among 12 countries worldwide for as many as 300 Irish organizations. Some money has gone toward community development, education, and cultural programmes in Ireland, while a large percentage has been forwarded to victims, prisoners, and community groups in Northern Ireland. 'What we have done in Northern Ireland is little known and understood,' says Aikins. 'It has helped to keep a lid on the Troubles and create an environment in which the peace process has developed.' Aikins was born and raised in Dublin, Ireland, but after graduating from Trinity College Dublin, he worked in Spain and France, followed by a later move to London

and then Australia. In Australia he became the founding director of the Australian Ireland Fund and set up The Ireland Fund in New Zealand. The 48-year-old executive lives in Boston with his wife, Claire, and their two children. He says, 'The thing that has fascinated me most is seeing the greatest Irish Empire in the world. The reawakening of the Irish Diaspora is one of the most exciting things to be involved in.'

ELIZABETH FRAWLEY BAGLEY

When Elizabeth Frawley walked into the offices of Ted Kennedy in 1974, could she have known then that she was taking the first steps in a political career that thus far has spanned more than a quarter of a century? Perhaps she did. As Elizabeth herself admits: 'Politics is in my blood'. Her father was a family court judge in New York and the eight Frawley children could not help but be aware of the build-up to election day every four years. Although her family was staunchly Irish-American—Elizabeth's grandmother hails from County Clare—her work with Kennedy introduced her to the complexities of Irish politics and the tireless work of one man in particular: 'I respect John Hume enormously,' Elizabeth says. 'I don't think people realise how intensely he has devoted every fibre of his being to his job. I hope that in his lifetime he sees peace.' Elizabeth's interest in

Irish affairs has not waned, even as her political career has taken off—she assisted the special advisor to the Camp David Peace Accords under the Carter administration, worked on the Dukakis presidential campaign, was the foreign policy adviser on the Clinton presidential campaign, served as the first female American Ambassador to Portugal and is currently the senior adviser for media programming and democracy in the Balkans under Secretary of State Madeline Albright. Elizabeth and her husband and children carry Irish passports and she has been a member of the Board of Directors of the American-Ireland Fund since 1990 and is the Honorary Chair of the 2000 American Fund Gala. Where next for this sophisticated political operator? Well, there is that 'dream posting'—the ambassadorship to Ireland. Watch this space.

Matthew Barrett

John Banville

JOHN BANVILLE

Born in Wexford in 1945, John Banville is one of the most prolific and respected of all modern Irish writers. Described as the most European of Irish novelists, his writing nonetheless retains a distinct Irishness. His first collection of short stories, *Long Lankin*, was published in 1970 and his first novel, *Nightspawn*, followed in 1971. Over the intervening years, his impressive body of work has won many awards—the James Tait Black

Memorial Prize for *Doctor Copernicus* in 1976, the Guardian Fiction Prize for *Kepler* in 1981, and the Guinness Peat Aviation Award for *The Book of Evidence* in 1989. He received a Lannan Literary Award for *The Untouchable* in 1997, a novel loosely based on the Cambridge spy ring of the 1930s, but, despite worldwide critical acclaim for this astonishing feat of storytelling, *The Untouchable* failed to make the Booker Prize shortlist— an omission that could be explained, it has been suggested, by the novel being too close to British establishment sensibilities for comfort. The elusive Booker Prize has not proved too great a distraction. His career began in journalism (at *The Irish Press*) and despite his great literary

successes he remains a popular and busy journalist. The highly respected Literary Editor of *The Irish Times* from 1988 to 1999, John was appointed Chief Literary Critic and Associate Literary Editor in March last year. His latest novel, *Eclipse*, has been described as 'an intense, relentlessly argued near monologue'.

MATTHEW BARRETT

Flamboyance is not a quality typically associated with bankers, but Matthew Barrett may be the exception that proves the rule. The debonair 56-year-old Chief Executive of Barclays Bank has hit the headlines for reasons other than his financial acumen—divorce from his wife of 25 years, marriage to former cover girl Anne Marie Sten and public relations disasters at Barclays have tended to overshadow what has been a phenomenally successful career in international banking. Born in County Kerry and educated by the Christian Brothers in Kells, County Meath, Barrett's career began quite unspectacularly when he joined the London branch of the Bank of Montreal as a lowly bank teller. He was transferred to Montreal HQ in 1967 and there began a slow and steady climb up the corporate ladder, until he was appointed Chief Executive Officer and Chairman in 1990. In 1994 Barrett became an Officer of the Order of Canada, the country's highest civilian honour and the following year he was named Outstanding Chief Executive Officer of the Year. His record at Montreal was certainly impressive—he presided over nine years of record profits, pioneered Canada's first electronic banking operation in supermarkets, and promoted the role of women in the bank. But a failed merger with the Royal Bank of Canada and his very public marital problems won the battle for headlines. Barrett moved to Barclays and London in October 1999, pledging to double economic profits every four years and cut costs by £1 billion by the end of 2003. The headlines soon followed—the decision to close 171 branches of Barclays on the same day drew condemnation from politicians and the public, and revelations of an online security breach that allowed one customer to access details of another person's account on the Internet have all been embarrassing own goals. At time of going to press, Barclays Bank was negotiating a £5.3 billion takeover of the Woolwich mortgage bank that will see 100 branches shut and 1,000 jobs lost, a move that has prompted concern among financial analysts. Barrett was unperturbed by the approaching storm. 'Some in the City appear to be a wee bit spooked about what we regard as a good business,' he said dismissively. Despite the inevitable criticisms from certain sections of the British press, Barrett is generally regarded as a first-class operator and motivator, and the natural choice to run the newly enlarged Barclays Bank.

Slim Barrett

SLIM BARRETT

The Sunday Telegraph has hailed him as the 'king of coronets'. His designs have graced collections by Chanel, Versace, John Rocha, Galliano and McQueen; his admirers include Madonna, Cher, Naomi Campbell and the late Diana, Princess of Wales. And his tiaras adorned two of the most high-profile brides last year—Victoria Beckham (Posh Spice) and Ffion Hague (Political Spice). Galway-born Slim Barrett has been based in London since 1983, steadily building a devoted clientele and attracting attention from around the world. His work has been exhibited at the Museum of Modern Art in Japan and Le Centre Pompidou in Paris, and both The Victoria & Albert Museum

in London and the Ulster Museum in Belfast feature Slim's work in permanent collections. The high point thus far in his glittering career was reached this past January when he was awarded the De Beers Diamonds International Award for his cascade necklace, which incorporates 336 brilliant-cut diamonds set in 18-carat gold. 'This is like getting an Oscar,' Slim beamed.

ANTHONY BARTON

Ireland may not be renowned for its wine production prowess, but it could arguably claim some share of the success enjoyed by Anthony Barton, heir and manager of Chateaux Langoa and

Leoville Barton in Bordeaux. Born in Straffan, County Kildare, in 1930, educated in England at the famous public school, Stowe, and later at Cambridge, Anthony Barton took over the family label on the death of his uncle, Ronald. There have been Bartons in Bordeaux since Tom Barton emigrated from Ireland in 1722, and Bartons at Chateaux Langoa since Hugh Barton bought the castle and vineyard in 1821. The family has survived the French Revolution, the Napoleonic Wars, and the Nazi occupation, not to mention French inheritance laws. While other estates broke up around them—an unfortunate consequence of the French legal requirement that property must be divided equally among direct

descendants—the Bartons kept their Irish passports and took foreign wives. Today, Barton wines are sold all over the world, Chateux Langoa has been restored to its former glory, and Leoville Barton wines are served at State dinners around the world. Yet the connection with Ireland has endured—Barton's office is decorated with a set of original hunting scenes from County Meath, his family hold Irish passports and Anthony admits: 'We are more Irish than French.' He recently visited his old home at Straffan (now the site of the K Club) with his daughter, Lilian Barton Sartorius, and declared himself pleasantly surprised at how little the grounds had changed over the years.

MAEVE BINCHY

'Oprah Winfrey called me at home one evening at 8pm,' Maeve Binchy says. '"This is Oprah Winfrey," she said. "Who is it really?" I asked, not wanting to seem like an eejit. I assumed it was a friend playing a joke.' This anecdote captures perfectly the essence of Ireland's best loved and best-selling author. Born in Dalkey, County Dublin, where she still lives, Binchy was the eldest child of a lawyer and a nurse. Her upbringing was traditional and Catholic. 'The nuns told us the world was full of lust and it was waiting for us,' she says. 'Of course it wasn't.' After graduating from University College Dublin, Binchy worked for a time as a teacher, and then a holiday in Israel inspired her to work on a kibbutz. While there, Binchy wrote letters to her father every week describing life in a land on the brink of war. When her father sold one of her letters to *The Irish Times* for £18, Binchy thought that she had made it. In 1968 she was appointed women's editor at *The Irish Times*. She tried her hand at fiction and her first book *Light a Penny Candle* was published in 1983. It was an immediate success. 'I was lucky to be 43 when I became successful,' Binchy says. 'I was already happy then, married to a man I love, the writer Gordon Snell. I didn't want yachts or diamonds. To me success meant I didn't have to worry about the phone being cut off.' Books such as *Evening Class*, *The Lilac Bus*, *Firefly Summer* and *Circle of Friends* (which became a very successful film) and her appearance on Oprah Winfrey's Book Club to discuss *Tara Road* have ensured that such worries are a thing of the past. Indeed, a readers' poll earlier this year ranked Binchy the sixth most popular author in the UK, ahead of Joyce and Shakespeare. Now aged 60, Binchy has decided to take things a little slower. Earlier this year she relinquished her regular newspaper column to concentrate on her new novel, *Scarlet Feather*, which was published recently. She is invariably modest about her success. 'I do not write poetry, I do not have a particular literary style, I am not experimental, nor have I explored a new form of literature. I tell a story that I want to share with my readers.' Many of her readers are women, drawn to stories that touch on the small tragedies and

Maeve Binchy

triumphs of daily life; some characters are strong, some are weak, like all of us. A reviewer once called Binchy 'a quiet feminist'. Binchy has kept the clipping, not because she values the political brownie points. 'I keep it,' Binchy laughs, 'because I was so pleased that anyone would call me quiet!'

James Bolger

JAMES BOLGER

Daniel and Cecilia Bolger left their home in County Wexford the day after they married, never to return. Their dream was for a better life amid the wide open spaces of New Zealand and with a great deal of hard work along the way, their dreams came true. Their son James Brendan was born in 1935, elected Prime Minister of New Zealand in 1990, and is acknowledged today as one of the great statesmen of his generation. James Bolger worked on his parents' 94-acre farm from a young age, and recalls rising at 4am to milk the cows and the sheer hard work of farm life. But love of the land was in his blood, and beef and sheep farming seemed like a good life for a young man. However, Bolger soon became embroiled in community affairs and farming organisations. 'I had a point of view I was willing to express', he recalls, with a hint of a smile. Elected to parliament in 1972, Bolger's rise to prominence was rapid—New Zealand's first Minister of Fisheries in 1977,

John Bowman

Minister of Labour and Immigration in 1978, President of the International Labour Organisation in 1983, Leader of the National Party in 1986, and Prime Minister in 1990. Under his seven-year-leadership New Zealand pursued an outward-looking foreign policy, and James is quick to credit his parents: 'Being the son of parents from the other side of the world certainly influenced me. They brought their values from Ireland and encouraged me to look outside New Zealand.' On his retirement as Prime Minister in 1997, James was appointed a member of the Order of New Zealand, the country's highest honour awarded to only 20 individuals living at any time in recognition of outstanding service to the people

of New Zealand. In 1998, James was appointed his country's Ambassador to the USA and lives in Washington, DC, with his wife Joan and two of their nine children.

JOHN BOWMAN

At a time when political platitudes seem the order of the day and spin doctors wield their ever-increasing power over the media, Ireland is indeed fortunate to count John Bowman among its leading political journalists and broadcasters. As chair of *Questions and Answers*, arguably Ireland's most important current affairs programme, Bowman directs questions from the audience to

Lara Flynn Boyle

the politicians and commentators that comprise the panel on any given programme. Woe betide any panel member who seeks to evade a difficult question. Bowman combines a sharp intellect and controlled manner with fastidious attention to detail—few broadcasters enter a studio better prepared than Bowman, and politicians know it. But Bowman is evenhanded—if he believes in giving politicians a hard time, he also resents 'the way some broadcasters, with very little interest in politics only highlight the scandals and encourage cynicism'. Born in Dublin and educated at Trinity College, Bowman has been involved with Irish current affairs programmes on radio and television for more than 30 years and has anchored RTÉ's coverage of general elections more times than he cares to remember. The sudden and tragic death this year of his son Jonathan, a popular journalist himself, was a devastating blow for the closely-knit Bowman family and the sympathy and support that followed from colleagues and members of the public alike is some indication of the respect and esteem in which John Bowman is held.

LARA FLYNN BOYLE

The day after she graduated from high school Lara Flynn Boyle left her native Chicago and moved to LA, determined to make it as an actress. Only four months later, she landed her breakthrough role, playing vixen Donna Hayward in the critically acclaimed television series *Twin Peaks*. Fame (and famous boyfriends) came fast and now, at only 30, Boyle is the star of the hit series *The Practice*. She remains admirably level-headed amid the starstruck environment of Hollywood, due in no small part to a staunchly Irish-American upbringing (her ancestors hail from Cork and Mayo). 'Being Irish was a big thing for me, particularly growing up in Chicago,' she says. 'In Chicago there are North Side Irish and South Side Irish. We were North Side Irish and proud of it'. She clearly remembers Irish dance lessons, St. Patrick's Day parades, and colourful stories from her grandfather—'all of the Irish stereotypes were alive and well within my family,' she laughs. In 1997 Boyle auditioned unsuccessfully for the lead role in the television show

James Brady

Ally McBeal, but David E. Kelley, who produces both shows, was so impressed by Boyle that a few months after her audition he decided to write her into *The Practice*, a drama centered around a small law firm in Boston. 'I was supposed to do this role,' Boyle says, 'And I will do it for as long as they'll have me.'

JAMES BRADY

His life story reads like the screenplay for a classic Jimmy Cagney film. Born in Brooklyn, New York, in 1928, the son of second generation Irish Americans (his maternal grandmother was a Kennedy from Castlebar in County Mayo) James

Brady worked as a copy boy for *The New York Daily News*, before joining the Marines to fight in the Korean War. On his return to the US, he turned his hand to journalism and covered the US Senate for three years. Tiring of the political rat race, he wrangled a foreign correspondent's gig and moved to Europe, where he says he 'learned about fashion at the knee of Coco Chanel'. After seven years as publisher of *Women's Wear Daily*—during which time he helped to create *W*, arguably the greatest fashion magazine in the world—Brady joined Hearst as publisher and editor of *Harper's Bazaar*, but was unceremoniously fired for trying to modernise too quickly that elegant old monthly. Rupert Murdoch knew a good thing when he saw

Jane Bradbury

it and Brady was soon editor of the supermarket tabloid, *Star*, and then editor of *New York* magazine. Now 72, Brady shows no inclination to slow down. He writes weekly columns for *Advertising Age* and *Parade* magazine and has carved out quite a reputation for his celebrity TV interviews. His latest book, *The Marines of Autumn*, was published earlier this year and acclaimed as the Iliad of the Korean War. What does this Boy's Own hero do to relax? He leaves his home in New York for his retreat in the Hamptons, where he says, 'I ski, fish and regularly capsize my canoe'. Naturally.

JANE BRADBURY

The life of this baker's daughter from County Kildare changed forever when she won a Ford Model competition in Dublin. Today 25-year-old Jane Bradbury is an internationally successful model, in demand by designers such as Dior, Gucci, Donna Karan, and Armani. She has graced the pages of *Vogue*, *Marie Claire* and *Elle*, and last year she was chosen as the face and spirit to relaunch *Allure* magazine. Bradbury made her European acting debut in Roman Polanski's *Ninth Date* and has just won her first starring role in *My Achilles Heart*, co-starring Paul Rudd. Bradbury credits her constant travelling with opening her eyes to some of the injustices in the world. She works with Children with Aids and the Sony Foundation for Autistic Children, but after a recent shoot in India, Bradbury hit on the idea of asking models to donate photographs taken on their travels for an auction to raise money for children in India. In Bradbury's case, beauty is not skin deep.

KENNETH BRANAGH

Although he is now 40 years old, Belfast-born Kenneth Branagh has never quite managed to shrug off the precocious luvvie tag that has dogged him since he first joined the Royal Shakespeare Company at the age of 23. While at the RSC he took starring roles in *Henry V* and *Romeo and Juliet*, but found the company too impersonal and decided to form the Renaissance Theatre Company, which now counts Prince Charles as one of its royal patrons. 'My definition of success is control,' Branagh says, which goes some way towards understanding why he often assumes multiple responsibilities on his projects—at only 29, he directed, adapted, and starred in the film version of *Henry V*; he directed, produced and took two lead roles in *Dead Again* in 1991; directed, produced and starred in *Peter's Friends* the following year, and surpassed himself this year by writing the screenplay, directing, producing and starring in *Love's Labour's Lost*! His driving force is to bring Shakespeare to the masses and he has been successful—his hit adaptation of *Much Ado About Nothing*, which featured an all-star cast that included Denzel Washington and Keanu Reeves, and his musical rendering of *Love's Labour's Lost* have certainly brought a new edge to the words of the Bard. There have been more mainstream acting successes such as *The Gingerbread Man*, *Celebrity*, and *Wild Wild West* and four Oscar nominations. His marriage to Emma Thompson broke up in 1995 and he is has an on-again-off-again relationship with Helena Bonham Carter. Spectacularly talented and driven, Branagh has been compared to Laurence Olivier and, like him, will no doubt remain a force to be reckoned with in theatre and film for many years to come.

Maura C. Breen

MAURA C. BREEN

As a child growing up on a predominately Irish street in Bridgeport, Connecticut, ('there were five other girls named Maura,' she laughs) Maura C. Breen thought of following in the footsteps of her father Hugh, who served as mayor of the town for five years before being appointed a State Superior Court Judge. Breen studied government and economics at Skidmore College in Saratoga Springs, New York, and even spent a summer working in Senator Chris Dodd's Washington office. But she chose a different path and today, as President and CEO of Bell Atlantic Communications, Inc., she is happy with her choice and is a role model for female executives in the US—in 1999 Breen was appointed to the Academy of Women Achievers by the YWCA of New York. Breen is responsible for leading the business unit that markets and sells the Bell Atlantic's long distance services to consumers as regulatory approvals are received. As Bell Atlantic merges with GTE this year, to create a combined company known as Verizon, Breen's role will expand. 'It's a challenge integrating two companies and growing our business across the country, but it's one I'm looking forward to,' she says. After graduation, Breen worked with the American Red Cross before joining a management programme with New England Telephone in 1978. Her rise through the telephone business was rapid and she credits her father's influence and her Irish heritage with helping her advance through the senior management ranks. 'I saw how my father treated people, his leadership skills, how people viewed him. He was able to handle criticism very gracefully and deal with all kinds of people. But the Irish and people of Irish heritage are usually friendly and down to earth. We don't tend to put on airs and we're very comfortable with ourselves and new situations'. Breen lives in Fairfield, Connecticut, with her husband, Jay, and their son, Ryan.

Patricia Breen

PATRICIA BREEN

Although Patricia Breen was born in New York, her father, John McCloskey, was adamant that she would have a good Irish Catholic education. So, when she was 13 years old, McCloskey took his daughter home to Ireland and entrusted her to the care of the nuns at the Sacred Heart Convent on Leeson Street, Dublin, and then to the University College Dublin. Breen eventually returned to the US and married Daniel Breen, a former Wall Street financier and President of the Fayez Sorafin Investment Company in Houston, Texas, who set up Breen Financial, an investment company for multinational pension funds. Today, Breen is regarded as one of the leading hostesses in the US and has been ranked one of the most stylish women in America by *America's Elite 1000*. The Breens entertain frequently at their elegant homes in Houston (regarded by *The New York Times* as one of the most fashionable cities in the US), East Hampton and Lyford Cay. However, Breen is unusual among the higher echelons of society hostesses—she raised six sons, Daniel, John, Thomas, Brian, Patrick and Michael, and she is proud of it. 'Raising my boys was my career,' she says. Her boys may be raised, but this energetic woman has no intention of slowing down—she serves on the boards of the Houston Ballet Company and the University of Texas Health Science Center, and is an active member of the Textile and Costume Institute. Breen is also the Executive Vice-President of

Pierce Brosnan

Garech Browne

The New York Post and *Newsday*. In 1986 he was awarded the Pulitzer Prize and the George K. Polk Award for newspaper commentary. Along the way, he has written numerous best-selling novels and appeared in several feature films. His family may have left Donegal for America in the late 1800s, but Breslin is clear about what his Irish ancestry means to him: 'It means maybe we get lucky once in a while and pull together a couple of phrases out of the mist that turn out well, despite our thirst, pomposity, and procrastination.'

PIERCE BROSNAN

'I left a Navan boy and came back a Navan man,' and with a broad smile, Pierce Brosnan accepted the Freedom of Navan and the adoration of the people in the small County Meath town where he had been born. Hollywood stars are thin on the ground in Navan, so the return of this prodigal son was an event not to be missed. Brosnan lived in the town until, aged 11, he rejoined his mother who had moved to England in search of work to support her children. Plunged into a tough London comprehensive school, Brosnan admits that he 'spent a long time trying not to be Irish' to overcome the stigma of being the only Irish kid in the class. Who could have foreseen that 'the Irish kid' would one day portray that most English of English gentlemen, James Bond. The road to superstardom was not an easy one. After several years hard graft in English theatre, Brosnan made the move to Hollywood, but real success eluded him until he donned the dinner jacket and knowing smile of Ian Fleming's James Bond. The world was shaken and stirred, and Brosnan was critically acclaimed as the best Bond since Sean Connery—which begs the question, are Celts only equipped to portray this archetypal English spy? There has been heartbreak along the way. His wife Cassandra was diagnosed with ovarian cancer and died in 1991, one day after the couple's eleventh wedding anniversary. Brosnan has been disarmingly candid about the devastating effect of her death on him and their three children: 'They lost their mother,' he says. 'And they will feel that loss forever. Losing Cassandra affected me profoundly, in so many ways, forever.

the Board of Trustees of the Houston Opera—in Houston, there is no greater social kudos. Breen's legendary hostess skills were called upon by The Ireland Fund which was looking for someone to host a gala dinner in Houston in aid of the Fund. Breen hosted the party with Senator Lloyd Bentsen, who had just left the Clinton administration, and the fundraiser was acclaimed as a runaway success. Breen is a regular visitor to Dublin and declares herself in awe of the energy and talent of the young people she meets and fascinated by the changes that have taken place since she lived there as a young girl.

JIMMY BRESLIN

Describe, if you will, your picture of the archetypal hard-nosed Irish-American newspaper man and the chances are you will have described Jimmy Breslin. He pulls no punches, and New Yorkers love him for it. For more than 40 years his words have provided a unique window into the characters and events that can only be found in the Big Apple. Jimmy Breslin started his newspaper career at the tender age of 16 as a copy boy and later worked as a sportswriter for *The New York Journal-American* and *The New York Herald Tribune*, and as a columnist for

But you live on. I have a life to live and children to bring up, and I wish it hadn't happened, but it did.' Success as Bond has enabled Brosnan to establish his own film production company, Irish Dream Time, which he hopes will 'spawn the careers of some wonderful actors and directors and a body of films to be really proud of'. And Brosnan has at last found happiness in his personal life, with television reporter Keely Shaye Smith and their son Dylan. Their wedding plans were postponed when Brosnan's son was involved in a motor accident earlier this year, but hopes of an Irish wedding later this year are still alive.

GARECH BROWNE

In 1965, Erskine Childers, then a minister in the Irish government and subsequently President of Ireland, asked Garech Browne, co-founder of Claddagh Records: 'Why are you making gramophone records of squealing pipes and old women wailing by the hearthside when it's an image of a modern Ireland we wish to present to the world?' It's a indication of how far we have come that Irish traditional music co-exists quite easily alongside U2, e-commerce and *Riverdance* as enduring images of modern Ireland. But it was not always so. And we must thank The Hon. Garech Browne for his tireless campaign to reawaken popular

interest in traditional music. Browne was born in 1939 into a life of privilege—the Brownes are one of the original Tribes of Galway, his father, now 99 years old, is the 4th Lord Oranmore and Browne and the longest ever sitting member in the history of the House of Lords at Westminster, and his mother was Oonagh Guinness of the famous brewery dynasty. Browne exhibited a wayward streak at a very young age—at 14, he ran away from Le Rosey School in Switzerland, calmly booking a seat on the next plane home and at 15, he left school for good. While living in India, he converted to Hinduism and when he eventually married at the age of 42, he chose a Rajput princess from Kathiawar. Browne recalls that after leaving school, 'My great friend Jimmy O'Dea always worried I would not find a direction in life.' That all changed around a kitchen table in 1958 when Browne and his friend Ivor Browne decided to produce an LP of Irish uilleann piping when all of the established record companies refused to risk such an uncommercial undertaking. In 1959, *Rí na bPíobairí* (The King of the Pipers) was released and with it the new wave in traditional music. The works of Beckett, Heaney and Kavanagh were recorded on its Spoken Word list and in 1963 the first of many albums from The Chieftains was released. Browne is delighted with the brave new Ireland of the 21st century. 'It has allowed many Irish people to think about themselves and who and what they are and it has created an awareness of the world—we read our poets, admire our painters, and listen to traditional and other forms of music and we have the courage to honour Daw Aung San Suu Kyi and support the Dali Lama'. Browne is busy as ever— he is preparing for the release of John Montague's epic poem, *The Rough Field*, restoring his mother's favourite home, Luggala Lodge in the heart of County Wicklow, arguing—as Sean O'Casey did before him—that the original flag of Ireland (the Irish harp on a a background of St. Patrick's blue) should be reinstated in place of the Tricolour, and continuing to hope for 'a happy and united Ireland with the Irish language restored to its rightful place'. And, of course, he is enjoying what he likes most—a glass or two of champagne and good conversation.

Ed Burns

Gabriel Byrne

ED BURNS

Ed Burns exploded on to the film scene in 1995 with his debut effort, *The Brothers McMullen*. The tale of three Irish-American brothers and their romantic tribulations in New York enjoyed phenomenal success, grossing nearly $15 million, far above its relatively meagre five-figure budget, and capturing the Grand Jury Prize at the Sundance Film Festival. Quite a success for the Long Island, New York native who had worked previously as a production assistant on *Entertainment Tonight*. Burns' next moves were to direct and star in two bigger-budget films, *She's the One*, with Jennifer Aniston and Cameron Diaz in 1997, and *No Looking Back*, with Lauren Holly and Jon Bon Jovi in 1998. Burns focused solely on acting with a starring role in Steven Spielberg's 1998 blockbuster, *Saving Private Ryan*, filmed partly in County Wexford, Ireland. The 32-year old Burns, whose ancestors hail from Westmeath, is reportedly developing a television sitcom tentatively called *The Fighting Fitzgeralds*. As he explained, 'A lot of the stuff I've written really makes sense as television, because it's intimate and deals with people dealing with people. I don't have time for the idea that making television is a step down from making movies. It's all just creation to me.'

JEAN BUTLER

From the moment she swept across the stage in that now-famous Eurovision *Riverdance* sequence in 1994, Jean Butler has been revered as the woman who brought beauty, sex appeal and street cred back to Irish dancing. That an entire Irish dance industry has sprung up in the wake of *Riverdance* is due in no small part to Butler. Born in New York, she was enrolled in Irish dancing classes at the age of four by a mother desperate to sustain links with her homeland, and she has been dancing ever since. She left *Riverdance* in 1996, appeared in the prisoner of war film *The Brylcreem Boys* (director Terence Ryan reportedly hailed her as 'an absolute natural on screen'), and launched her new show, *Dancing on Dangerous Ground* in London and New York this year. Developed and choreographed by Butler and her partner Colin Dunne, the show met with poor reviews and

bankruptcy was eventually declared, but this is bound to be only a temporary setback for this talented and determined woman.

GABRIEL BYRNE

Over the past decade, Gabriel Byrne has made quite a place for himself in Hollywood. He first appeared in the 1990 gangster film *Miller's Crossing*, and then in *A Dangerous Woman* and *Cool World*. He also appeared in *Enemy of the State*, *Stigmata*, and his latest film with Arnold Schwarzenegger, *End of Days*. All in all, he has

been in more than 50 movies. But according to Hollywood standards, Byrne was a late-bloomer. As a Dublin youngster, he briefly considered becoming a priest, and even attended seminary school at age 12, but then turned to teaching in his early twenties. At the unlikely age of 29, Byrne gave up academia for a full-time career in acting, and soon joined the Project, a theatrical group of talented unknowns that included Liam Neeson and Neil Jordan. Within three years, the handsome actor set off to London to make his motion-picture debut in *Excalibur*, and after a successful nine years he arrived in Hollywood. Aside from

Jean Butler

Patrick Byrne

Mariah Carey

his family's history in County Cork, and cycled three times across the USA. And then there is his business life. Byrne has served as Chairman, President and CEO of both Centricut (a manufacturer and distributor of industrial torch parts) and Fechheimer Brothers (a manufacturer and distributor of uniforms), and he has recently bought Overstock.com (which buys overproductions of consumer goods and sells them online at huge discounts). Cancer struck first in 1985 and has recurred twice, but 20 operations and 12 years' remission later, Byrne is bullish about the future – he predicts Overstock.com 'will make more money in the next five years than Amazon' and as for Byrne himself? He would like to lead the life of a country squire in some remote corner of a green country. Watch out, County Cork, the Byrnes could be coming back!

acting, Byrne has produced several films, including Oscar-nominated *In the Name of the Father*, and now heads up his own production company, Plurabelle Films. To add to that, he published his early personal memoirs, *Pictures in My Head*, in 1994. Now 50, Byrne lives in Los Angeles, and visits his two children by his ex-wife Ellen Barkin in New York. He returned to the theatre this year to perform Eugene O'Neill's *Moon for the Misbegotten*. A new prime time TV show, *Madigan Men*, is due for release later this year, adding yet another string to the bow of this great Irish actor.

PATRICK BYRNE

'If you tell a man he is to be hung in the morning, it tends to focus his mind tremendously'. Patrick Byrne quotes Samuel Johnson when asked how his bout with cancer affected his outlook on life. However, in truth, Byrne has never had a problem with focusing his mind. Still only 38, he studied moral philosophy at Cambridge as a Marshal fellow, received a PhD in philosophy from Stanford, speaks five languages (including Mandarin), holds black belts in hapkido and tae kwon do, pursued a brief career as a professional boxer, researched

 MARIAH CAREY

'Diva' doesn't mean what it used to—songstresses from the past must surely be turning in their graves as teenage pop stars lay claim to the title. But their wrath must be abated by Mariah Carey, a true diva of the old school. As Carey says: 'There's never been anything else in my life that inspired me. I can't remember a time when I didn't want to be a singer.' Born in Long Island, New York, in 1970, Mariah Carey is arguably the most successful female singing star in the world today, achieving more number one hits than anyone since the Beatles. It hasn't been a smooth journey. Her parents' marriage (her mother is Irish-American, her father American/Venezuelan) was over by the time she was three years old. Then began years of financial troubles as her opera singer mother, Patricia, raised Mariah and her brother and sister against the odds, not least of which was racial prejudice. Mariah recalls: 'Coming from a racially mixed background, I always felt like I didn't really fit in anywhere. I always felt like the rug could be pulled out from under me at anytime. Singing made me feel special.' Teenage bands, amateur demos, odd jobs and backing singer gigs led up to the life-changing moment when record company boss Tommy Mottola heard one of Mariah's tapes. And the rest is history—marriage to Mottola in 1993, platinum albums, Grammy awards, and sell-out tours until the fairy tale unravelled a little when Mariah and Mottola separated in 1997. The last few years haven't been easy—divorce, law suits, interminable tabloid speculation and accusations of prima donna behaviour may have taken their toll, but her close relationship with her mother and her sense of humour (traces of her Irish ancestry perhaps) have seen her through: 'Even when I'm in a moment of intense despair I'll think of some joke and I'll laugh', she explains. The new millennium is looking good for this diva.

Mary Higgins Clark

DARREN CLARKE

This hasn't been a bad year for Darren Clarke. Victory at the Andersen Consulting Matchplay in February (made all the sweeter by his defeat of Tiger Woods and the $1 million purse) was followed in June by a win at the English Open, prompting commentators to report that he is 'elevating his game to an altogether higher level'. The 32-year-old golfer from Dungannon in Northern Ireland turned professional in 1990 and achieved a breakthrough win at the Belgian Open in 1993, when he beat the then World Number One Nick Faldo. Since then Darren has been making sure and steady progress, winning five tournaments on the European Tour before the successes

of this year. He credits Butch Harmon, the coach he shares with Tiger Woods, with helping him scoop the English Open. The straight-talking coach may have called the 17st golfer a 'fat ****', but Darren isn't complaining: 'His advice did the trick, so he can call me whatever he wants in future if it always has that effect.' Despite the financial temptations of the US Tour, Darren has no plans to base himself Stateside. 'There is a lot more to professional golf than just making money. It's about where you want to live, and I want to be home with my family.' Home for Darren is Sunningdale in Northern Ireland, where he lives with his wife Heather and son Tyrone. The arrival of their second child is eagerly awaited in the autumn, rounding off what really hasn't been a bad year, all told, for Ireland's golfing hero.

MARY HIGGINS CLARK

The story of Mary Higgins Clark reads similar to that of her best-selling novels. As she says, 'I write about nice people whose lives are invaded'. Although today she is described as America's Queen of Suspense, with 22 bestsellers to her name, her life was anything but a fairy tale growing up. Clark was born and raised Irish Catholic in The Bronx, New York, and lost her father at age ten. Her husband died when she was 36 years old, leaving her to raise her five children. Nothing, however, stopped the Queen of Suspense from pursuing her dream as a writer. In addition to supporting her children writing radio scripts, she rose early in the morning to work on her books at the kitchen table. Clark had a pile of rejection slips from previous work she had submitted before her 1975 suspense novel, *Where are the Children?*, became a best-seller. Her success continues 25 years later, at 72, with her latest novel, *Before I Say Good-Bye*. In connection with this book, Clark most recently visited Ireland, the land from where her family emigrated. The inherited flavour of her immigrant father from County Roscommon, the stories about her grandparents—from County Mayo and Sligo—and the Irish characters that surrounded Clark's childhood permeate her writing. 'They spoke with such lyricism and directness,' says Clark. 'Their style has influenced the way I developed as a writer.' A regular diner at Jimmy Neary's pub and restaurant in New York City, Clark has weaved the establishment into a number of her novels, much to the delight of the owner and regular customers. Clark has been a strong influence on her daughter, Carol, who is also a best-selling writer of suspense novels. Clark has also remarried. As in her novels, there has been a happy ending.

BILL CLINTON

Not since Kennedy has a US President been regarded as the harbinger of dreams for so many Americans. When Bill Clinton swept into the Whitehouse in 1993, it seemed to signal a new order, a fresh start—the man from Hope, Arkansas, was young, smart, charismatic, trendy (well, he played saxophone), and he was passionate. Ironic then, if not tragic, that this very passion, when misdirected, would almost prove his undoing. The rumours of serial womanising that dogged his presidency culminated in the Starr investigation and Clinton's impeachment on charges of perjury and obstruction of justice. The frenzied media reports of his antics in the Oval Office will overshadow his achievements for some time to come. And there were achievements—not least of which was his part in the peace process in Northern Ireland. From the decision to grant a US visa to Sinn Féin leader Gerry Adams to the innumerable phone calls and words of encouragement to Northern Irish politicians on the eve of the Good Friday Agreement, Clinton will be remembered by many as a positive force for change in Ireland and as a warm and popular

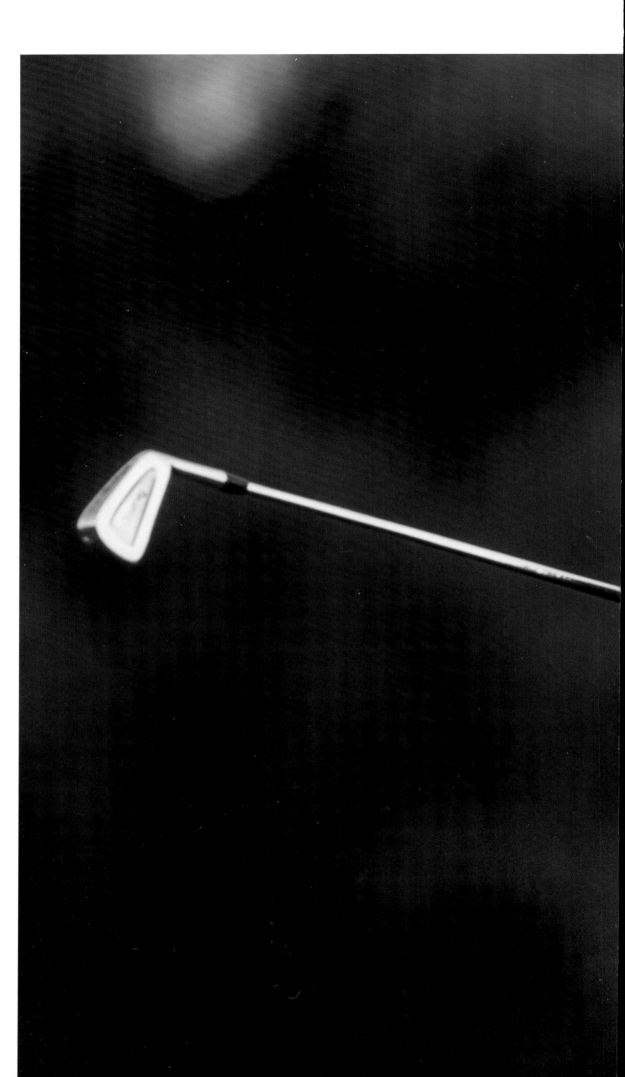

Darren Clarke

Irish American president (he traces his roots to County Fermanagh). The US has benefited, too, from his presidency—Clinton has presided over a near-unbroken run of prosperity and he has managed to balance the US budget for the first time in many years. Nor should we forget his influence on other political figures—the style of leadership adopted by British Prime Minister Tony Blair bears more than a passing resemblance to Clinton's. As he nears the end of his term in office, the spotlight has fallen on his wife, Hillary, as she campaigns for a seat in the U.S. Senate. His presidency did not—perhaps could not—deliver what it promised, but Clinton survived it.

MICHAEL COLGAN

The announcement earlier this year that the rights to film the entire Beckett canon have been awarded to Michael Colgan and Alan Moloney by the Beckett estate is another landmark in the extraordinary career of Michael Colgan. Born in Dublin in 1950, Colgan has been at the very heart of Irish theatre for the best part of 30 years. As artistic Director at The Gate since 1984, Colgan has spearheaded award-winning Gate productions around the world—Beckett's *I'll Go On*, O'Casey's *Juno and the Paycock*, Wilde's *Salomé*, and Friel's *Molly Sweeney* are just some of the award-winning productions that have delighted audiences around

the world. Colgan won the *Sunday Independent* Arts Award in 1985 and 1987 and a National Entertainment Award in 1996, and has been working on the Beckett project since 1991. With a budget of £4.5 million, directors of the calibre of Anthony Minghella, David Mamet and Neil Jordan, and big-name actors like Michael Gambon and Julianne Moore, this ambitious plan to bring all 19 stage plays written by Beckett to cinema and television screens is an extraordinary endeavour. But Colgan is confident. 'It sounds arrogant,' he says, 'but having known Beckett and having lived with his work, and unlike anybody else, having produced all of these plays at least once on stage, I think it would be better for me to do this than anyone else.' Married to the talented and beautiful actress Susan Fitzgerald, Colgan is a superb ambassador for contemporary Ireland.

DAVID COLLINS

'What gives me the edge over other designers is that I never repeat myself, I am never satisfied with what I've done and I have other interests apart from design'. And that, according to David Collins, architect and designer to the stars, is the secret of his success. Born in Dublin, Collins studied architecture and worked for a spell at an architectural practice in London, a period he dismisses as too boring to talk about. The break came in the mid-1980s when he was asked to do some residential design work for friends, one thing led to another and in 1985 David Collins Architecture and Design was born. His vision was brilliant in its simplicity—to create a one-stop design shop incorporating architects, interior designers, furniture designers and graphic designers. The hallmarks of Collins' style lie in his attention to detail, texture, lighting and colour—whether that be the edgy design and muted glamour of Marco Pierre White's Quo Vadis in Soho, the aluminium leaf wall paper (hand-painted in China) that line the walls of the private dining rooms at the Mirabelle, or the after austerity decor ('by that I mean the decorative edge to minimalism,' he explains) of the Montevetro building in London. 'I find boredom mentally exhausting' says Collins, 'and I am

Bill Clinton

David Collins

Eileen Collins

Michael Colgan

driven by fear of failure'. With plans to open an office in New York, restore the grandeur of the Russian Astoria Hotel in St. Petersburg and publish a book on new design in hotels—not to mention rumours of a songwriting contract—Collins may rest assured that neither boredom nor failure are likely to figure large for him in the foreseeable future.

EILEEN COLLINS

Eileen Collins has accumulated some historic frequent flyer miles. The Elmira, New York native became the first woman ever to command a Space Shuttle mission in July of 1999, when she and her crew led the Columbia on a 118-hour flight that featured the deployment of a telescope that enables scientists to study exotic phenomena such as exploding stars and black holes. The historic assignment wasn't the first venture into space for Collins. That came in 1995, when she became the first woman pilot of a Space Shuttle during the first flight of the Russian-American Space programme. She flew again in 1997, during a nine-day mission that included a rendezvous and dock with the Russian Space Station Mir. The 43-year old, who has spent over 530 hours in space during her three missions, can trace her Irish heritage back to Counties Clare and Cork. A graduate of Syracuse, Stanford and Weber Universities, Collins attained the rank of

Lieutenant Colonel while serving in the US Air Force. Collins was selected for the astronaut program while attending the Air Force Test Pilot School at Edwards AFB in California, from where she graduated in 1990. Today, she is one of three female pilots at NASA, and one of just 34 women among the 247 astronauts to fly on the Shuttle. Collins is married to Pat Youngs, a Delta Airlines pilot and they have a daughter, Bridget Marie.

SEAN CONLON

It would be an understatement to call him Chicago's most eligible bachelor. In fact, it would make Sean Conlon blush. Despite his meteoric rise in the hardnosed Chicago real estate market, this native of Kildare has a reticence for superlatives, especially the kind reserved for single, handsome millionaires. At just 30 years of age and only eight years since his arrival in the US, Conlon's commercial success might frighten someone lacking the genuine Irish self-effacement that keeps him grounded. One of Chicago's most successful real estate tycoons, Conlon is also its youngest and one of the new generation of Irish immigrants who come with the view that it is easier to own the building than to build it. After breaking all records for individual US sales for three years running, Conlon, with partners Tim O'Neil and Frank Parkinson, subsequently formed his own company, Sussex & Reilly (the maiden names of his mother and Parkinson's mother). In the fluid markets of Chicago real estate, they are the talk of the town. Conlon has brought his siblings to the US to share in what is fast becoming the city's most exciting commercial venture. One brother, a member of the Garda Síochána, and a school age sister, remain in Ireland. This former janitor turned 'uber salesman' got where he is the old fashioned way—hard work. Eighteen-hour days, he admits, wrecked his marriage and his health while making his fortune, at a time when most twenty-somethings are still busy sending out resumés. His personal ownership of prime real estate is daunting. His new four-storey baronial mansion in Chicago's Old Town neighbourhood is reminiscent of another era of Chicago commercial booms when young men like Marshall

Field and Potter Palmer became household names in the decades of Chicago rebirth following the Great Fire of 1871.

THE CORRS

They are almost too good to be true. Beautiful, charming, and talented, The Corrs have cornered the market in feel-good pop music with an Irish twist. Raised by musical parents on a diet of classical music, reels, and rock and roll, the four siblings from Dundalk first played together in public in 1990 when they auditioned for a part in Alan Parker's film, *The Commitments*. Although unsuccessful, Jim, Sharon, Caroline, and Andrea decided to take the show on the road and see what happened. What happened, of course, is that Jean Kennedy Smith, the US Ambassador to Ireland, attended one of their gigs, invited them to perform in Boston at the festivities for the 1994 soccer World Cup, where they charmed their way into the office of the vice-president of Atlantic Records and walked away with a record deal. Their first album, *Forgiven Not Forgotten*, sold two million copies and they eclipsed U2 by being the first Irish band to reach Number 1 and Number 2 simultaneously with two of their albums. Decried by some purists for their interpretation of traditional Irish music, The Corrs are defiant: 'Who knows what traditional music began like? Music is about expression. It's art. It has to grow.' In 1999 they scooped the award for Best Group at the Irish Music Awards in Dublin and were voted the Best International Group at the Brit Awards, the UK's equivalent of the Grammys, but the year ended on a sad note when their mother died suddenly. Their third album, *In Blue*, was released this summer and they have been asked to act as artists' spokespersons for the European music industry. The Corrs are the glamorous ambassadors of modern Irish music, marching in step with the Celtic Tiger. They can rock and they can reel, and we cannot get enough of them.

BRIAN CRONIN

New York has been good to Dublin-born graphic artist Brian Cronin. Discouraged by the lack of

The Corrs

Brian Cronin

opportunities for graphic artists in Ireland in the early 1980s, Cronin sent examples of his work to his mentor, the artist and designer Milton Glaser, and asked him whether he thought there would be any work for him in the US. Encouraged by Glaser's response, Cronin and his wife Siuin packed their bags and moved to New York in 1985. And they haven't looked back since. Born in 1958, Cronin studied at the National College of Art and Design in Dublin and says he chose graphic design over fine art because 'I was attracted to art that was accessible to everyone'. The polished, stylised forms in Cronin's work are reminiscent of Art Deco, but he is fascinated with adding flaws to the image, by using collage or emulating cheap colour printing processes. The effect is spectacular. And in demand. Cronin's work has appeared in *Time*, *Newsweek*, *Rolling Stone*, *Art and Antiques*, *The Washington Post*, *The Los Angeles Times*, *The Wall Street Journal*, *GQ*, *French Cosmopolitan*, *Le Monde*, and *Esquire*. Cronin has also won two gold medals at the Society of Publication Designers Annual Exhibition and admits to feeling 'very honoured' at being asked to exhibit his work at the Irish Museum of Modern Art. At present he is working on a series of paintings about memory and hopes to make an animated film. When asked about the inspiration behind his work, Cronin says: 'I'm inspired by honesty in work. Anything that comes from the heart inspires me to delve deeper and see

what I can find. And I will always have an Irish perspective, whether I am aware of it or not. An old New Yorker I met recently said to me, 'You're not Irish for nothing.' I'm not sure what that means, but it sounds about right.'

SEÁN CURRAN

Hailed as the Buster Keaton of modern dance, Seán Curran is astounding audiences around the world with his virtuoso performances and innovative choreography. Born in Boston, Curran is the only child of Irish parents—his mother is an accomplished fiddle player from Roscommon and his father is a proud Kerry man and host of the popular radio show, *The Sound of Erin*. Curran has been dancing since he was a child—his first dance class was in Irish step dancing at a community hall. He joined the Bill T. Jones/Arnie Zane Dance Company in 1984 and travelled the world for ten years as their principal dancer, winning a New York Dance and Performance Award for his performance in *Secret Pastures*. Curran left the company following the death of his mentor, Arnie Zane, to explore his own dance ideas. A three-year gig with the Off Broadway musical *Stomp* encouraged him to launch his own dance troupe, the Seán Curran Company. Since then critics have raved about the powerful emotion of Curran's dancing. His Irish identity is important to him. 'Part of my Irishness is a need and desire to tell stories and I think I am telling a story,' he says. 'Put a person on a stage and there's a story'.

ELEANOR 'SIS' DALEY

In 1969, when plans were afoot to tear down Chicago's central public library building on Michigan Avenue, a real urban treasure of architecture and design overlooking Grant Park, Eleanor 'Sis' Daley, wife of the then Mayor Richard J. Daley put her foot down. It was a rare use of the public prerogative of the consort. 'I told Dick that something had to be done,' she says simply. She led the charge that ultimately saved a rare landmark. Today, under the administration of her son, Mayor Richard M. Daley, this building, the largest mosaic building in the world

outside the Haggia Sophia in Istanbul, is busier than ever as the Chicago Cultural Center. Anytime plans surface to name the building in her honour, Eleanor Daley exercises an emphatic veto. 'Don't be ridiculous,' she says. Finding her name on a public building would be out of character for this youthful 94 year old, who still can be seen, surrounded by her devoted family, making not infrequent public appearances. As any Chicagoan knows, 'Sis' Daley's real legacy is her family. Their success in politics, law, or the number of fields in which they work brings deep pride to this mother of seven and grandmother of 18. Her grace, humour and Catholic faith are undaunted. The wife of Mayor Richard J. Daley for more than 40 years, 'Sis' continues to wow Chicagoans. She still waves to a crowd and receives a special Chicago respect no one else in town calls forth. The granddaughter of immigrants from Limerick and Tipperary, Eleanor Guilfoyle Daley is a Chicago treasure.

MAYOR RICHARD M. DALEY

When he laughs, there is no mistaking whose son he is—Mayor Richard M. Daley of Chicago is the son of legendary Major Richard J. Daley. As Mayor, Daley enjoys an unheralded popularity, having managed over his ten years in office of cementing old-fashioned Chicago politics with inclusive politics. In a city that to many invented the brash, big city machines of yesteryear, Daley has knitted together a more modern and vibrant style for his own reign. Its faces are as young as they are ethnically diverse and lifestyle accepting. Despite having a name that is virtually synonymous with Chicago politics, this Mayor Daley treads lightly on the memory of his father who ruled Chicago with an iron fist from 1955 until his death in 1976. Daley's frequent linguistic *faux pas* have an endearing, old neighbourhood quality to them. It gives him a impish character that appears far closer to his third generation County Waterford immigrant Irish roots than any member of his family. All Chicago knows that for Richard M. Daley, family comes first. Rare is the weekend in which public duties are permitted to interrupt a trip to the Daley family compound in Grand

Richard M. Daley

Beach, Michigan. But a look at the physical transformation of Chicago and its financial growth tells the real story of Daley's Mayoral success. In a city described as the most livable big city in the nation, Daley presides with a nod and a wink, and often the laughing echo of a treasured father whose legacy is not yet ended.

WILLIAM DALEY

There is hardly a more savvy or graceful minister of state in the Clinton government than Bill Daley. He was the skilled architect who secured passage of the NAFTA Treaty in the early days of the Clinton administration. His fancy footwork in three nations on behalf of the less than popular trade agreement brought confidence and understanding to its debate. This Daley, son of one Chicago Mayor and brother-confidante of another, sailed through the international mine fields with aplomb, managing to keep his dignity and his crisp well-tailored suits unwrinkled. He is a skillful diplomat, filled with tough charm, with none of the traditional phoniness that frequently abounds in such waters. He is a man's man, well liked, respected by Chicago colleagues and still in touch with his old neighborhood roots. Like his brother, he comes with a strong handshake, a memory for faces and names—a throwback to his Bridgeport neighborhood's Irish roots where people still take time for hellos and a chance to

William Daley

talk about the Chicago White Sox. As Secretary of Commerce Daley led President Clinton's most aggressive trade initiatives around the world. His frequent visits to China have given him exposure usually reserved for the Secretary of State. Daley's interest in the Irish peace initiative has taken him to Ireland on both sides of the border, exercising critical support for economic development in the North. His experience and drive make him a most trusted political ally for Democrats in Washington. In a surprise move, Daley took control of the Gore Presidential Campaign in July 2000, a move that many feel was an attempt by the Democrats to rescue Gore Presidential hopes. If Gore is successful, many Washington commentators

believe that Daley could be the next Whitehouse Chief of Staff.

BARBARA DAWSON

As Director of the Hugh Lane Municipal Gallery of Modern Art, Barbara Dawson is one of the most influential women in the Irish art world. Under her direction the gallery embarked on an ambitious programme of temporary exhibitions with a particular emphasis on contemporary art. Dawson's most recent coup was the acquisition of Dublin-born artist Francis Bacon's studio, which was transported from London to Dublin. A subsequent exhibition, Francis Bacon in Dublin, was acclaimed as being one of the most important exhibitions ever held in Ireland. Born in Carlow in 1957, Dawson is a graduate of University College Dublin and Trinity College Dublin, and launched her career in the art world as a research assistant at the National Gallery of Ireland. She joined the Hugh Lane Municipal Gallery in 1988 and was appointed director in 1991. Untiringly passionate about art, Dawson is the author of *Turner in the National Gallery of Ireland* and was responsible for the publication of *Images and Insights*, the first colour catalogue featuring selected masterpieces from the Hugh Lane collection. Dawson lives in the heart of Dublin with her husband, Paul, and their two children, and is regarded as a breath of fresh air in the rarefied climes of the art world.

DANIEL DAY-LEWIS

Daniel Day-Lewis is considered one of the greatest character actors of his time. He spent five months carrying a primitive flint rifle to prepare for his starring lead in 1992 film, *The Last of the Mohicans*, and for his role as John Proctor in the 1996 film, *The Crucible*, he spent several weeks planting fields with primitive 17th-century tools. During his Oscar-winning performance as the crippled Christy Brown in *My Left Foot*, Day-Lewis refused to actually walk on the set. And in his last film to date, *The Boxer*, he went so far as to study with Ireland's former heavyweight champion for two years, and then injured his back as a result of the film. With over a dozen films to his name, including *In the Name of the Father*, Day-Lewis is a hard act to follow. Because of his intense performances, Day-Lewis has taken several sabbaticals from his acting career—the last of which ended only recently. The 43-year-old actor is currently rehearsing for an upcoming Scorsese film, *Gangs of New York*. He plays an Irishman who challenges an early 19th century New York activist who tries to calm Irish and Italian gang violence with a gang of his own. His role of an Irishman is all too familiar to him. Although born and raised in London, Day-Lewis is proud of his Irish roots, which he traces through his father, Cecil, England's Poet Laureate from 1968 until his death. Now living for part of

the year in County Wicklow, the low-key actor has been strongly influenced by long summer holidays in the family home in County Mayo. His sister, the food writer and broadcaster Tamasin Day-Lewis writes fondly of their times there in her best selling book *West of Ireland Summers— Recipes and Memories from an Irish Childhood*. Day-Lewis is married to director and actress Rebecca Miller, the daughter of another writer, Arthur Miller. With two young children, one by Miller, the line of talent in the Day-Lewis family is bound to continue.

DERMOT DESMOND

Dashing Desmond, Whiz Kid, The Original Celtic Tiger, High Roller—can any man really merit such headlines? In the case of Dermot Desmond, the answer is a resounding yes. Born in Cork in 1950, this flamboyant and spectacularly successful financier has set the standard for budding Irish entrepreneurs. He joined the Dublin office of Citibank in the 1970s as a junior clerk and left as a credit analyst. A brief sojourn as a lending executive at the International Bank of Ireland was followed by a stint on a World Bank

Barbara Dawson

Daniel Day-Lewis

project in Afghanistan and, on his return to Dublin in 1981, he set up a moneybrokering firm, National City Brokers. Within four years, NCB controlled 40 percent of a market previously dominated by a handful of long established Dublin companies. The old boys' network that was Irish stockbroking at the time crumbled before him. He sold NCB to Ulster Bank in 1994 (Desmond's share was reportedly upwards of £10 million) and now describes himself as an 'eclectic investor'—his investments include Celtic Football Club, London City Airport and a string of Irish companies. However, it is his role in developing the International Financial Services Centre in Dublin that Desmond describes as 'the best thing I've been involved in'. The idea of an offshore financial services centre was dismissed by sceptics, but Desmond's argument won the support of the then Taoiseach Charles Haughey and provisions for the centre were laid down in the 1997 Finance Bill. Today, the IFSC is championed as a model for innovative thinking, creating thousands of jobs and massive revenue for the government. But it hasn't all been plain sailing—his bloodstock venture with Vincent O'Brien failed and, as the dubious activities of Charles Haughey continue to be revealed, all those who were involved in business with him, however innocent they be, cannot help but be a little tainted by association. Desmond will undoubtedly survive. Friends speak of his boundless enthusiasm, loyalty, innovation and, above all, love for all things Irish. He cites three essential elements for a happy life: 'something to do, someone to love, and something to hope for'. Desmond has his work to do, his family to love … and there's always that next deal.

CHRISTOPHER DODD

Senator Christopher Dodd can be counted among several American politicians who have kept a close eye on Northern Ireland's peace process. He travelled with President Clinton on his historic trip to Northern Ireland in 1995, commemorating the first period of peace in a generation, and played a part in two other official trips promoting trade in 1994 and 1996. Dodd also voted

Dermot Desmond

for a $50 million contribution for Ireland to help implement the Anglo-Irish Agreement of November 1985, and worked with British and Irish parties to secure a restoration of the 1994 IRA ceasefire and the holding of serious party talks. It should come as no surprise, therefore, that when the IRA pledged to reveal its secretly stored weapons to international arms inspectors in early May, thus paving the way for restoring the local government in Northern Ireland, Dodd was elated. 'Spring is a time for new beginnings and clearly this breakthrough is a positive step forward,' he said. Raised in Willimantic, Connecticut, Dodd followed the political footsteps of his father, the late Thomas Dodd, who had served as a

two-term US senator. The younger Dodd won his first Senate seat in 1974—only 36 years old, he became the youngest person ever elected to the Senate in Connecticut history. Dodd served a two-year stint as chairman of the Democratic Committee, and, today, at 56, Dodd is the senior Democratic leader in the senate, and has carved a niche for himself as an advocate for children's issues. The third generation Irish American has also focused much attention on international policies, with an emphasis on South America as well as Ireland. Dodd explained, 'As a world leader the United States must work to facilitate international peace and prosperity and ensure the human rights of all people.'

Ken Doherty

Christopher Dodd

KEN DOHERTY

Deafening cheers rang out around his native Dublin and throughout Ireland when he raised the Embassy World Championship trophy in The Crucible back in 1997. Ken Doherty was the first player from the Republic of Ireland to win the world title and the only player ever to have won both the Amateur and Professional World Championship, and he was accorded a hero's welcome when he returned triumphant to his home town. President Mary Robinson described him as 'a role model for the youth of the country' and the 250,000 people who lined the streets of Dublin to welcome him apparently agreed. Born in 1969, he turned professional in 1990, having twice been the Republic of Ireland Amateur Champion, the World Under-21 Champion and the World Amateur Champion. Doherty won the Regal Welsh in 1993, the Regal Scottish Masters in 1993 and 1994 and the Dr Marten's European League in 1995, but a major win eluded him until the Embassy World Championship in 1997. Since then he has remained among the top players on the circuit, although his world ranking slipped from 3 in 1997 to 7 earlier this year. However, his victory at the Malta Grand Prix may have been a turning point. 'This is really special to me because it's been so long since I last won a ranking title. I won't be resting. I'll keep practising and hope I can pick up another trophy.' So do we, Ken.

MOYA DOHERTY AND JOHN McCOLGAN

The worldwide success of *Riverdance*, which transformed Irish dancing from a local and sometimes frowned upon art to that of a global trend, can be attributed in no small measure to John McColgan and Moya Doherty. It was as executive producer on the Eurovision Song Contest in 1994 that Moya commissioned *Riverdance* in its original seven-minute format. The public response was unprecedented and Moya joined ranks with producer/director John McColgan and developed this concept into a full-length stage production. Since its inception *Riverdance* has gone from strength to strength and has received rave reviews all around the world, not least for its debut performance on Broadway. When Michael Flatley left the show, some believed that it would not survive without him, but Doherty and McColgan were undaunted and *Riverdance* continued to develop, incorporating other musical and dance styles. Though still very much infused with its Irish flavour, the show's metamorphic quality has ensured that it never loses its sense of originality. It would be easy to accredit its success to luck but the real reason rests with Doherty and McColgan's experience in the entertainment and television industry. McColgan is a former producer/director with RTÉ and recipient of a prestigious Jacob Award for his work in entertainment programming. Doherty's career background is no less impressive—she worked as a journalist in Britain and Ireland and won awards for her contribution to television. Along with McColgan, Doherty is a Director of Tyrone productions. Doherty and McColgan are partners in both their business lives and in their private lives and have recently bought a house in Howth, County Dublin.

MICHAEL DOLAN

Young & Rubicom were recently acquired by the Sorrell WPP Group, the largest advertising agency group in the world. For a group that clearly needs a major presence on Madison Avenue, what better acquisition than New York's largest agency. Advertising publications reporting on Dolan's appointment referred to his diverse career background as a distinctive plus—a PhD in medieval literature, an MBA in finance, and a previous life as a management consultant. He also worked in a snack food venture, and closer to the ground, in a construction and mining business. The advertising agency world is a world of attrition. As one cynical advisor said, 'you win some, you lose some, depending on a complete range of factors, change of management, new advertising by the opposition, the aggressive poaching of clients by competitors, and of course the ultimate arbiter, does advertising really work?' After a rather academic kick-off to his career, Dolan specialised in learning old English, French, and his thesis included a dissertation on Chaucer. But realising the importance of a more financial-based flavour to his career, Dolan achieved a MBA from Colombia University, and worked as a management consultant for some of the top companies in the US including J. P. Morgan, and Booz Allen & Hamilton. Dolan joined Y&R in 1966. His strong financial background has ensured not only that the creative juices of Y&R run freely, but that the profitability of the company has soared. Today operating margins are up to 12% from a miserable 5% when he first joined the company. Colleagues speak well of the IrishAmerican. Stephen Heyer, Dolan's former boss at Booze Allen & Hamilton, 'Clients love him, he is just the kind of guy you are willing to bet the brand on.'

Moya Doherty

John McColgan

Kathi Doolin

KATHI DOOLIN

As vice-president and publisher of *Departures* magazine, Kathi Doolin is one of the most influential figures in US publishing. Originally created in London by Irish publisher Kevin Kelly for American Express Gold Card holders, the luxury lifestyle magazine was subsequently transported to the even wealthier pastures of the US, where it was exclusively available to platinum card holders. Doolin's father hails from County Waterford and Doolin grew up in the Pacific NorthWest, before attending Portland State University. Doolin started her career in advertisement sales and became the first female division sales manager at *People* magazine. She moved to American Express in 1991 and was appointed advertisement director within a year. Under her three-year tenure as publisher, the circulation and revenue at *Departures* magazine has increased dramatically—the readership tops 460,000 and a full page advertisement will set you back $49,000—that is, if you can manage to net one of these coveted pages.

TOM DONOHUE

As President of the US Chamber of Commerce since 1997, Tom Donohue leads the world's largest business federation representing three million companies and organizations. 'The Chamber under Donohue will be more aggressive and lively than at any time in its history,' said *Industry Week* magazine. 'Nobody has mastered the new Washington game better than Tom Donohue,' said *The Washington Post*. Prior to his current position, the 62-year old Donohue was president and CEO of the American Trucking Associations, where he was the driving force in making the ATA one of the most powerful and vocal lobbies in Washington, DC, tripling the revenue base and increasing membership by 100 percent. Before heading the ATA, Donohue was deputy assistant postmaster general in Washington DC; regional assistant postmaster general in San Francisco and New York; and vice-president of Fairfield University. The New York City native earned a bachelor's degree from St. John's University and a master's

Maureen Dowd

degree in business administration from Adelphi University. He and his wife Liz reside in Potomac, Maryland, and have three sons.

BARRY DOUGLAS

Since he first came to international attention in 1986 when he won the Gold Medal at the Tchaikovsky Piano Competition (only the second westerner to do so), Barry Douglas has developed a maturity that places him, both technically and artistically, among the best in the world. Born in Belfast, Douglas studied in London and lives in Paris, but home for him is at the piano. He has collaborated with conductors such as Ashkenazy, Masur, and Slatkin, performed with the philharmonic orchestras of London, Berlin, Philadelphia, and Tokyo, among countless others. His performances are uniformly described as 'fiery', 'riveting', 'remarkable', 'triumphant', but his ability to illuminate the music fully and maturely without falling prey to sentimentality is perhaps Douglas' greatest gift.

MAUREEN DOWD

Maureen Dowd has quite simply changed the image of newspaper columnists. Her acerbic wit lights up the pages of *The New York Times* and she wields more influence than anyone since Walter Lippmann. Peggy Noonan, author and former speech writer for Ronald Reagan, credits Dowd with changing political reporting in the US. Dowd's father left County Clare when he was 16 years old. 'He told me his mother cried so hard, he cancelled the trip three times,' says Dowd's mother, whose own grandparents hailed from County Mayo. Dowd's father became a cop on Capitol Hill and was elected the national president of the Ancient Order of Hibernians. Dowd was born in Washington, DC, in 1952 and was crowned Little Miss Ireland when she was two years old. 'Being Irish was such a big part of our family. It's ingrained in me,' Dowd says. She attended the Catholic University in Washington and, after graduating with a degree in English literature, started her career as an editorial assistant at the *Washington Star*, where she worked her way

Barry Douglas

up to become a sports columnist, metropolitan reporter and feature writer. She moved to *Time* magazine in 1981 and to the Washington bureau of *The New York Times* in 1986, from where she covered two Presidential campaigns. In 1996 she was appointed a columnist at *The New York Times*—her column 'Liberties' now appears twice weekly. A Pulitzer Prize finalist in 1992, Dowd won the coveted award in 1999 for her 'unsparing columns on the hypocrisies involved in the Lewinsky affair and the attempt to impeach President Clinton'. Neither fools nor hypocrites are suffered lightly. As many of her colleagues in the media were caught up in the moralistic grandstanding of Congress in the aftermath of the tragic shooting

at Columbine High School, Dowd's voice was a wake-up call: 'Before they go ahead and hang the Ten Commandments in the schools, they should make sure they are hanging where they are broken daily—Congress and the White House. They might also consider adding an 11th: Thou shalt not pander.'

ROMA DOWNEY

When Roma Downey was a child growing up in Derry during the turbulent 1960s, the last thing she ever dreamed of was starring in a hit television show in the US. But that's exactly what happened. The beautiful actress, who first came to

Roma Downey

fame in the US with her portrayal of Jackie Kennedy in *A Woman Named Jackie* in the late 1980s, now stars in *Touched By An Angel*. Consistently rated among the top ten television shows, the CBS programme now in its sixth season attracts an estimated 25 million viewers each Sunday night. Downey plays the character of Monica, a guardian angel who intervenes in the lives of people in crisis. Downey has built a career based on far more than just her stunning looks. She earned a bachelor's degree at Brighton Art College in England and attended the London Drama Studio, where she starred in productions of many classics, including the plays of Shakespeare, Shaw, and Chekhov. Downey toured

the United States with Dublin's famous Abbey Players in a production of *The Playboy of the Western World* and was nominated for the Helen Hayes Best Actress Award in 1991. Her additional stage credits include the Broadway production of *The Circle* opposite Rex Harrison, and Off Broadway productions of *Love's Labour's Lost*, *Tamara*, and *Arms and the Man*. Downey's additional television credits include starring roles in the films *A Child Is Missing* and *Borrowed Hearts: A Holiday Romance*, both on CBS, and *Getting Up and Going Home*. Her three-year marriage to second husband director David Anspaugh failed in 1998, leaving Downey to care for their daughter, Reily. 'It's a big responsibility when you have

a career and a wee one,' she says. 'It's even harder when you have to do it alone. But I do it, because my child needs me and depends on me.' Despite her success in the US, Downey is quick to acknowledge the strong ties she maintains with her homeland. 'I have a terrific fondness for Ireland. My national identity is very important to me and I am very proud of it. I am an immigrant, and I'm a long way from home, but America has been very good to me, and I'm very grateful for the generosity this country has shown me and the good fortune I've had here. I'm like a walking cliché; I came over here in search of the American dream, and I feel like I found it. I am very blessed.'

DOMINICK DUNNE

'I'm afraid of nothing. Why should I be? I'm rich and famous. And I did it all myself'. Indeed he did. Regarded as the premier chronicler of the powerful and notorious, 74-year-old Dominick Dunne came to writing late through a combination of chance and tragedy. Born into a wealthy Irish American family—his grandfather fled Ireland during the potato famine and made his fortune in the US—Dunne was drafted during World War II and awarded a Bronze Star for saving the life of a wounded soldier. From the Battle of the Bulge to the Battle for Ratings, Dunne moved to LA and worked in TV and film there for 25 years, moving in the same gilded circles as Lana Turner, Princess Margaret and Frank Sinatra (who once paid a waiter $50 to punch Dunne in the face). But he always suspected it wouldn't last. Alcohol and drugs took their toll, his marriage broke up, one of Dunne's stinging remarks about a Hollywood power broker was published, and suddenly it was all over. Work dried up, the phone stopped ringing, and Dunne retreated to a cabin in Oregon, where he attended AA meetings and began to write his first novel, seemingly content to live in splendid isolation. The suicide of his younger brother, Stephen, catapulted him from his idyll and he moved in to his son's apartment in New York where he wrote *The Winners* and began work on *The Two Mrs Grenvilles*. In 1982, his daughter, Dominique, was strangled by her former lover. 'It changed my life,' Dunne recalls. Tina Brown, then Editor at *Vanity Fair*, suggested that he might find it cathartic to cover the trial of his daughter's murderer. Dunne has been writing for *Vanity Fair* since that first commission. His coverage of the most spectacular trials, from Claus Von Bulow to the Menendez brothers, and books such as *Another City, Not my Own* (based on the O. J. Simpson trial) are infused with passion and remind us that, amid the media hype, these trials are about the victims and their familes. In 1999 Dunne changed direction and published *The Way We Lived Then*, a memoir of his years in Hollywood, featuring many of his own photographs. 'I don't think you should keep doing the same thing. There's so much that is fascinating'.

EAMON DUNPHY

Every nation needs a conscience, and in Ireland today Eamon Dunphy is the voice of our conscience. His Today FM radio show, The Last Word, lays bare the injustices of our legal system, the inadequacies of our healthcare provision, and the duplicity of our elected representatives— not to mention the sheer bloodyminded ineptitude of those who endeavour to manage our national football team. This is but the latest incarnation for this former professional football player, journalist, television presenter, and rock biographer. Born in 1945, Dunphy played with Manchester United, York City, Millwall, Charlton and Reading and holds 23 international caps for Ireland.

After 17 years playing professional football in England, Dunphy returned to Ireland in 1977 and became one of the most controversial and well-read columnists on *Magill* magazine and the *Sunday Independent* (Ireland's biggest selling and most influential Sunday newspaper). Although considered by many as a rather eccentric choice, his biography of U2—entitled *The Unforgettable Fire*—confounded critics and was an international best seller in 1985. Always controversial and outspoken, this straight-talking Dubliner pulls no punches and, whatever the arena, you can be sure that he will continue to challenge the Establishment and champion the underdog.

Dominick Dunne

Eamon Dunphy

PAUL DURCAN

Poet Paul Durcan has been at the heart of Irish cultural life for more than 30 years. Described as 'the most capacious and generous mind in contemporary poetry', Durcan was born in Dublin to parents from County Mayo and studied archaeology and medieval history at University College Dublin before moving to London and a string of jobs as dishwasher and security guard before publishing his first book, *Endville*, in 1967. Since then he has amassed a formidable body of acclaimed work, winning the Patrick Kavanagh Award in 1974 and the Whitbread Poetry Award (for *Daddy, Daddy*) in 1990. 'Poetry is music', Durcan says, 'Poetry is born of speech and it is through recitation that the narrator brings forth a fuller meaning to his verse.' To that end, Durcan has travelled the world, reciting his poetry to audiences spellbound by his mesmerising voice. His poetry records the trials and triumphs not only of his life but of Ireland itself—*The Divorce Referendum, Ireland, 1986* captured the tension between church and state at that time ('I have come to this temple today to pray/And to be healed by, and joined with, the Spirit of Life/Not to be invaded by ideology/I say unto you, preacher and orators of the Hierarchy/Do not bring ideology into my house of prayer') while *Woman of the Mountain* captured the hopes of the nation as Mary Robinson was elected President of Ireland ('Mary, the day you become Uachtarán na

héireann/Come see me in my sweet shop under the mountain/I'll embrace you with all my wings, all my prayers). New York poet Samuel Menashe has said of him: 'Ireland has a voice in Paul Durcan'. And we count ourselves very lucky.

 EDWARD MICHAEL EGAN
New York has a new Archbishop, its ninth, who comes from a long tradition of ecclesiastical Irishmen who have guided the most important Archdiocese in the US. The 68-year-old Egan, installed on 18 June 2000, is a native of Oak Park, a fashionable collar suburb of Chicago, brimming with successful Irish, proud of

their manicured mansions and achieving children. Archbishop Egan is 'to the manor born', as they say, but a gentle shepherd, sensitive to the realities of modern Catholic life, proud of his Irish roots not only from his Egan relations but his mother's Costello family roots. He is an elegant Irishman, his genteel manners layered with the added refinement of a Roman education preceding his ordination there in 1957. Back home, Egan's career brought him into close collaboration with Chicago Cardinals Albert Meyer and John Patrick Cody. In 1971, Egan returned to Rome where he served as a judge at the Sacred Roman Rota, the Vatican's version of the Supreme Court. He returned to the US in 1985

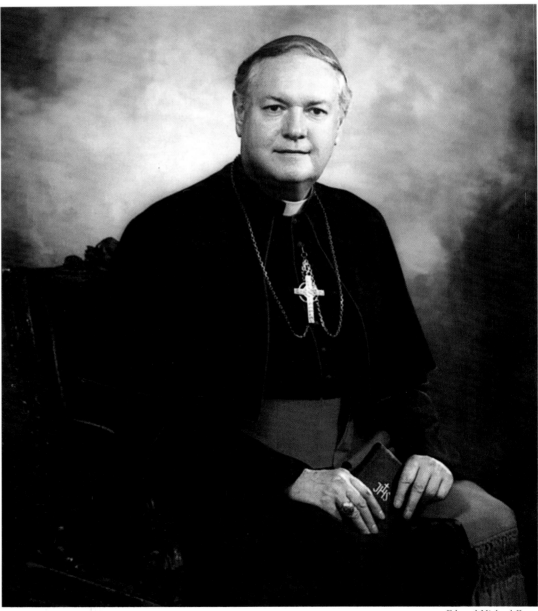

Edward Michael Egan

Paul Durcan

following his ordination as a bishop and served as Auxiliary Bishop of New York under the late Cardinal John O'Connor. He was appointed Bishop of Bridgeport, Connecticut in 1988. Archbishop Egan is a classical scholar who quotes Virgil, Horace and Homer with dignity and humour. His ability at the keyboard has filled many rectories and Episcopal residences with the airs of Bach and the classic Irish songs of Thomas Moore. He is a bright man of soul and intelligence, conservative, whose Spanish is as tasteful and accomplished as his Italian and French. A renaissance man at ease on the subway, he undoubtedly will soon become a Prince of the Church, in an influential office that has, over time, grown accustomed to the personalities of its Cardinals who call St. Patrick's Cathedral home.

RÓISÍN EGENTON

In a rapidly changing Ireland, it is somewhat reassuring that some things remain constant. It has been ridiculed for being too corny and criticised for its lack of political correctness, but year after year for the past 42 years, the Rose of Tralee Festival has attracted crowds to the Tralee Dome and netted huge television audiences. This year, a record 1.5 million television viewers tuned in to watch 23-year-old New York Rose Róisín Ryan Egenton be chosen from among the 28 women from around the world who were chasing the title. Egenton's Irish-born parents, Michael and Katherine and her brother Cormac were the first to congratulate her as she declared herself 'overwhelmed but looking forward to the next year'. A health insurance advisor from Fanwood, New Jersey, Egenton is a frequent visitor to Ireland and dreams of living and working here permanently. But first comes her reign as the millennium rose.

ENYA

Her album sales around the world top an incredible 33 million, making her one of the most successful female artists of all time, but her jealously guarded privacy and reluctance to dance to the media tune means that this low profile musician can enjoy a relatively quiet life in her £2.5 million

Roisin Egenton

house in County Dublin. Born in Gweedore, County Donegal, Enya (christened Eithne) first came to public attention in 1980 when, aged only 19, she joined her sister, two brothers, and twin uncles in Clannad. Musical differences within the group resulted in Enya leaving to launch her solo career in 1982. Although she wrote the score for David Puttman's film *The Frog Prince* and the soundtrack for The Celts, a major BBC television series, her first major commercial success didn't come until 1988. The single *Orinoco Flow* from the album *Watermark* sold nine million copies worldwide (half of those in the US), and went platinum in 14 countries. Her follow-up album, *Shepherd Moons*, went platinum in 18 countries

and netted her a Grammy. A second Grammy followed in 1995 for her album, *The Memory of Trees*. Enya works slowly (just one of her hauntingly beautiful melodies can take months to perfect), but for her millions of fans around the world, the wait is always worthwhile.

IVAN FALLON

Born in 1944, Ivan Fallon is one of six sons of the poet and playwright, Padraic Fallon. Fallon decided against following his father into the arts and opted instead to study business at Trinity College Dublin. After graduation, he worked briefly at *The Irish Times*, before

Enya

Ivan Fallon

Sarah Flannery

MARIAN FINUCANE

Hers is the most recognisable female voice in Ireland. Every weekday afternoon for 13 years, Marian Finucane's soothing voice, sympathetic manner and warm sense of humour encouraged listeners to phone in and share their thoughts and worries on her RTÉ radio show, *Liveline*. She became an institution, a trusted listener, a voice for many (women particularly) who felt trapped in

Marian Finucane

moving to London in 1966 to pursue his burgeoning career in financial journalism. Fallon found success on Fleet Street. He worked on the *Sunday Express*, *Daily Mirror* and the *Sunday Telegraph*, until Rupert Murdoch appointed him Deputy Editor of *The Sunday Times*, a position he held for ten years. When Andrew Neil was seconded to Sky Television in 1989, Fallon was appointed Acting Editor of the paper. In addition to this demanding role (*The Sunday Times* employs more than 200 journalists and its circulation tops 1.4 million), Fallon found time to write a biography of DeLorean, which became the first business biography to be a Book of the Month choice in the US. Biographies of Saatchi & Saatchi and

the billionaire Jimmy Goldsmith followed DeLorean onto the best seller lists around the world. In 1981, Fallon won the coveted Wincott Award for his outstanding contribution as a financial journalist and in 1991 he was named Financial Journalist of the Year. A change of course came in 1994 when Fallon moved to South Africa as Group Editorial Director of Independent Newspapers, where he oversaw the launch of several new titles, including *Business Report*. Now Chief Executive and Chairman of iTouch, the Independent's subsidiary responsible for developing services for mobile telephony around the world, Fallon is forging ahead amid the sunny climes of Johannesburg.

their homes and silenced by their lives. So much so that an Irish opinion poll in 1993 ranked her the third most popular woman, behind Mother Theresa and Mary Robinson. Finucane was born in Dublin in 1950 and worked for a while as an architect, before joining RTÉ as a continuity announcer in 1974. Her break came when she was chosen to present a books programme and in 1985 she began presenting *Liveline*, RTÉ's first public access programme, which attracted a daily audience of 400,000. Finucane keeps a low profile, preferring to do her job and drive home to the farm in County Kildare that she shares with her second husband, John Clarke, and her son, Jack. 'I don't do the glitterati scene,' she says. 'I love being with friends. Friends, by definition, are people you like. So I spend time with people I like rather than with people I don't know.' The death of her nine-year-old daughter Sinead from leukaemia in 1990 shook her to her core and she still prefers not to talk about it. In 1999 Finucane took over the morning radio slot relinquished by Gay Byrne after 25 years and listenership figures released this year show that she is attracting 389,000 listeners every morning. So what next for this doyenne of the airwaves? Many regarded Finucane as a presidential hopeful three years ago (a suggestion that Finucane found hilarious), but a seat in the Senate might not be out of the question.

SARAH FLANNERY

When 16-year-old Sarah Flannery won the Esat Young Scientist of the Year Award in 1999 for her cryptography project, so complex that the adjudicators had to call in outside experts to verify her astonishing achievement, she was catapulted on to the international stage. University places, job offers, book deals, television crews, and reporters camped out on the doorstep disturbed the usually peaceful Flannery home overlooking the River Shournagh in Blarney, County Cork. 'The only way I could deal with it was just to get on with it,' she says. The discovery of a flaw in her encryption formula, the Cayley-Purser Algorithm, that left data vulnerable to attack, was a low point for her, but she still managed to walk away with one of the three first-place prizes at the EU Young Scientist Competition in Greece. Two years on, Flannery remains as down-to-earth as ever, no doubt due to the steadying influence of her father David, a maths lecturer at the Cork Institute of Technology and her mother, Elaine, a lecturer at the Institute of Biology and Microbiology, and her

four younger brothers. Flannery's book, *In Code, A Mathematical Journey*, co-written with her father and published earlier this year, was serialised in *The Telegraph* and she has spoken at conferences from Singapore to Stockholm. But Flannery is no precocious maths prodigy cooped up in a study poring over computer print-outs and mathematical formulae. The fresh-faced teenager plays basketball, Gaelic football, is passionate about horseriding. Now that the hurdle that is the Irish Leaving Certificate is out of the way (she did very well, but typically won't sing her own praises), Flannery is looking forward to studying mathematics and computing at Cambridge later this year.

MICHAEL FLATLEY

How did the tabloids fill their pages before Michael Flatley blasted onto our consciousness six short years ago? His court cases, his egotism, his houses, his highs, his lows, his girlfriends—these have certainly been the Flatley years. When he was unceremoniously fired from *Riverdance* in 1985, a more sensitive man might have packed his dancing shoes in his bag and returned to his home town of Chicago, cursing *Riverdance* and an unappreciative world. Not Flatley. He sued the producers of *Riverdance*, claiming the show could not have been created without him and he was therefore entitled to 2 per cent of the gross

Bill Flynn

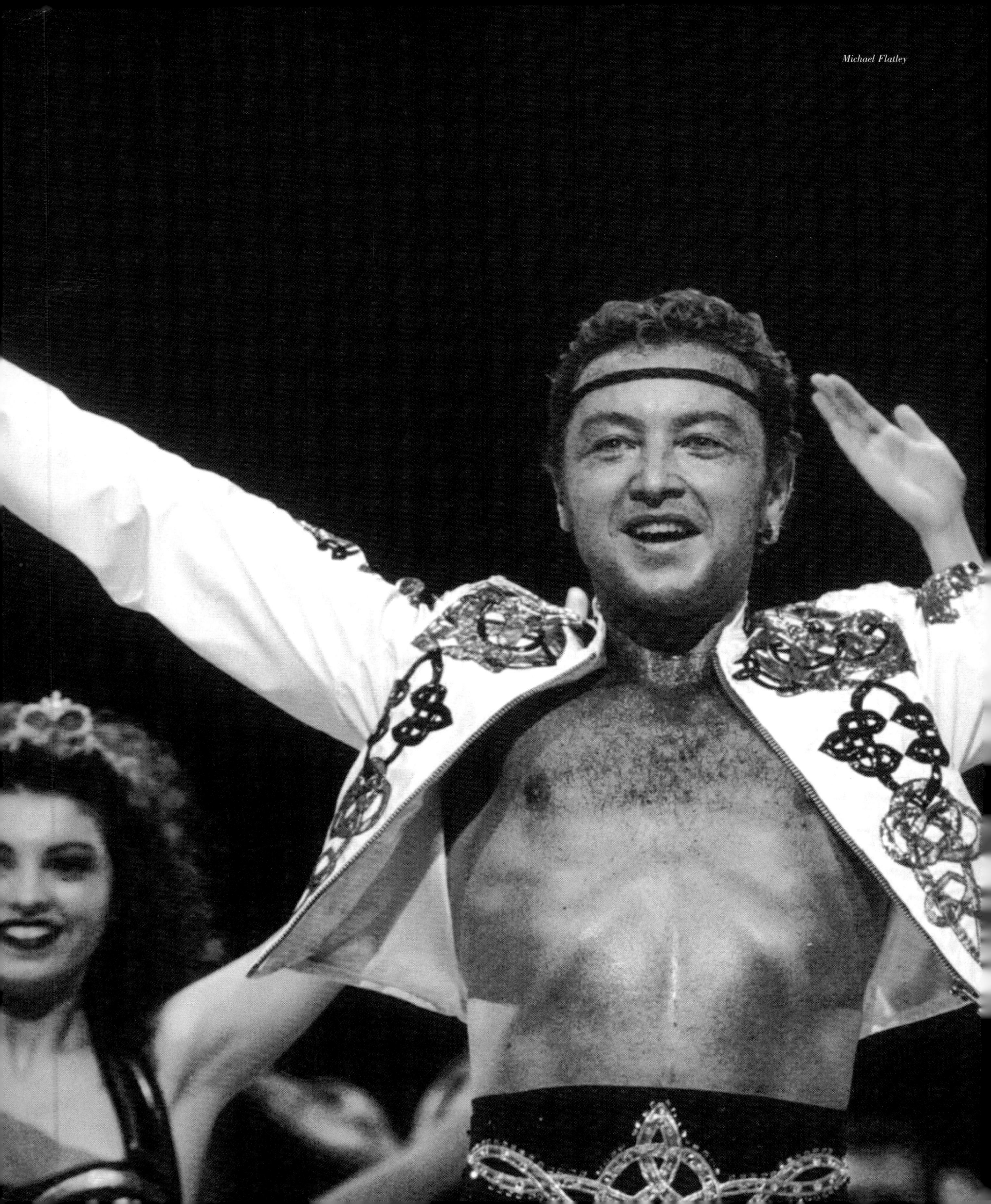

earnings of the *Riverdance* shows—given the phenomenal success of *Riverdance*, this represented a cool £80 million (the case was settled in 1999 for an undisclosed amount). Then he had the audacity to develop a rival show, *Lord of the Dance*, which thumbed its nose at *Riverdance* and was staggeringly successful. His latest offering, *Feet of Flames*, is breaking records around the world. Then, in Cannes earlier this year, he announced that he will start filming a $20 million motion picture later this year. 'I don't fancy myself as the next greatest actor in the world but I think I could make a hell of a movie star,' he replied when asked about his acting credentials. Media reports of him draw a picture of an egotistical manipulator, but people close to him speak of his charm and generousity, and point out that he pushes himself harder than any one who works for him. Ronan Hardiman, composer of the music for *Lord Of The Dance*, makes an interesting point: 'He came here to Ireland, invested a large degree of his own money, and created an entity that now employs 300 Irish people worldwide. Not only employed them, but gave them the opportunity of a lifetime to perform in one of the hottest entertainment entities to hit America in the last decade.' One of the wealthiest men in the world, it is unlikely that he will retire to his Georgian house in Castle Hyde, County Cork and tend his garden. Not while there are stages, and blondes, and camera flashes, and breath left in his body. Love him, or loathe him, Flatley is here to stay.

BILL FLYNN

Bill Flynn is no run-of-the-mill company chairman, no more than Mutual of America is a run of-the-mill insurance company. For more than 50 years, the New York-based company has generated life insurance and retirement plans for not-for profit organizations. And, for the best part of 20 years, Bill Flynn has guided its evolution into one of the financially strongest life insurance companies in the US. He has also been one of the driving forces behind the peace process in the North of Ireland—many believe it was Flynn, as Chairman of the National Committee on Foreign Policy, who convinced President Clinton to grant

the Sinn Féin leader Gerry Adams a visa to visit the US in 1985. It was Flynn, too, who brought John Hume, Adams, and Alliance Party leader, John Alderdice together in 1994 to discuss the Downing Street Declaration. Six months after that meeting the IRA announced its first ceasefire. Flynn's father left Ireland in the early 1900s, travelling first to British Columbia, then Alaska, then Montana (where he learnt the engineering trade that would see him and his family through the worst of the Depression) before finally settling in New York. Now in his seventies, Flynn remains a dynamic and respected businessman and philanthropist, brimming over with excitement when he speaks of Ireland. 'People around the world love the Irish, because they're hardworking, they're intelligent, and they put great stock in schools and learning, and they can do business anywhere. Ireland will be one of the wealthiest nations in the world within 25 years.'

EILEEN AND KATIE FORD

Eileen Ford is the tough, straight-talking woman who has been described, by all accounts, as the grandmother of the modelling industry. Her own grandmother hailed from Longford and kept her brogue until the day she died (Ford claims that her own Longford accent can be pretty impressive). In 1946, Ford was a graduate of law and pregnant with her first child when she took on the job of secretary for two model friends who were frustrated with their agencies. Her hard work on behalf of her friends attracted others to become 'Ford Models', and soon her husband, Jerry Ford (his grandparents came from Mayo), joined the business. While back then their models earned $25 an hour, today's Ford Models net multimillion dollar contracts and worldwide fame—Jerry Hall and Kim Basinger are just some of the women who have been on Ford's books. By 1995, when Ford's daughter, Katie, took over her parent's modelling business it had mushroomed into an international multi-million dollar business. Although 44-year-old Katie originally had no intention of taking over, she proclaims, 'Some people may know this business as well as I do, but nobody knows it better. I've lived in it my whole life.'

Lincoln Center Festival in the US. An Honorary Senior Fellow of University College Dublin and a member of the American Academy of Arts and Letters, the Royal Society of Literature and Aosdána (the Irish academy of artists and writers), Friel lives quietly in Donegal and is undoubtedly one of the foremost playwrights in the world.

Eileen and Katie Ford

BRIAN FRIEL

Irish Minister Dr Jim McDaid has anointed Donegal as 'Friel Country' and dreams of developing the area into a leading tourist attraction. What the notoriously reticent Brian Friel (who was born in Omagh in Tyrone, by the way) thinks of this grand plan is not on the record. Born in 1929, Friel studied to become a priest, but changed his mind and spent ten years as a teacher. In 1958 his first radio plays were produced by BBC Belfast and in 1962 *The Enemy Within* was produced at the Abbey Theatre in Dublin. Friel is credited with playing a leading role in the revival in Irish theatre that began in the late 1950s—he co-founded the Field Day Theatre with Seamus

Heaney and Seamus Deane—but his first major success didn't come until 1964 with *Philadelphia, Here I Come*, a play that looks at the emigrant's experience and has been performed more than 300 times on Broadway alone. His range has been applauded for being as ambitious as it is diverse, underlined by work such as *Faith Healer* (1979), *Translations* (1980), *Making History* (1988), *Molly Sweeney* (1995) and *Volunteers* (1998). *Dancing At Lughnasa* (1990), with a screenplay by Frank McGuinness, was a hugely successful film starring Meryl Streep and brought his work to the attention of a wider audience. In 1999 he was awarded a Lifetime Achievement Award by *The Irish Times* and a Friel Retrospective has been featured at the

NOEL & LIAM GALLAGHER

The undisputed bad boys of rock 'n' roll, Noel and Liam Gallagher have entertained and shocked in equal measure since they burst on to the English music scene in a cloud of cocaine and an explosion of testosterone in 1993. Oasis were hailed as the new Rolling Stones, the voice of a disaffected and disillusioned generation. And what a voice. Their records sold in the millions, but their music often came second to gleeful tabloid reports of decadent lifestyles and assaults on anyone unfortunate enough to get in their way—fans, reporters, flight attendants, not to mention other band members, have all felt the fury of a Gallagher outburst. The brothers Gallagher were born in Manchester to Irish parents, who separated when their three sons were considered old enough to cope with the break-up. The brothers are extremely protective of their mother, Peggy, but severed all ties with their father many years ago. Their troubled childhood has been well documented—not least by the third Gallagher son, Paul, who wrote a book on the subject—but Noel recalls marvellous summer holidays in County Mayo, where they visited their grandmother for six weeks every year. At the height of their fame in the mid-1990s, Liam and his wife Patsy Kensit were hailed as the superstars of swinging London, while Noel's wife Meg Matthews brought new meaning to the term born to shop. The past couple of years have been troubled ones for the Gallaghers—two of the original members left the band, their world tour crashed as Noel refused to perform, critics have panned their recent songs, and both their marriages have failed. Yet they continue to fascinate. The combination of Noel's songwriting and Liam's voice is an explosive one. When it works, the Gallaghers can rock the world.

Brian Friel

Noel and Liam Gallagher

Christopher Galvin

CHRISTOPHER GALVIN

With sales of $33 billion in 1999, it's clear that Christopher Galvin, CEO of Motorola Inc, heads a global leader in integrated communications solutions and embedded electronic solutions. And this past July, the Illinois-based company reported record sales of $9.3 billion in the second quarter of 2000. Galvin said of that achievement, 'This is our eighth consecutive quarter of delivering on our promises to achieve a significant turnaround, improved profitability and a strategic refocusing of Motorola around wireless, broadband and the Internet.' Few are more experienced in this highly competitive market than Galvin. His career with Motorola started 33 years ago with a summer job. He joined the company on a full-time basis in 1973 and rapidly climbed the corporate ladder. In May 1988, he was elected to the Board of Directors of Motorola, Inc and elevated to an Executive Vice-President in May 1989. In January 1990, he was appointed Senior Executive Vice-President and Assistant CEO, and was elected President and CEO in December 1993 and Chairman of the Board in June 1999. Galvin, who holds a bachelor's degree form Northwestern University, Illinois and a master's degree from the Kellogg Graduate School of Management at Northwestern, is also actively involved in civic affairs. He is a director of the Illinois Coalition for science and technology, a trustee of Northwestern University and the American Enterprise Institute, and a member of the Business Council.

James Galway

JAMES GALWAY

'My grandfather played the flute. My father played the flute, so naturally I played the flute', 60-year-old James Galway offers, by way of explaining how he started out on his half century in music. As a child in Belfast, Galway played the penny whistle in the local Orange band, before switching to the flute and studying at the Royal College of Music and the Paris Conservatory. He began playing professionally at the Sadlers Wells Opera and the BBC Symphony Orchestra and in 1969 he was appointed Principal Flute at the Berlin Philharmonic. Six years later, Galway launched his solo career and since then he has travelled the world, performing at The White House, Buckingham Palace, Madison Square Garden and to sell-out concerts from Tokyo to Zurich. Ask him to choose a highlight, and his performance at the Nobel Peace Prize Ceremony, when John Hume and David Trimble received their awards, would be near the top of the list. 'I've played to many audiences all over the world, but that was something really fantastic,' he says. His view on the political situation in Northern Ireland is devastatingly simple: 'It will all end in Ireland when the people who hate stop passing it on to their children'. Galway hails from a staunch Protestant background (his father worked in the shipyard and played in the Apprentice Boys Band), but he says his family decided several years ago that they wouldn't play again in Orange bands. 'After much thought, we came to the conclusion that it wasn't

Michael Gambon

at the Royale Theatre in New York. A recipient of many drama awards over the years, in 1998 he received the KBE for his services to the theatre.

BOB GELDOF

Unpredictable, irreverent, unkempt, Bob Geldof is an unlikely hero. But he is one, nonetheless. In the 1984 Geldof spearheaded the Band Aid, Live Aid and Sports Aid campaigns to help the starving people of Ethiopia—Geldof's impassioned pleas to pick up the phone and make a donation became one of the defining images of that decade. Before Live Aid forever changed the public's perception of him, Dublin-born Geldof enjoyed massive success as the controversial lead singer of the Boomtown Rats and was always a good bet for an off-the-cuff remark that would outrage some sector of Irish society (usually the clergy), although he did display uncharacteristic reticence during his very public split from his wife Paula Yates in the 1990s. Knighted for his work on Band Aid (which raised $150,000,000) and nominated three times for a Nobel Peace Prize, today the 46-year-old lives in London and is an extremely successful businessman. Planet 24, the television production company founded by Geldof and his partners in 1992 is responsible for launching the careers of such media darlings as Chris Evans and Denise Van Oughten and for changing the face of 'youth' programmes with shows like *The Word* and *The Big Breakfast*. 'I'm as proud of Planet 24 as anything else I've done,' Geldof says. 'This one company managed to shift the way television looked, so that nowadays our screens are awash with Planet 24 "wannabe programming".' Last year, Carlton Communications bought Planet 24 for an estimated £15 million (Geldof's share was reported to be in the region of £5 million). But once a crusader always a crusader. Geldof's latest mission is the Jubilee 2000 Campaign to cancel Third World debt—earlier this year a tee-shirt clad Geldof travelled to Rome with Bono to meet the Pope in an attempt to enlist his support for the campaign. What's next for Sir Bob? 'Astrophysics', he says, tongue firmly in cheek.

right. It's as simple as that.' Today, when he is not touring, Galway lives in Lucerne in Switzerland with his third wife Jeanne, also a flautist, but Belfast is still home. Retirement is unthinkable: 'I'm busy teaching myself to do new things every day. I'll never get tired of this profession.'

MICHAEL GAMBON

With his lugubrious features and shambling gait, actor Michael Gambon's physique is tailor made for tragedy. In a career that spans over forty years, Gambon has played both the clown and the hero and has garnered many awards for his virtuoso performances. Born in Dublin, his family moved

to London when he was five and Gambon spent most of his childhood in Camden Town. He left school at 15, gained a Vickers engineering scholarship and then at 21 became a fully qualified engineer. However, he was drawn to the theatre and he began his career as an actor under the tutelage of Michael MacLiammoir and Hilton Edwards at the Gate in Dublin. A man of many talents who has crossed the divide between theatre and the cinema, he has also created memorable role in television. His *tour de force* performance in Dennis Potter's TV series *The Singing Detective* earned him a BAFTA Award. He has graced the stage of the National Theatre, London, and in the US starred in productions on Broadway and

Bob Geldof

THOMAS GERNON

'I grew up with a great interest in geography and geology, aroused during travels with my parents to Paris, Venice, Naples, and Sicily. Certainly those trips brightened up the usually tedious geography lessons and speculation of what lies beneath the landscape geologically was really the inspiration for my project,' says the 17-year-old winner of the Millennium Esat Telecom Young Scientist of the Year. Thomas Gernon scooped the award for his project 'The Geography and Mathematics of Europe's Urban Centres', the first time that a project in the social and behavioural sciences was awarded the top prize. In recognition of his achievement, Gernon was honoured with a joint civic reception from Louth County Council and Dundalk Urban District Council. What is next for the young scientist? Gernon will represent Ireland at the European Contest for Young Scientists later this year and hopes to study paleontology and geology at university. 'I have plenty more mountains to climb and summits to reach,' he says. We wish him luck on his journey.

THOMAS GILLIGAN

You can hear the banter of his second generation Kerry origins in his speech. Ancient Order of Hibernians President Thomas Gilligan is passionate about the Order, an organization whose roots stretch back to 1836, to a time when Irish Catholic immigrants went from being unpopular to being physically threatened in the US. The Order was a lifeline for many Irish immigrants in the mid-19th century. Unwanted for employment in Protestant businesses, the swelling numbers of poor immigrants faced angry 'Nativists', who wanted to be rid of the Papists they perceived as the ruination of the US. The Order was a defensive, protectionist organization that saved many an Irishman from a beating, starvation and sometimes death. The Ancient Order of Hibernians continues to flourish today, though its role is far less protective. For many Irish Americans, their involvement with the Order is the ultimate commitment to their sense of Irishness. It is an honourable, fraternal, and committed organisation that, when harnessed to its full potential, can be an influential lobbying

force. Gilligan is nearing the end of his first four-year term and is already eyeing another run for the presidency. The Connecticut native, now long transplanted amid the sand and palms of Fort Lauderdale, Florida, knows the value of Irish fraternal bonds. It has been more than 20 years since he and a group of other Irish Floridians established a 'Division', as the local groups are known, in Fort Lauderdale. Appreciative of the Order's southern origins, Gilligan is quick to point out that a Division was started in Pensacola, Florida, back in 1898, though it had disappeared from that remote location by 1902. Gilligan has been married for 22 years and is the father of two teenage sons, Brian and Patrick.

LORETTA BRENNAN GLUCKSMAN

Life can be surreal at times. Just ask Loretta Brennan Glucksman. Despite growing up in a staunchly Irish-American family (Loretta's maternal grandfather left Leitrim when he was 12 years old and went to work in the coalmines of Pennsylvania; her paternal grandparents left Donegal in the 1830s and opened a brewery in Pennsylvania that was successful until the Depression), her Hungarian-Jewish-American husband Lew was the first to awaken in her a deep love of Ireland and a real sense of her Irishness. She hasn't looked back since then. Together the couple established Ireland House, a centre for Irish studies at New York University, in 1993.

Thomas Gilligan

Al Gore

Thomas Gernon

Now President of the American Ireland Fund (she was the obvious choice to succeed Dr. A. J. F. O'Reilly), Glucksman has enjoyed an enormously successful career in journalism, public relations and local government, winning journalistic awards and well-earned praise for her pioneering work along the way. Her work at the American Ireland Fund is enormously important to her: 'The American Ireland Fund is much more than a link to my heritage. It has connected me with modern Ireland.' The Fund is part of an international network stretching from Australia to Mexico that raises funds (more than $100 million to date) to promote projects in Ireland that foster peace and reconciliation, culture and the arts, education and community development. The current renaissance in Ireland is 'exhilarating' says Loretta, and her hope is that 'the enormous cultural wealth of Ireland will be accessible to and enjoyed by all the people of Ireland'.

ALBERT ARNOLD GORE, JR.

Reaching for the highest office in the land is a bold and risky business. Vice-President Al Gore insists he's up for the job. That's not too hard a stretch for a man who as a boy was the most well known youth in Washington, D.C. The son of famed Tennessee Senator Albert A. Gore, young Al grew up amid the high politics that found him at home from Capitol Hill to Embassy Row. What few know is that he possesses a distinguished Irish lineage going back to the days of Elizabeth I. The first Gore came to Ireland at the beginning of the

Lord Gowrie

17th century and was rewarded for his service with a large estate in County Donegal which became known as Manor Gore. From this ancestor, Paul Gore, came Arthur Gore the first of the Earls of Arran. Another son, Francis, became the ancestor of the Sligo Gore-Booths who count Constance Gore-Booth, known as the Countess Markiewicz, an Irish Patriot, among their family. Other relations of the Gores include William Gore, an 18th century Bishop of Limerick and their cousin Sir Ralph Gore who served in Parliament and was created the 1st Earl of Ross. He was married to Catherine Connelly, the daughter of Speaker Connelly who built historic Castletown House outside Dublin. She was a cousin of Lord Edward Fitzgerald, the 18th century patriot. Still another branch of the Vice-President's family, the Gores of Newtown Gore in County Mayo produced an Attorney General of Ireland and a Chief Justice of the King's Bench. The Gores have left a distinguished record of public service in Ireland. It is no accident that the American Gores have left the air similarly honoured by their achievement.

LORD GOWRIE

Lord Gowrie is a highly influential figure at the very heart of English politics and arts. Born in Dublin, he grew up in an elegant Georgian house on the banks of the River Liffey in County Kildare. The house, Castle Martin, is now the home of Dr. A. J. F. O'Reilly. Gowrie (Grey to his friends) also spent summer holidays in Donegal where he managed to acquire *cúpla focal*. He later studied at Oxford and Harvard, where he became a fellow and tutor in English and American literature. On his return to London, he lectured at University College London, before joining Edward Heath's administration. In 1974 he was appointed the Opposition Spokesperson on economic affairs in the House of Lords and five years later he joined the government as a Minister of State, a role he held in the department for education and the department for Northern Ireland. Gowrie was appointed to the Privy Council in the New Year's Honours List in 1984 and joined the Cabinet later that year. In 1985, he resigned his office and concentrated on the arts, most notably as chairman of

Bernadette Greevy

Sotheby's in Europe, chairman of Andrew Lloyd Weber's Really Useful Group, chairman of the Arts Council of England and chairman of the Serpentine Gallery. Now 61-years-old, Lord Gowrie has been a member of the board of the Ireland Fund of Great Britain since its inception. When he has time to relax, he reviews books for *The Daily Telegraph*.

BERNADETTE GREEVY

Her voice has been her fortune and our great fortune as a nation. Dublin-born Bernadette Greevy is internationally recognized as one of the finest mezzo sopranos in the world and has

been described as 'one of the noble and beloved artists of our time'. The petite woman with the big voice has enthralled audiences around the world and is particularly renowned as a Mahler singer. 'Singing was always something I was good at,' she says, and her talent was encouraged by her musical family and her school (The Holy Faith in Clontarf), and later through the intensive atmosphere of Feis competition. Greevy studied at the Guildhall School of Music in London, supporting her studies by working for a cosmetics firm, and made her debut at the Wigmore Hall 'It started me off,' she recalls, 'and I never looked back.' Tragedy struck in 1983 when her husband, Peter Tattan, died suddenly of a heart attack:

'My personal life was destroyed. Peter's death was so unfair. I still think it is.' But she had a 14-year-old son to care for, and she buried herself in her work: 'My voice is where I go when I need strength. It is my core being. And it has never let me down.' As founder and artistic director of the Anna Livia International Opera Festival, Greevy is primarily responsible for bringing the ten-day opera festival to Dublin this past summer. The Government contributed £300,000 towards the festival with the remainder of the cost met by the corporate sector, private funding and the box office. 'I thought it would be nice to show ourselves off at a time when there are many visitors, as well as giving Irish singers an opportunity to perform with their international peers while giving home audiences a chance to applaud our existing talent.' None should be applauded louder than Bernadette Greevy.

THE HON. DR. DESMOND GUINNESS

The Hon. Dr. Desmond Guinness has been the driving force behind the preservation of Georgian Ireland's architectural heritage since he founded the Irish Georgian Society in 1958. The son of Lord Moyne (the poet and novelist and vice-chairman of the Guinness Brewery) and Lady Mosley (one of the famous literary Mitford sisters), Guinness has restored the 12th century Leixlip Castle, which he bought in 1958, to its former glory. Over the years, the Castle has served as a retreat for international stars such as Mick Jagger and Jerry Hall. Guinness also bought Castletown House, regarded by some as the greatest country house in Ireland. 'I bought Castletown in 1967 to save it from the developers, who had bought it at auction and left it empty.' The house now falls under the protection of the State. Long considered one of the most handsome men in Ireland (his impossibly blue eyes are reputed to stun at several paces), Guinness and his good friend Desmond Fitzgerald, the Knight of Glin and President of the Irish Georgian Society, are regular visitors to the US, where their combined charm and passionate commitment to Ireland's architectural heritage persuade WASP ladies and Irish Americans alike to make generous donations to their cause.

PETE HAMILL

Pete Hamill has written eloquently on so many topics for so long now it's almost easy to take his talent for granted. But then you read his memoir *A Drinking Life* (1994), his recollections of Frank Sinatra in *Why Sinatra Matters* (1998), or even if you dip in and out of his collection of stories in *Piecework* (1995), and you realize that a wordsmith of his stature does not come along often. Whether during stints at newspapers like *The New York Post* and *Daily News*, or in countless articles covering people and places around the world for national magazines, his writings have managed to capture the human element of the famous while also attaching a sense of glory to the more common. This son of Belfast-born parents is perhaps most well-known for his vivid insights into his native Brooklyn and New York City, mixing haunting memories of a city landscape long gone with the contemporary kaleidoscope of immigrants that still walk its streets today. And as always, his work is tinged by his Irish heritage, directly when writing about Northern Ireland, or even indirectly when talking about American immigration policies. So it's no surprise to hear him describe what his ancestral

Pete Hamill

background means to him. 'For an American also to identify himself as Irish is to embrace a link to an imagined past and the culture that is woven into that past.' In the 1960s, this charming hard-drinking Irish man, together with the Clancy Brothers and assorted Irish musicians, poets, cops and firemen, made The Village fashionable. Many smart New Yorkers gravitated to the Village's Irish bars. Jackie Onassis, a close friend of Hamill's was one of the many charmed by this charismatic Irish group. These experiences were part and parcel of his best selling auto-biography, *A Drinking Life*. Today Hamill is a supporter of all things Irish. He is highly regarded by his fellow New Yorkers as a quintessential New Yorker and his good friend John Scanlon, the distinguished New York PR guru remarked, 'Hamill will go a long way to introduce young talent or to promote young Irish writers and his name carries a lot of clout.'

KEVIN HAND

EMAP plc is one of the most powerful media companies in the world. In the UK alone, EMAP produces 150 consumer titles, 100 business-to-business publications, and owns nearly 20 AM and FM radio stations. The company entered the US market in 1999 with its purchase of Petersen Companies and plans to double its share of the market. Kevin Hand is Group Chief Executive of this media giant. Although born in the UK, Hand has fond memories of holidaying in Ireland every year until his early twenties as a result of his parents' determination to maintain their links with Ireland (his mother hails from Killarney). Hand qualified as a typographic designer, but spent three years in public relations at Link House before joining EMAP in 1983 as Circulation Director and then Chief Executive of the Consumer Division, where the number of titles increased from 40 to 90 and the market share from 6% to 13% in seven years. In 1990 Hand concluded a deal with Bayard Presse in Paris for the purchase of *Le Chasseur Francais*, thus launching EMAP International's strategy. EMAP then went on to buy *Les Editions Mondiales* (including titles such as *Modes & Travaux* and

Kevin Hand

Auto Plus) as well as several titles from *La Famille Hersant*. Hand was appointed President and Director General of the newly created EMAP France, and spent four years there with his wife Fiona and their four daughters before being named Group Chief Executive of EMAP plc in July 1998. Earlier this year, EMAP launched EMAP Digital, another stage in 49-year-old Hand's mission to make EMAP the most exciting media company in the world.

CHARLES HANDY

Although hailed by the British press as Britain's greatest management guru, Charles Handy is in fact Irish. Born in County Kildare, the son of an archdeacon in the Church of Ireland, Handy was educated at Trinity College Dublin, Oxford, and the Institute of Technology in Massachusetts. He has found success in many different arenas, as an oil company executive, economist, professor at a London business school, former chairman of the Royal Society of Arts and a regular contributor to the BBC's religious humanist programme *Thoughts for Today*. However, it is as an author and business philosopher that Handy is most acclaimed. Books such as *Waiting for the Mountain to Move*, *Gods of Management*, *Beyond Certainty*, *The Hungry Spirit*, *Understanding Organisations* (now in its fourth edition) are all landmark studies, prompting Tom Peters,

the US business guru to say of Handy: 'His lucid, exciting, and shocking descriptions of tomorrow's organisations brings us closer to understanding competitive reality.' Handy's Irish roots have been a source of inspiration. In his book, *The Age of Unreason*, Handy uses the three-leaved shamrock to illustrate how businesses today comprise three different groups of workers, each with different expectations, each managed differently, paid differently, and organised differently, but coming together to mutual advantage. He describes how the third leaf of the shamrock represents the flexible labour force (part-time and flexible workers), the fastest growing sector in the employment market. In Handy's brilliant hands, the humble shamrock has become a key symbol for today's greatest business minds.

JOSEPHINE HART

Acerbic journalists who have seen and heard it all before have professed themselves spellbound by her charm. Former colleagues in the hard-nosed advertisement industry speak of her cleverness, ambition and, again, her charm. Mullingar-born Josephine Hart started out in advertising sales on *Campaign* magazine (one colleague remembers her as the best saleswoman he has ever known), enjoyed a hugely successful career in publishing (she was Director of Haymarket Publishing and

Josephine Hart

Seamus Heaney

founded Gallery Poets) before going on to produce a number of West End plays, including Noel Cowards *The Vortex* and Irish Murdoch's *The Black Prince*. But it is as a novelist that she is perhaps best known. Her first novel, *Damage*, was published in 1991, remained on *The New York Times* bestseller list for 14 weeks, was translated into 25 languages, and subsequently made into a successful film starring Jeremy Irons and Miranda Richardson. Her latest novel, *The Stillest Day*, has been hailed as 'an elegant and mesmerically compelling psychological thriller'. Married to Maurice (now Lord) Saatchi, Hart is credited with being a driving force behind his phenomenal success.

SEAMUS HEANEY

Seamus Heaney is quite simply our greatest living poet, though he would perhaps shrink away from such an accolade. Described by Robert Lowell as the most important Irish poet since Yeats, Heaney is a quiet and unaffected man—when he received the Nobel Prize of Literature in 1995 he declared that such an award 'was not just beyond expectation: it was simply beyond conception'. Born in County Derry in 1939, the eldest of nine children, Heaney won a scholarship to St. Columb's College, a Catholic boarding school in the city of Derry, some forty miles away. While future moves to Belfast, California, Wicklow, and Boston would take him further from his birthplace, rural County Derry is the 'country of the mind' where much of Heaney's poetry is still grounded. Heaney taught for a time in Belfast following his graduation from Queen's University and began writing poetry, coming to public attention as one of a group of poets (including Michael Longley and Derek Mahon) who were subsequently recognized as a 'Northern School' within Irish writing. *Death of a Naturalist* and *Door into the Dark* were published in the late 1960s , but in 1970 Heaney and his wife, Marie Devlin (a writer in her own right and one of the immensely talented County Tyrone Devlins), moved to California where Heaney was appointed a visiting lecturer at Berkeley. Those heady days in California may have contributed to his decision, on his return, to resign his lectureship at Queen's University and move to

County Wicklow to work full time as a poet and freelance writer. The political situation in the North of Ireland has always influenced his work, no more so than in the harrowing years of the 1970s, and Heaney has admitted the difficulties of 'conducting oneself as a poet in a situation of ongoing political violence and public expectation'. In *Exposure* he wrote: 'How did I end up like this?/I often think of my friends'/Beautiful prismatic counselling/And the anvil brains of some who hate me/.../Rain comes down through the alders/Its low conducive voices/Mutter about letdowns and erosions/And yet each drop recalls/The diamond absolutes./I am neither internee nor informer;/An inner émigré, a grown longhaired/And thoughtful; a wood-kerne.' Heaney moved back to academia when he was appointed Head of the English Department at Carysfort College, a teacher training college, until, in 1982, he was appointed Boylston Professor of Rhetoric and Oratory at Harvard University, a position that allows him to spend eight months at home without teaching in exchange for one semester's work at Harvard. In 1989 Heaney was elected for a five-year period to be Professor of Poetry at Oxford University. In 1999 his translation of the Anglo-Saxon epic *Beowolf* was hailed as a masterpiece. The accolade bestowed by the Nobel Prize Committee perhaps best sums up Heaney's importance: '[His] works of lyrical beauty and ethical depth exalt everyday miracles and the living past'.

MARGARET HEFFERNAN

Ireland's leading business woman keeps a low profile and jealously guards her privacy, but her omission from this celebration of Irish success is unthinkable. Born in 1942, Heffernan joined the family supermarket business in 1956 and, as Chief Executive of Dunnes Stores, now presides over the largest privately owned supermarket chain in the country, employing more than 5,000 people. Dunnes Stores occupies a unique place in Irish retailing—a supermarket-cum-drapery business, it dominates the mass end of the market. 'Dunnes Stores Better Value Beats Them All' was the mantra of the famous founder Ben Dunne Sr and Dunnes has stayed true to this simple

Margaret Heffernan

philosophy, in their time seeing off often fierce competition from European competitors. The revelations of the financial dealings between her brother Ben Dunne and Charles J. Haughey (Haughey has admitted that he received more than £1.3 million from Dunne when he was leader of Fianna Fáil and Taoiseach of Ireland) have been a source of embarrassment, but Heffernan has emphatically denied any knowledge of their dealings, and her recent High Court victory, which overturned The Tánaiste Mary Harney's appointment of an authorised officer to examine the company's books, was surely sweet. Heffernan's charity work—she founded the People in Need organisation in 1989, which has raised in excess of £10 million—and her business acumen have earned her the admiration and respect of many in Ireland.

JOHN HUME

On the last day of the last millennium a poll in the *Irish Independent* rated John Hume as the man of the millennium. There could have been no other result. For more than 30 years this former schoolteacher from Derry has been the inspiration and the backbone of the ongoing struggle for peace and reconciliation in Northern Ireland. From the civil rights marches of the 1960s and the barricades of the 1970s to the tentative negotiations of the 1980s and the all-party discussions of the 1990s, Hume has been the north star, the guiding

John Hume

a process. But that we have come this far is due in no small part to John Hume. Now in his 63rd year, he remains an inspiration: 'I want to build an Ireland of partnership where we reach out to the marginalised and dispossessed, where we build a future that can be as great as our dreams allow.' His announcement in August this year of his intention to resign his seat in the Northern Ireland Assembly due to ill health was cause for a still regrettably rare moment of absolute agreement in Northern Ireland, as all shades of political opinion united to acknowledge his immense contribution to the peace process and to agree that the Northern Ireland Assembly would not be the same without him.

EDDIE IRVINE

He is the poster boy for a brash new Ireland. As a Formula One driver, Eddie Irvine is already steeped in the glamour that surrounds that exalted sport, but his antics away from the race course have elevated him to the status of icon for all young boys who dream of yachts, and helicopters, and race cars, and girls, girls, girls. Born in Newtownards in Northern Ireland in 1965, Irvine was just 17 years old when he competed in his father's Crossle FF1600 Chassis. He moved up through British Formula Three and F3000 in the late 1980s before making his Formula One debut driving for Sasol Jordan in 1993, achieving sixth place in Japan to become the first driver since Jean Alesi to score points on his Formula One debut. Since then Irvine's fortunes on the track have been mixed—he took his first podium finish in 1995, finished 7th in the championship in 1997, and 4th in 1998. But in 1999 his dreams came true when he won the Australian Grand Prix. It seemed as though the year would end in spectacular style as Irvine won the inaugural Malaysian Grand Prix in October, but only two hours after celebrating his win with the traditional champagne shower, race officials ruled that both Irvine's and second-placed Schumacher's cars had infringed FIA regulations. Irvine has now moved from Ferrari to Jaguar, to whom he is contracted until the end of 2002, but this year has been rather a

light for the countless and often nameless people who worked tirelessly for peace. At the height of 'The Troubles', that terrible euphemism for such a bitter and bloody conflict, Hume was as likely to be shot by the IRA as by loyalist paramilitaries. And still he persevered. Through accusations of sectarianism and naivety, his message was clear— there can be a peaceful and peacefully negotiated solution to the conflict. He saw the potential for US involvement and won the support of Senator Ted Kennedy and leading Irish Americans. A long-serving member of the European Parliament, his clarity of thought and unimpeachable integrity not to mention his impressive linguistic skills (a rarity among Northern Irish politicians) won him

many admirers. Hume's recognition that there could be no peace in Northern Ireland unless Sinn Féin were brought into the political mainstream coincided with Gerry Adams' realisation that the armed struggle would never end in victory. Hume's courage in taking the decision to work with Adams and introduce him to the highest ranking officials from Whitehall to the White House cannot be overstated. Hume was pilloried in certain sections of the press, both in Ireland and around the world. He ran the risk of losing his grass roots support. But he persevered. In recognition of that perseverance and courage, Hume was awarded the Nobel Peace Prize in 1998. There have been triumphs and tragedies, and the peace process is still that—

troubled one—he failed to finish in Australia, stalled at the start grid in Canada, pulled out of the Austrian Grand Prix complaining of stomach pains, and finished fourth in Monaco. Despite this, Irvine's tanned face and trademark sunglasses dominate gossip columns around the world and his off-the-cuff remarks continue to entertain and offend in equal measure. For the playboy of the North, it's a case of damn the begrudgers. 'I'm very happy with my life,' Irvine says. 'What the newspapers write is really not my problem. I come to the race circuit to work. Away from the circuit I do my own thing and I have a lot of fun.'

Eddie Irvine

EILEEN IVERS

One minute she is playing a plaintive air that silences the audience with its spare beauty. The next she is off the stage and into the crowd, encouraging all sorts of dancing with her electrifying musical talent. That's what you get when you attend a concert featuring Eileen Ivers, widely recognized as the pre-eminent exponent of the Irish fiddle in the world today. The Bronx native began playing the fiddle at the age of eight and went on to win seven All-Ireland fiddle titles and an eighth on tenor banjo. A founding member of the all-woman folk group, Cherish the Ladies, Ivers' talents were exposed to a worldwide audience when she participated in the first touring production of *Riverdance*. She has toured throughout the US and around the world. Her first Sony Classical recording, *Crossing the Bridge*, was released in 1999 to critical acclaim. Featuring rhythms and beats from around the world, Ivers and her band have created a sound that takes Irish traditional music to new heights. Ivers plans to release her next album in the fall of 2000.

DEREK JETER

Professional baseball players are often judged on their skills in five categories—hitting, throwing, defence, running speed, and mental toughness. Derek Jeter, who plays shortstop for the New York Yankees, gets high marks in each of those categories. And he is just 24 years old. The native of Kalamazoo, Michigan, was the sixth overall pick in the 1992 Major League Baseball draft, and has since led the Yankees to three world championships in his first four full years in starting lineup. He won the American League Rookie of the Year Award in 1996 and is sure to pick up more accolades for his playing prowess in the future. Off the field, the 195-pound Jeter attracts innumerable female fans thanks to his All-American good looks (his Irish ancestry comes through his mother's side of the family), and even dated singer Mariah Carey for a while. And while it's rare enough these days to find professional athletes who accept the mantle of role model, Jeter not only does so gracefully, he also started the 'Turn 2 Foundation' in 1996, an organization formed to support and create activities and programmes designed to prevent and treat teenage substance abuse.

BARBARA JONES

Dare to question Judge Barbara Jones about her Irish roots, and the reply is swift, 'With a mother named Peggy O'Neill, how Irish do you think I am?' Her Irish ancestry is a source of pride to her, and not without good reason. Her family were harbour pilots in Cobh, County Cork, an esteemed occupation that made the family the focus of envy and admiration among their neighbours. Both her

Eileen Ivers

Barbara Jones

mother and her grandmother, Madeline Nash, were born on Albert Terrace, in Cobh, County Cork. Her great-grandfather, Charles Nash, was the harbour pilot charged with bringing the *Lusitania* into port when the ship was blown up. Jones' grandfather, Alexander O'Neill, moved to Brooklyn, New York, in 1926, and one esteemed family profession was swapped for another— Jones' uncle, Desmond O'Neill, carved out a distinguished reputation as an undercover officer with the Alcohol, Firearms and Tobacco Authority. Jones is continuing the family tradition of proud public service. A graduate of the Temple University School of Law in 1973, Jones has devoted her life to the practise of law. She has been a Special Attorney in the honours programme of the US Department of Justice, assigned to the Manhattan Strike Force against Organized Crime and Racketeering and served ten years as the Assistant District Attorney for the Southern District of New York, during which time she swore in the late John Kennedy Jr. In 1984, Jones was appointed chief of an Organized Crime Strike Force, the first women to hold such a position. While a federal prosecutor, Jones specialized in racketeering prosecutions and was responsible for the conviction of such high-profile figures as Anthony 'Tony Pro' Provenzano, Russell Bufalino, and Frank 'Funzi' Tieri, then head of the Genovese La Costra Nostra Family. When not on the frontline of law and order, Jones has lectured on trial advocacy at the Fordham University School of Law, served as chair of the Council on Criminal Justice of the Bar of New York City, and in 1998 she travelled to Ireland as a member of the Committee on International Human Rights. For the past four years, Jones has served as a Federal District Judge, presiding over such high-profile cases as the Autumn Jackson extortion trial involving Bill Cosby, and the antitrust case brought by the US Department of Justice against Visa and Mastercard. A leading light in the US justice system, Jones is as passionate about fighting the good fight as she is about her Irish roots.

EDDIE JORDAN

Dublin-born Eddie Jordan has come a long way since he jettisoned his career in banking and founded Eddie Jordan Racing in 1980. His wife Marie, a former Irish basketball international supported this drastic move, both morally and financially—in the early days, she took a job in a factory to help keep Eddie on the road as he tried to break into the motor racing world. He entered Formula One with the creation of Jordan Grand Prix the following year and his team proved to be the success story of the season by finishing 5th in its first season of competition. In 1998, Damon Hill won for Jordan at Spa and his team stole fourth place in the Constructor's Championship, breaking the McLaren-Ferrari-Williams-Benetton stranglehold on Formula One. Critics who dismissed him as a lightweight have been forced to eat their words. 'I am often accused of not being a serious operator,' says the 52-year-old Jordan, 'and that can hurt me. But I know what we have achieved and when I look at Jordan's history, from our victories in Formula Ford, F3 and F3000, to victory in Formula One, I feel very proud.' His flamboyant style of management may not be to everyone's taste—his propensity for remarks such as 'I own you. I have made you' and his hectic social calendar of rock concerts (Jordan harbours dreams of becoming a professional drummer), soccer matches, and golf tournaments may not be a style recommended in management textbooks. But it works. Jordan is the second most recognised Formula One brand after Ferrari. And he is undoubtedly the best dealmaker in the business— he personally negotiated the $12.5m Deutsche Post contract that bumped his year 2000 sponsorship up to $57.5 million and he reportedly earned $40m from the $65 million sale of a half share of his team to venture capitalists Warburg Pincus. Recognition for placing Ireland on the Formula One map came in 1999, when he was named one of the 1999 People of the Year for his contribution to Irish society and he has been appointed a Sporting Ambassador for Ireland. Jordan has no intention of resting on his laurels: 'I, and the team around me, believe in what we are doing. The question is, how far can we go? I believe we can go all the way.' Unless, that is, U2 suddenly find themselves in desperate need of a drummer.

NEIL JORDAN

Sligo-born film maker Neil Jordan actually began his career as a novelist—in 1979, his collection of stories, *Night in Tunisia*, won the Guardian fiction prize and he has since published three novels to critical acclaim. But it is as a film maker that he is best known. Films such as *Mona Lisa* (1986), *We're No Angels* (1989) and *Interview with a Vampire* (1994) have established him as one of the most successful film makers in the world. He won a Best Screenplay Oscar for the controversial film *The Crying Game* (1992) and provoked further controversy when he decided to tell the story of Irish patriot Michael Collins. 'I have never lost more sleep over the making of a film than I have over *Michael Collins*,' he recalls, 'but I'll never make a more important one. In the life of one person you can tell the events that formed the north and south of Ireland as they are today.' Starring Liam Neeson in the title role, the film was denounced in some quarters as pro-IRA, a charge rejected by Jordan. Nominated this year for a Best Director Oscar for *The End of the Affair*, he is undoubtedly a big player in Hollywood, but media-shy Jordan lives in Dublin, preferring the glittering waters of Killiney Bay to the star dust of the Hollywood hills.

Eddie Jordan

Neil Jordan

ROBBIE KEANE

K It's every young boy's dream—kick a ball around after school, play in the English premiership, and be snapped up by a European club. But for Robbie Keane, the dream became a reality. Keane's footballing skills have taken him from a housing estate in Dublin to the glamour of Milan in only a few short years. Still only 20 years old, Keane signed to Inter Milan in July this year for a staggering $20 million. 'When I used to kick a ball around the back streets of Dublin, I could never have imagined that one day I would pull on the legendary blue and black striped shirt of Inter Milan. It's a dream come true,' Keane says in wonder. Born in Dublin in 1980, Keane played for one of the leading schoolboy clubs, Crumlin United, before moving to Wolverhampton Wanderers, despite interest from

far bigger clubs in the UK. He signalled his arrival in spectacular style by scoring twice on his first team debut in 1997, adding a further ten goals over the course of the season. In 1998 he made his international debut for the Republic of Ireland and, in only his second appearance on the international scene, he was named Man of the Match for his outstanding performance against Argentina. In 1999 he moved to Coventry for a fee of £6 million, making him the most expensive teenager in the Premiership, and showing no sign of the pressure on him he calmly scored twice on his debut there. His move this year to the rarefied atmosphere of Inter Milan is a massive undertaking—a new language, a pressured environment and strong competition for a place on the frontline—but this down-to-earth Dubliner is determined to show Italy what he can do on the pitch.

ROY KEANE

He may be the bad boy of the English Premiership, but Cork-born Roy Keane is also its brightest star, as evidenced by Manchester United's decision this year to pay their skipper a reported £50,000 a week to keep him at the club for the next four years. Amazingly, as a teenager Keane failed to get an apprenticeship with any English League club and began his footballing career with Cobh Ramblers before Brian Clough took him to Nottingham Forest when he was 18 years old for fee of £10,000. The bigger clubs soon sat up and paid attention and in 1993 Manchester United paid a then club and English record fee of £3.75 million for him. Keane's ball winning skills, drive, determination and late runs into the box to score vital goals have made him an irreplaceable figure in United's midfield and, at

Robbie Keane

Roy Keane

the end of the 1996/97 season, when Eric Cantona retired from professional football, Keane took over the role of team captain. He is also captain of the Republic of Ireland team, first capped by Jack Charlton in 1991 and now holding 46 caps for his country. Keane is an aggressive player and has suffered more than his fair share of injuries and sendings off (seven times in his Manchester United career), but he is the heart of the team, and they know it. Former captain Bryan Robson said of him: 'He is already an Old Trafford legend. He is absolutely top class. He is quality.' That was recognised this year when both the Football Writers and the Professional Footballers Association voted Keane Player of the Year.

PAUL KEATING

Undoubtedly the most controversial Australian Prime Minister in recent years, Paul Keating almost single-handedly reignited the simmering republican issue in Australia when he dared to put his arm fleetingly around the Queen of England's lower back and then, to the horror of the press who designated him The Lizard of Oz, he left Windsor early to meet Charles J. Haughey at a Gaelic football match. As Prime Minister of Australia from 1991 to 1996, Keating presided over (some would claim stoked) the bitter constitutional debate that divided Australians until they voted last year to retain the Queen as head of state. Keating was born in Sydney in 1944, leaving school at just 15 to work at Sydney City Council. He joined the Australian Labor Party the same year and became the President of the New South Wales Youth Council when he was 22. Spells as Minister for Northern Australia and Treasurer culminated in his election as Prime Minister in 1991. Two years later he led the Federal Government to an historic fifth term of government and Keating declared it a victory for the true believers in a compassionate and visionary Australia. Those true believers turned against Keating in spectacular style just three years later when they elected conservative John Howard, in every way his diametric opposite. Keating relinquished the leadership of the Labor Party and resigned from parliament. Observers attribute the massive swing against him to the

electorate's bitterness at policies that saw wage-earners suffer a 25 percent cut in their incomes, while the combined wealth of the top 200 richest Australians rose from $A5 billion to $A25 billion during his time in office. Keating did, however, address the issue of land rights for the Aboriginal people in the Native Title Bill in 1993 and he developed trade links with Asia that ended Australia's traditional dependence on Europe and the US. Although retired from public life, Keating hit the headlines in 1998 when his 23-year marriage broke up amid rumours of extramarital affairs (vehemently denied by Keating and his wife, Annita), and again in 1999 when he bitterly lamented the result of the constitutional

referendum and warned that the pressure for an Australian head of state would continue, as the monarchy was now 'irreversibly broken'. The fight continues for this Wild Colonial Boy.

RONAN KEATING

In the mid-1980s, a group of teenagers appeared on the *Late Late Show* television programme and mimed and danced gleefully, without any regard for timing or rhythm, to the great amusement of the audience and viewers around the country. 'They can't sing and they can't dance', pronounced the host, Gay Byrne. And that should have been that. But today those teenagers, known

Paul Keating

collectively as Boyzone, are pop star millionaires. They may or may not have plans to break up this year (depending on which media hack you speak to), but lead singer, Ronan Keating has already eclipsed the group and is an international star in his own right. And somehow, somewhere along the line, an initially contemptuous Irish public has accorded the 23-year-old Dubliner a grudging respect. His first solo effort, *When You Say Nothing At All*, for the soundtrack of *Notting Hill*, was a massive hit and his first solo album went straight to Number 1 in the UK album chart. And music is only one of the strings to his bow. He co-manages Westlife, the successors to Boyzone's throne, and he has launched himself as a television star—Keating presented the National Entertainment Awards and the Eurovision Song Contest in 1997, and is by now a regular host of the MTV Music Awards. He married his long-time girlfriend Yvonne Connolly in 1998, and lives with her and their son Jack, who was born last year, in Kildare. The couple expect their second child in February 2001, an event that will no doubt be covered in minute detail by the glossies, whose pages Ronan and Yvonne inhabit with astounding regularity. The second single from his solo album is aptly entitled *Life is a Rollercoaster*. Maybe so, but Ronan Keating is firmly in control of this ride.

Ronan Keating

KEVIN KELLY

'You know, I don't like computers. Computers as things frustrate me. But I'm interested in computers and their consequences because they're the greatest philosophical instruments that we have made so far.' So speaks Kevin Kelly, former 'editor of edge' at *Wired* magazine, hippy philosopher, Internet guru, and prophet. Born in Pennsylvania in 1952 and raised in New Jersey, Kelly is the eldest of five children in an Irish American Roman Catholic family—his parents opted for good Irish names for all their children, Kevin, Brian, Sean, Colleen, and Michael. Kelly's great-grandparents left Ireland and settled in the coal mining region of eastern Pennsylvania before the turn of the century. In 1965, Kelly's father took him to his first computer show. 'I was so underwhelmed,' Kelly recalls. He was also underwhelmed by college, dropping out in the early 1970s to read and travel for ten years. On his return to the US, Kelly moved to the West Coast, stumbled into magazine editing and became interested in technology. The two interests collided on *Wired*, the first mainstream magazine to chart the emerging digital culture and the first organization to set up a commercial website and in the process invent banner ads. Kelly was involved with the launch of the magazine in 1993 and was Editor-in-Chief for six years, before stepping down last year when the title was bought by Condé Nast. Kelly helped to set up The Well, one of the first public teleconferencing facilities and now viewed as a model of online community, published two books, *Out of Control* and *New Rules for the New Economy*, and is a member of the Global Business Network, a think tank specializing in future scenarios for global-minded businesses. All of which has established him as the 'chief guru of the Internet age'. This former hippy is now in great demand on the global conference circuit, hired by big business and the military alike. When not travelling, he lives in San Francisco with his wife and three children, whose regime is stricter than might be expected—no television, music practice each day, grace at meals, prayers at night. Old values in a new age, but in keeping with the enigma that is this non-drinking, non-smoking hippy philosopher technophile who hates computers.

Thomas Keneally

THOMAS KENEALLY

When the Irish Australian writer Thomas Keneally made a stop in Beverly Hills, California, on his way home from a film festival in southern Italy he met the owner of a luggage store who would change his life. A survivor of the Holocaust, the man told him a story that later became the subject of Keneally's novel, *Schindler's Ark*. Not only did *Schindler's Ark* win the Booker Prize and the *Los Angeles Times* Prize for Fiction after it was published in 1982, but the rights to his book were sold to Steven Spielberg and made into the critically acclaimed and Oscar-winning film, *Schindler's List*. Keneally was already established as a writer of almost two dozen novels, plays and children's books before the film was released, but its global success provided him with the financial freedom to spend the next five years researching and writing his latest book, *The Great Shame: And the Triumph of the Irish and English Speaking World*. In this 712-page work of non-fiction, Keneally uses the story of his own ancestor (John Keneally) to give a true account of Irish convicts who were transported to Australia. A committed Republican ('there's definitely a tradition of republicanism in the Keneally family,' he smiles), Keneally is convinced that, despite the results of last year's constitutional referendum, it will only be a matter of time before Australia becomes a republic. At a lunch in honour of Irish President Mary McAleese, Keneally said: 'We need an Australian version of Mary McAleese, someone who at least spiritually has been a communicant across the borders of sect and race, someone who understands her country and its place in the world in a profound manner, in which our present head of state, with all the best intentions on earth, could not possibly do.' Although born in New South Wales and now living with his wife, Judith, in Sydney, Australia, Keneally is a tremendous fan of Ireland and has written several books about the land of his ancestors. After all, he was raised Catholic by Irish people in the full-blown Jansenist tradition. 'It gave me what every writer needs,' says Keneally. 'A sense of the inevitability of original sin.' Now 65 years old, the writer insists, 'I am going to write until they pull my plug.'

PATRICK KELLY

Dr. Patrick Kelly has performed more than 3,000 brian tumour operations at the renowned Mayo Clinic and New York Medical University Medical Center. His fame, however, doesn't rest on the number of operations but rather on the type of operations he has performed. Kelly is a pioneer in modern medicine, responsible for developing and using a minimally invasive, computer-assisted stereotactic surgical procedure for the brain, for which he was awarded the prestigious Scoville Prize by the World of Neurological Sciences in 1997. Using this process, the image of the brain is transferred into a computer, enabling neurosurgeons to precisely target the site of a tumour. This method has since been adopted by the international neurological community and has made the business of removing malignant growths far less traumatic for patients. Kelly currently serves as the Ransohoff Professor and Chairman of the Department of Neurological Surgery at the New York University School of Medicine. Although he lives in Manhattan, New York, with his wife, Carol, and their daughter, Caitlan, Kelly hankers after a home in County Galway, the land of his ancestors. In collaboration with his colleagues in the Irish medical profession, Kelly hopes to establish a neurological centre in Galway that will serve all the people of the West of Ireland.

Louise Kennedy

LOUISE KENNEDY

She has been described as a postmodern magpie with an exquisite eye. Designer and style goddess Louise Kennedy embodies the very best of contemporary Ireland—successful, talented, innovative, stylish, and great fun. Born in 1960 in County Tipperary, Kennedy's passion has always been fashion. After graduating from the Grafton Academy, she took a leap into the unknown and set up her own fashion business in 1984, with the help of a £10,000 loan from her father. Only five years later she won the coveted *Late Late Show*/Ulster Bank Designer of the Year Award, and it's been onwards and upwards since then. Kennedy dresses some of the most high profile women in the world—her clients include Meryl Streep, Mary McAleese, Mary Robinson, Cheri Blair, Sophie, Countess of Wessex, and most recently, Sarah Macaulay was photographed wearing a Kennedy shantung silk dress and coat at her wedding to the British Chancellor of the Exchequer, Gordon Brown. In 1998 Kennedy opened a 'lifestyle salon' in an early 19th century house on Merrion Square in Dublin. Kennedy's headquarters and home (she lives on the top floor) displays her range of clothes and the glassware she designed for Tipperary Crystal, as well as interior accessories, books, *objets d'art* and gifts from a diverse range of English and Irish designers. Earlier this year, she opened a shop in exclusive Belgravia in London. But, for all her success and glittering client list, one of the highlights (certainly one of the greatest challenges) of her career to date came this year, when she announced that she would redesign the traditional blue-and-gold jerseys of the senior Tipperary hurling team. Her father, Jimmy, from Puckaun, outside Nenagh, was a four-time all-Ireland medallist, three times with Tipperary, and once with Dublin while studying in University College Dublin and Kennedy herself is fiercely proud of her Tipperary roots. 'I have a great sense of being from Tipperary, because of my dad and being involved with Tipperary Crystal,' she says. Irish hurlers are not usually regarded as fashion icons, but, with a little dash of the Kennedy magic, you never know.

RORY KENNEDY

As the youngest of Robert and Ethel Kennedy's eleven children, 31-year old Rory Kennedy's determined personality stood out even among the strong-willed Kennedy clan. That doggedness is serving her well these days in her career as a documentary film-maker. After graduating from Brown University, she started her film-making career with *Women of Substance*, a documentary about pregnant drug addicts. In 1999, Kennedy directed the prizewinning documentary *American Hollow*, which followed a year in the life of the Bowling family, a poor yet tightly knit Appalachian family living in rural Kentucky.

The next project for Kennedy, who lives in New York City with her husband Mark Bailey, is a documentary tracing mental illness in a Mississippi family. And while her famous last name has brought with it both opportunity and tragedy, it's clear that Rory Kennedy is forging her own path by focusing on topics such as human rights in her own distinctive manner. As her brother Douglas said, 'Rory can get into a person's humanity quicker than anybody I've ever met— whether it's a top executive, a recovering crack addict, or a young mother in Appalachia,' he said. 'It's a quality that people say my father had. Rory has that more than anybody in our family.'

Ted Kennedy

TED KENNEDY

Few politicians in US history have seen more professional and personal successes and tragedies than Ted Kennedy. First elected to the US Senate in 1962 to finish the term of his brother Jack, few match Kennedy's political longevity, and his role in relations between America, Ireland and Northern Ireland, is almost immeasurable. His early championing of John Hume has been a crucial element in contemporary Irish history. Kennedy opens every door in the US and he strove mightily to ensure that John Hume's message was getting through. He was also instrumental in ensuring the appointment of his sister Jean Kennedy Smith as Ambassador to Ireland, despite a vitriolic British anti-Kennedy press campaign, Kennedy and his sister made a huge contribution to the resolution of the Troubles in the North and to the ultimate signing of the Good Friday Agreement. Whether it be supporting a visa for Sinn Féin leader Gerry Adams or providing assistance to President Clinton on Irish issues, Kennedy's efforts to support peace and encourage investment in Ireland have been steadfast even when the spotlight did not shine as brightly on the Emerald Isle as it does these days. Currently seeking re-election in his native Massachusetts, Kennedy is the Senior Democrat on various Senate committees and probably the most liberal of American Senators, and his influence on issues such as civil rights and health care is far-reaching. The graduate of Harvard and the University of Virginia Law School also serves as a trustee of the John F. Kennedy Center for Performing Arts in Washington, DC. The youngest of nine children of Joseph and Rose Kennedy may never have reached the office of President as many would have hoped, but he has surely earned his reputation as a hard-working Senator who deserves recognition for a lifetime of service to his own country, as well as to the land of his ancestors.

PAT KENNY

This past year has been rather difficult for Ireland's most important broadcaster. In 1999, Pat Kenny achieved a long-cherished ambition and succeeded Gay Byrne as host of that Irish institution, the *Late Late Show*. But it hasn't been an easy ride. Unfairly criticised by the media for being a stiff and uncomfortable chat show host, Kenny has also had to face up to falling audience figures—an inevitable, if hopefully temporary, reaction to the departure of Byrne. Born in Dublin fifty something years ago, Kenny won a scholarship to study chemical engineering at University College Dublin and spent a year in Atlanta, Georgia, after gaining another scholarship to study thermodynamics there. On his return to Ireland, he took up a lecturing post at Bolton Street College in Dublin, but auditioned for RTÉ in 1972 and was plucked from 500 applicants to join Montrose. Kenny made an immediate impression as an incisive presenter of current affairs programmes on both television and radio (still his greatest strength) and was lauded as 'a crisp, competent and extremely talented performer'. His Saturday night prime time show, *Kenny Live*, went some way towards proving he could handle the lightweight stories as well as the serious issues. Colleagues speak of a 'genuinely pleasant and generous team player' but one who, too, is very sensitive to criticism. However, all agree that he is

Daryl Kerrigan

Pat Kenny

one of the most hardworking broadcasters in the country—in addition to the weekly *Late Late Show*, Kenny presents *Today with Pat Kenny* on radio and is a director of Pro-media, an independent television production company.

DARYL KERRIGAN

The New York fashion cognoscenti is falling at the feet of a young Dublin designer. Daryl Kerrigan (or Daryl K, as she is known) received the Perry Ellis Award for New Fashion Talent from the Council of Fashion Designers of America in 1996 and was recently named as the creative consultant to Tommy Hilfiger's women's collections. However, like all overnight success stories, Daryl's rise to fame has come only after years of hard work and little reward. A graduate of the National College of Design in Dublin, Daryl moved to New York in the mid-1980s, but recalls: 'I couldn't get a job in design even after I graduated so I worked as a waitress for a year, then I quit and got work in the movie business as a wardrobe assistant and then designer. But you can't be that creative in movies.' So in 1991 with the help of her boyfriend and business partner, Paul Leonard from Rush, in County Dublin, Kerrigan opened a shop selling her own designs, which combine, she says, her Irish roots and her Manhattan lifestyle. The success of the business prompted Daryl to open a flagship retail store, wholesale showroom and design studio in lower Manhattan and last year, due to tremendous demand, Daryl opened a boutique in Los Angeles. All of which leaves little time for trips back to Ireland, but Daryl says: 'I do try to get home once a year. I love going, although I usually need a holiday after I've been there!'

PETER KING

'Being Irish means fighting hard for principle, not taking yourself too seriously, and knowing that somewhere, somehow, the world is going to break your heart.' So says Congressman and native New Yorker Peter T. King. And anyone who has seen him in action during his four terms in the US House of Representatives can testify that he is

Peter King

to drag him out of the saddle to make him give up', Kinane recalls. Kinane himself is now in his 41st year and shows no inclination to retire from racing. Now with trainer Aidan O'Brien, Kinane believes he has found in *Montjeu* and *Giant's Causeway* two of the greatest horses he has raced since his first victory at the age of 15 on *Muscari*. Softly spoken and self-effacing, Kinane has enjoyed phenomenal success and has been champion jockey in Ireland on 11 occasions. When he is not racing, Kinane retires to the peace of the farm in Punchestown, County Kildare, where he lives with his wife Catherine and their daughters Sinead and Aisling. Does he have any ambitions left? 'Just one,' he says, 'To do it all again.'

 LOUIS LE BROCQUY

Described as Ireland's most distinguished living painter, Louis Le Brocquy was born in Dublin in 1916 and has been a dominant force in the Irish art world for more than five decades. This self-taught artist left the family business in 1938 and studied the museum collections in London, Paris, and Venice before returning to Ireland to co-found the Irish Exhibition of Living Art in 1943. His discovery of decorated Polynesian ancestral skulls in the Paris Musée de L'Homme inspired his acclaimed series of head images, initially anonymous but later depicting artists such as Yeats, Joyce and Beckett. At the request of Beckett himself, Le Brocquy illustrated *Stirrings Still* and designed the set and costumes for *Waiting for Godot*. His work is exhibited in public collections around the world, including those at the Guggenheim Museum in New York, the Musée d'Art Moderne in Paris, the City Museum of Contemporary Art in Hiroshima and the Irish Museum of Art in Dublin. He has been awarded numerous honorary degrees and was made Chevalier de la Légion d'Honneur and Officier des Arts et des Lettres. In 1994, he was elected Saoi Aosdána in 1994 in recognition of his outstanding contribution to the arts in Ireland, an award that can only be held by five artists at any one time. Married to the artist Anne Madden since 1958, Le Brocquy continues to live and work in Ireland.

indeed a fighter for the principles he believes in, especially when it comes to issues involving his constituents back home in Long Island or the peace process in Northern Ireland. Currently serving on the Committee on Banking and Financial Services, as well as the Committee on International Relations, King is a power broker in the Republican party and a frequent commentator on Northern Ireland. The 55-year old is a graduate of St. Francis College in Brooklyn and the University of Notre Dame Law School. He was comptroller of Nassau County prior to entering politics. A lifelong resident of New York, King and his wife Rosemary have two children. One of the Greener Irish American politicians,

King reputedly advised the previous Taoiseach that he should be a little more concerned with the Nationalist position rather than bending over backwards to accommodate the Unionists.

MICHAEL KINANE

Ask Michael Kinane why he decided to pursue a career as a jockey, and the reply is immediate. 'I didn't know how to do anything else. I could ride a horse before I could walk. And then there was the influence of my father.' Kinane's father, Tommy was a leading National Hunt jockey for many years, winning the Champion Hurdle at Cheltenham when he was 47 years old. 'They had

Louis LeBrocquy

DENIS LEARY

There are no in-betweens when it comes to the irreverent and often profane Denis Leary. You either love him or you don't. But there's no denying the many talents of this hard-working Irish-American. As an actor, writer, comedian, director, and editor, Leary has starred in, written and directed numerous feature and television films, written a one-man stage show (*No Cure for Cancer*) that won the Edinburgh International Arts Festival's Critics Award, and appeared in memorable commercials for MTV and Nike, among others. The 42-year old grew up in Worcester, Massachusetts in an Irish Catholic family. Leary started doing theatre with the New Voices and Charlestown Working theatre companies, and soon went to Emerson College where he founded their Comedy Workshop. He made his acting debut in *Strictly Business* in 1991, and has since worked with notables such as Robert DeNiro and Dustin Hoffman (*Wag the Dog*), Sylvester Stallone (*Demolition Man*), Danny Glover (*Operation Dumbo Drop*), and Pierce Brosnan (*The Thomas Crown Affair*). However, his breakthrough role came as the foul-mouthed thief Gus in *The Ref*, which also starred Judy Davis and Kevin Spacey. His directing skills also earned him a 1997 Cable Ace Award for Best Director of a Comedy for a Showtime movie called *Lust*. Leary traces his Irish roots back to Killarney, where he is currently on the look-out for a holiday home for his German-American wife and family. He travelled to Ireland in 1997 to film *The Matchmaker*, and in 1998 he starred in and produced *Monument Avenue*, a film based on the real life story of murder and crime by the Irish mob in South Boston. With many projects in the pipeline at his own production company, Leary is a multi-talented force to be reckoned with in the coming years.

MICHAEL LONGLEY

Michael Longley is one of Ireland's finest living poets. Born in Belfast in 1939, Longley read classics at Trinity College Dublin, and began writing poetry at the age of 23, but unlike other writers of his calibre Longley did not choose an academic career; instead, he worked for the

Michael Longley

Arts Council of Northern Ireland. The crowning achievement in his poetic endeavours came in 1991 when, after a 12-year silence he published *Gorse Fires*, a collection of some of his finest poetry that was to earn him a Whitbread Poetry Prize. Not as prolific as many of his poetic contemporaries Longley believes that silence is important and that poetry should only be written 'when you have something to say'. Having lived through the Troubles in Northern Ireland it seemed appropriate that his poem *Ceasefire* should be published in *The Irish Times* on the day the first IRA ceasefire was announced. His Dublin-born wife Edna, is herself an esteemed writer and critic and has made an immense contribution in bringing to light a more balanced view of Northern Ireland

Protestants. Now aged 60, Longley's retirement from the Northern Ireland Arts Council has afforded him more time to write—his latest contribution being *The Weather in Japan*—thus guaranteeing the public that this poet's splendid work will continue to grace the shelves of Irish bookshops.

CORA VENUS LUNNY

In many ways a classic teenager (she describes her hobbies as 'laughing, eating, and socialising'), 18-year-old Cora Venus Lunny is also an inspirational violinist who has already given recital and concerto performances to rapturous audiences around the world. Born in Dublin to German-Irish parents, Lunny has been playing the violin since

Cora Venus Lunny

she was three years old, studying with such luminaries as Eugene Sarbu and Vladimir Spivakov. In 1998 she was named RTÉ Musician of the Future, the youngest finalist in the history of the competition. Despite travelling around the world to study and perform, Ireland is still home for this bubbly teenager: 'Ireland is one of those rare places where heritage is not banished to museums. The old lives alongside the new, and that delights me. As a classical musician I strive not only to revere great composers of the past but also to honour the music of the present.'

PETER S. LYNCH

Tall, grey-haired, softly spoken, and bespectacled, Peter S. Lynch is the most successful forecaster and investor in the US. 'Investing is a lot like scuba diving,' he says. 'It's potentially dangerous, but rewarding when you're prepared. If you can swim with the markets, stay calm as prices are buffeted about, negotiate the deep drops, and learn to operate in different environments, you've got what it takes to become a successful investor.' Lynch has what it takes. Under his management from 1977 to 1990, the assets of the Fidelity Magellan Fund increased from $20 million to $14 billion. Born in 1944, Lynch received a bachelor of science degree from Boston College in 1965 and an MBA from The Wharton School at the University of Pennsylvania in 1968. Lynch served as lieutenant in the US Army for two years, before joining Fidelity in 1969 as a research analyst. During his tenure at Fidelity, he served as a managing director of Fidelity Investments, executive vice president and director of Fidelity Management & Research Company, and leader of the growth equity group. Today, Lynch is Vice-Chairman of Fidelity Management & Research Company, a member of the Board of Trustees of the Fidelity Funds, and a bestselling author—his first book, *One Up On Wall Street*, was translated into Japanese, Swedish, Korean, German, Spanish and French and his second, book *Beating The Street*, remained at No. 1 on *The New York Times* best seller list for eight weeks. In 1997, he produced a CD ROM entitled *The Stock Shop*, which provides research tools

for investors keen to examine companies for their own stock portfolios. Regarded as the number one money manager of his time, *The New York Times* wrote that 'Peter Lynch's investment record places him in a league of his own.' Lynch is the recipient of numerous awards, including the Wall Street Week Hall of Fame in 1990, Fortune's National Business Hall of Fame 1991, and the United Way of Massachusetts Bay Leadership Award in 1997. He holds a string of honorary doctorates from Boston College, Emmanuel College, Merrimack College, Skidmore College, and the University of Massachusetts. Despite his enviable reputation on Wall Street,

Lynch remains an essentially private person. He lives in Boston with his wife, Carolyn, and their three daughters and recently bought a house in Ireland. Lynch is a committed supporter of the Archdiocese of Boston (not many church finance committees can count a Wall Street legend among their members), devotes both time and money to charity, a commitment recognised by The Ireland Fund, the National Catholic Educational Association, and the Massachusetts Society for the Prevention of Cruelty to Children, among many others. In the often cut-throat world of investment banking, Lynch is viewed as the hero of the small investor. His philosophy is simple:

John Magnier

'Observe the local business developments and take notice of your immediate world, from the local mall to the work place you, too, can discover potential successful companies before the analysts do.'

JOHN MAGNIER

As managing partner of Coolmore Castlehyde in Fethard, County Tipperary, John Magnier presides over the world's preeminent nursery of thoroughbred talent. With studs in the US, Australia and Ireland, stallions of the calibre of Sadler's Wells, Stravinsky, and Danehill, customers that include Queen Elizabeth and the Aga Khan, the training genius of Vincent O'Brien and now Aidan O'Brien, and the expertise, salesmanship and minute attention to detail of Magnier himself, it is patently clear how and why Coolmore has secured its extraordinary reputation for breeding champion racehorses. Now a multimillionaire and tax exile (he shares homes in Switzerland, Spain and Barbados with his wife Susan and their five children), Magnier has had a colourful past. Born in 1948 in Fermoy, County Cork, his family's involvement with horse breeding dates back to the 1850s and Magnier acquired his first stud farm in the 1970s. His longstanding relationship with former Taoiseach Charles Haughey (who nominated Magnier to the Seanad in 1987) has been the target of intense media scrutiny over the past few years, no doubt a source of great irritation for a man who likes to play his cards close to his chest. Earlier this year, Magnier was awarded a Hall of Fame award from the Irish Thoroughbred Breeders' organisation and used the occasion to criticise the 'handful of amateurs' (in this case, the Turf Club) who opposed the amalgamation of the Irish Horseracing Authority, Racecourses Association and the Turf Club in return for the betting tax being put back into racing. 'Unless everyone wakes up, and then stands up, a handful of amateurs, and by that I mean people who do not rely on this business for their living, are going to cost professional trainers, jockeys, breeders, agents, stable staff and a mass of others their livelihoods.' Strong words from the man known as 'The Boss' in south Tipperary.

Rev. Edward A. Malloy

REV. EDWARD A. MALLOY

Now in the third year of his five-year term as President of his alma mater, the University of Notre Dame in Indiana, Rev. Edward A. Malloy has been an educator for the best part of 30 years. He is a rarity among university presidents—he continues to teach, conducting a seminar for first-year undergraduates each semester, and he makes his home in a student residence hall on campus. Malloy's ancestors emigrated from County Mayo in the 1890s and he was born in Washington, DC, in 1941. He was ordained in 1970, holds a bachelor's and two master's degrees from Notre Dame and a doctorate in Christian ethics from Vanderbilt University—in 1998 Vanderbilt honoured him with the establishment of a chair in Catholic studies in his name. However, Malloy is not content to restrict himself to the rarefied atmosphere of academia. He is actively involved in social issues, particularly in efforts to combat substance abuse—he was a member of the National Advisory Council on Alcohol Abuse and Alcoholism, President Bush's Advisory Council on Drugs and he currently chairs the National Commission on Substance Abuse and Sports. With its history of Irish influence, it is appropriate that Notre Dame should be headed by this Irish educator. 'To be Irish,' he says, 'is to be the inheritor of a grand tradition of culture, religion, and courageous resistance to oppression.'

John Mahoney

JOHN MAHONEY

Although it is for his depiction of Marty Crane, in the hit television comedy *Frazier* that he is most often recognised, John Mahoney's real passion is for the theatre. Mahoney decided to tread the boards later than most—prior to his acting career he worked in health publishing but soon after enrolling in acting classes he was offered a part with the Steppenwolf Theater Company. Born in England, Mahoney has spent most of his life in Chicago, a city he believes is the greatest theatre town in the US. And it was as a member of the Irish Rep of Chicago that he recently took part in the Galway Arts Festival, where his portrayal of James Tyrone in Eugene O'Neill's *Long Day's Journey into Night* was considered the highlight of the festival. The grandson of a County Cork émigré, Mahoney feels a strong empathy with the Irish. 'There's an emotional bond I have with Ireland that I just don't have with England,' he says. 'Perhaps it's because no other people combine tragedy and comedy like the Irish'.

PATRICK MASTERSON

Philosopher, university president and confidante of politicians and presidents, Patrick Masterson was born in Dublin in 1936. His path to academic excellence began at University College Dublin where he achieved First Class Honours, First Place and a Travelling Scholarship in Philosophy in 1960. He returned to his alma mater when he joined the staff in 1963 and was appointed President some 23 years later. In 1994 he moved to Florence as the newly appointed President of the European University Institute. His lengthy list of academic qualifications and awards is staggering—PhD (Louvain), Doctor of the University of Caen, Trinity College Dublin, and New York University, Grande Oficial da Ordem do Mérito da Republica Portuguesa and Grande Ufficiale della Republica Italiana. Masterson is regarded as an accomplished networker, whose contacts hold positions of power and influence around the world—friends say world leaders, film stars and financiers often rub shoulders around the dinner table at the house Masterson shares with his elegant wife Frankie and their four children.

Patrick Masterson

MARY MCALEESE

'The theme of my Presidency is building bridges', declared Mary McAleese at her inauguration as President of Ireland. But, ironically, her campaign to get there had been more notable for its rancour and divisiveness. In the run up to the Presidential election in 1997, one columnist wrote that her success would 'show if we really are a tolerant pluralist and inclusive society as we claim' while another spectator claimed that she was a 'tribal time bomb'. Still another wrote, 'She is, like Thatcher, tougher, more able, more single-minded than those around her. She is in a class of her own. That is why she scares the living daylight out of me. She'll make mincemeat of the elected politicians of Dáil Éireann'. Despite all this, McAleese was elected by the highest margin in the history of the State, an election that was for many reasons a groundbreaking moment in the evolution of the Irish nation—only the second woman ever to hold the highest office in the land, McAleese was also the first president from Ulster. Her political sympathies (Nationalist, Catholic) may have caused dissent in some quarters, but her sharp intelligence and ambition cannot be questioned. Born in 1951 in Rostrevor, County Down, McAleese was a successful barrister, professor of law at Trinity College Dublin, RTÉ journalist, Pro-Vice-Chancellor of Queen's University in Belfast and active campaigner for

peace and inter-community cooperation before her nomination by Fianna Fáil as the next president. Over the three years thus far of her presidency, her political intelligence, subtlety and genuine ease with people has won over many of her critics—for her first overseas trip, McAleese opted not for a visit to Boston or London, where she would be almost guaranteed a warm welcome from the Irish Diaspora. Instead, she visited Irish troops in Lebanon, an often demoralised group trying to keep the peace in an alien and forgotten desert, and earlier this year, she become the first Head of State from the Republic to attend a general assembly of the Presbyterian Church in Belfast. McAleese is leading by example and is undoubtedly the president we need in these changing times. 'With the millennium wind at our backs', she said this year, 'we are capable of ultimately reaching peace and prosperity in Ireland. We have come a long way, we are entitled to celebrate.'

NORA MCANIFF

So what's it like to work at the most popular magazine in the world? Well, 41-year old Nora McAniff can tell you. She was appointed president of *People* magazine in October 1998, becoming the youngest person ever to hold this position. She had previously served as publisher of the weekly magazine since September 1993. During her tenure, *People* was named *Advertising Age*'s 1997 Magazine of the Year and was ranked No. 1 on *Adweek*'s list of the Ten Hottest Magazines of 1996. During her tenure she has overseen the successful launch of *People En Espanol*, its Spanish-language spin-off; *Teen People*, a new magazine for teens; and *People*'s 25th anniversary issue, its most profitable ever. Her upbringing in Queen's, New York, was a staunchly Irish American one. 'I grew up in a large Irish community in Queens, New York, so I just assumed that everyone had freckles, all moms cried when they listened to *My Wild Irish Rose* and that the Irish jig was part of everyone's dance repertoire. It took me a while to finally catch on.' In 1982, armed with a degree in marketing from Baruch College, she started with Time Inc as a marketing information manager. A number of sales jobs within the company

Mary McAleese

followed before McAniff was appointed to the position of New York advertising director of *People* in 1990. In December 1992, McAniff was promoted to publisher of *Life*, becoming the company's youngest woman ever to hold that title. She moved to *People* as publisher nine months later. McAniff, who was honoured as one of Crain's NY Business's Forty Under Forty in 1993, entered the American Advertising Federation's Hall of Achievement in 1994. She served as president of the Advertising Women of New York from 1997 to 1999, and lives in Manhattan and Bridgehampton with her husband. 'To this day,' she says, 'I cherish Irish linen, The Chieftains and The Wolfe Tones and I have finally come to realize and accept that my freckles won't all connect for a year-round tan.'

TERENCE McAULIFFE

Would it be fair to say that without Terence McAuliffe there would be no Democratic Party? He is, without a doubt, the reigning king of the Democratic fundraising machine. So fashionable is McAuliffe in the US that he was the subject of an eight-page feature article in the highly influential *Vanity Fair* magazine and a front page lead story in the *Wall Street Journal*. As finance chairman for the Clinton/Gore Reelection Committee in 1996, McAuliffe pulled together a record-breaking $43 million in eight months. And just this past Spring he chaired the biggest Democratic fundraising gala in history with 13,500 attendees and $26.5 million raised. Not only has the 43-year-old entrepreneur served as national finance chairman for the democratic national committee in 1994 and for Richard Gephardt's presidential campaign in 1988, but he has been the money-man behind campaigns as far back as President Jimmy Carter's days. At a 14-year-old in Tipperary Hill, New York— where the Irish predominate so much that the green light uniquely sits above the red— McAuliffe was a moneymaker. He quit his job as a golf caddy and began a driveway sealing company. 'I thought I was not making enough of my life,' he says. McAuliffe has since been involved in more than three dozen companies, and has

spent 21 years helping the Democratic Party. Most recently, the father of four received the first annual award from the Irish American Democratic Committee for his years of dedication to the party, and his good friend, President Bill Clinton, was there to present it to him. His ancestors came from County Tipperary and Cork, and McAuliffe holds a fondness for Ireland, which he visited with the president on his historic 1995 trip. McAuliffe plans a return trip to Ireland with Clinton to play on the hallowed greens of Ballybunion Golf Course. McAuliffe is a powerful force in political circles and should not be ruled out as a future ambassador to Ireland.

NATASHA McELHONE

Natasha McElhone has co-starred in a string of hit films over the past few years. She performed with Robert De Niro in *Ronin*, Jim Carrey in *The Truman Show*, Anthony Hopkins in *Surviving Picasso*, Kenneth Branagh in *Love's Labour's Lost*, and most recently with William Hurt in *The Touch*. Between films, 27-year-old McElhone likes to take long breaks to spend time with her half-Irish husband, Martin Kelly, a specialist in cranial-facial reconstruction. The couple had their first child in May this year, a son they named Theodore Augustus Kelly. McElhone was raised in Brighton and London, where she studied at the London

Natasha McElhone

Academy of Music and Drama, and, although she still lives there when not filming, visits to her Falcarragh-born mother Noreen and step-father Roy Greenslade at their beautiful home in County Donegal are welcome escapes from the pressures of the acting world. 'I love Ireland,' McElhone says, 'I usually visit Mum several times a year.' With two, possibly three, films lined up for later this year, McElhone may not have a great deal of time for retreats to the delights of Donegal.

GENERAL BARRY McCAFFREY

General Barry McCaffrey saw the horrors of war firsthand during his 36 years in the US Army, which included 13 years of overseas service and four combat tours, Yet the battle he leads today, fighting the use of illegal drugs in the US, may be equally as difficult. As Director of National Drug Control Policy since 1996, McCaffrey controls a multi-billion federal drug control budget and develops the US National Drug Control Strategy. Some may say it's a losing battle, but McCaffrey pushes forward with a steely determination that would make his ancestors from Donegal and Cork proud. A graduate of the US Military Academy, McCaffrey holds a Masters degree in civil government from American University and has taught at West Point. McCaffrey served as Commander-in-Chief of the US Armed Forces Southern Command coordinating national security operations in the Latin America region and retired as the US Army's most highly decorated and then youngest serving four star general. McCaffrey acknowledges the legacy of his Irish ancestors. 'Their children and grandchildren all have a strong Catholic faith, an enormous loyalty to family, and a love of literature, poetry and music.'

MITCH McCONNELL

As Chairman of the Senate Foreign Operations Committee, US Senator Mitch McConnell travelled to Northern Ireland and the Irish Republic in 1997 to review projects of the International Fund for Ireland. It was relatively familiar ground for the Kentucky native, who has vacationed in the North looking for relatives from generations ago.

Mitch McConnell

McConnell's entry into politics started during his school years, when he served as student body president at both the University of Louisville and at the University of Kentucky's College of Law. In 1991, McConnell established a non-partisan scholarship programme at his alma mater to encourage future leaders from his home state. Today, the staunch Republican is known as a strong supporter of his party's platform and equally as proud of his Irish heritage, which he traces back to James McConnell, an immigrant from County Down in the 1760s who fought in the American Revolution. The 58-year old McConnell is married to Elaine L. Chao, former president of the United Way of America and director of the Peace Corps. They have three daughters.

TED McCONNELL

Ted McConnell considers himself to have the best of both worlds. He has been appointed by the Canadian government as an observer of the International Fund for Ireland, which supports areas seriously affected by the Troubles in Northern Ireland. Given that he was born and raised in Belfast, 'It is terrific for me to be able to make a contribution to the whole peace process,' says McConnell. And, as an old school friend and admirer of his said, 'There are not many fellows from the Glen Road who hurled for the Antrim minors and ended up a multi-millionaire, but it couldn't happen to an nicer fellow.' McConnell is also the Honorary Counsel General for Ireland in Toronto for the province of Ontario, and thus

General Barry McCaffrey

serves as a representative to Ireland in Canada. 'I can serve Ireland—the land of my birth—and Canada—the land of my adoption,' he says. The 68-year-old law graduate first arrived in Canada in 1956. Rather than returning to his homeland, he became an investment banker with Citibank, and then, in 1975, started his own investment management firm, E.J. McConnell and Associates. Since selling the business to Barclays Bank in 1994, McConnell has continued to work as a consultant and receive various accolades for his role as an Irishman in Canada. He was honoured at the Irishman of the Year in Toronto in the early 1980s and Irishman of the Year in Eastern Canada in 1989. To top his awards, McConnell served as Toronto's Grand Marshall for the Saint Patrick's Day Parade this past year. As the founder of The Apostles of Ireland, a group of Irishmen, from north and south, who provide a forum for Irish politicians in Toronto, he is glad to give back to his homeland in multiple ways. Taking his own motto from that of Belfast—'For so much, what shall we give back?'—McConnell says, 'Life has been good to me, so I owe something back.'

FRANK MCCOURT

From his apartment on the Upper East Side of Manhattan, in New York City, Frank McCourt has come long way from the cramped room he first rented when he arrived in the US in 1949. 'To arrive here was like emerging from an Irish womb. I might have had the English language, but I was unequipped—no education; no self esteem,' he says. Years later, McCourt more than made up for his perceived shortcomings when he published his very first book and autobiography, *Angela's Ashes*, which won the 1997 Pulitzer Prize and made the best seller list for an astonishing 200 weeks. In an hilarious and at times brutally honest account of his years of physical and spiritual poverty growing up in Limerick, Ireland, McCourt's childhood experiences have been transformed into a work of art or a flight of his imagination, depending on whose opinion you accept. Today, at 69, the author gives credit to his five-year-old granddaughter for inspiring his

straight-forward writing style. McCourt's follow up autobiography, *Tis*, which also became a best seller in 1999, adopts a similar style to depict his years in New York City, where he obtained a college degree without having attended high school, and then worked for 30 years as an English teacher. His younger brother, Malachy, who also lives in New York, followed on the success of *Angela's Ashes* with his own memoir, *Monks Swimming*, in 1998. McCourt said at the time, 'Our younger brother Alphie is threatening to write a book as well. We should be stuffed and mounted.' *Angela's Ashes* was made into a successful movie in 1999.

TONY MCCOY

Weighing more than ten stone and standing just over 5ft10" in height, Tony McCoy's physique appears at odds with preconceived ideas of how a jockey, let alone a champion jockey, should look. But a brief perusal of his resumé will quickly dissipate such misconceptions. Within the space of a few short years McCoy has become one of the greatest jockeys in the history of the sport. In 1997 he became only the fourth jockey to complete the 'Big Double' in the same year, achieving victories in both the Champion Hurdle and the Cheltenham Gold Cup. Aged only 24, McCoy had been riding in Britain for less than five

Martin McDonagh

Frank McCourt

seasons. During this period he joined the Grand National winning trainer and fellow Irishman Toby Balding. McCoy's record of 175 victories in 1995/1996 was surpassed the following year when he rode 190 winners. Even that success was dwarfed by his 1997/1998 performances when he rode a staggering 253 winners, creating a new world record. Son of Peadar and Clare McCoy, Tony was reared in Moneyglass, County Derry, and it was a mere seven miles down the road at Cullybacky that he embarked on a career as a jockey with horse owner, Willie Rock. McCoy freely admits to his lack of interest in school while growing up, preferring the rough and tumble sports of Gaelic football and horse riding. In retrospect McCoy believes that he should have pursued his education a little further, but at present he has little time for anything besides horse racing. These days McCoy shares a house near Farrington with Limerick jockey, Barry Fenton. Although McCoy is a non-smoker and non-drinker, and has no romantic ties at present, McCoy's life is far from hermetic. In between his hectic horse racing career, he spends his leisure time golfing, clay pigeon shooting and enjoying good-natured banter with his old friends about racing and Gaelic football. Despite his phenomenal career to date, McCoy plays down his achievements. 'In the world of horse racing,' he says, 'you're only ever a mistake away from having your backside in the mud.' Let's hope this young Irishman manages to stay in the saddle, and continues to do himself and Ireland proud on the race track.

MARTIN MCDONAGH

He is one of the most successful of our modern playwrights, lauded as 'a born storyteller with a precocious sense of dramatic structure But this London-born second generation Irishman dismisses such hyperbole. 'All this is icing. I didn't write the plays for this. The most important thing for me is that someone pays to see one of my plays and then, without any baggage, comes and tells me they liked it,' he says. And the thousands who have laughed and cried at performances of *The Beauty Queen of Leenane*, *The Lonesome West*, or

Siobhan McDonagh

Margaret McDonagh

The Cripple of Inishmaan could indeed be said to like his work. Lacking the propensity for pomposity that afflicts some of the more established stars of the theatre world, McDonagh claims he honed his craft at the altar of Australian soaps and wrote *Beauty Queen* in a week. That was a good week's work—*Beauty Queen* caused a sensation when it opened on Broadway in 1998 and proceeded to win four Tony awards. *The Lonesome West* continued the run of success by opening straight onto Broadway and netting four Tony award nominations. Still only 30, McDonagh is second only to Shakespeare as the most performed playwright in the US and his plays are being staged in more than 38 countries around the world. As he puts the finishing touches to his screenplay *Barney Nenagh's Shotgun Circus*, McDonagh's shooting star shows no sign of slowing down.

MARGARET AND SIOBHAN MCDONAGH

Margaret and Siobhan McDonagh are leading lights in Tony Blair's government. The two sisters joined the Labour Party as teenagers and have

forged their way through the ranks—Siobhan became a councillor at 21, one of the youngest in Britain, and Margaret is the first woman and youngest ever person to hold the position of General Secretary of the Labour Party. Siobhan cannot explain where the love of politics originated. 'Our parents left Ireland in the years following the War—my dad worked as a builder and my mum was a psychiatric nurse on night shifts for as long as I can remember. Neither was particularly political, but they voted Labour and encouraged us to read the newspapers and take an interest in the world around us.' Although their parliamentary and constituency responsibilities keep them extremely busy, the two sisters try to visit Ireland regularly and confess to being astounded by the changes that have occurred since they spent their long summer holidays here 30 years ago. 'There's a such a new sense of confidence and a notable sense of purpose, although I find it amusing that trendy Londoners are rushing to sample the cooking that we yearned to leave behind—to this day the smell of boiled ham can induce nausea in me from a half a mile away,' Siobhan laughs. Chances are, boiled ham is not often on the menu at the State dinners attended by the McDonagh sisters.

WILLIAM J. McDONOUGH

As President of the Federal Reserve Bank in New York, William J. McDonough is one of the most senior bankers in the US, probably second only to Alan Greenspan, the most influential central banker in the world. An indication of McDonough's financial clout came in 1999 when he brokered over one weekend a $3.5 billion bail out of Long-Term Capital Management, which came perilously close to being forced to liquidate billions of dollars of investments to meet minimum capital requirements—such a liquidation would have had potentially devastating effects on the entire western capital system. As one New York investment banker remarked at the time, 'McDonough is one tough cookie but he carries an enormous amount of leverage.' McDonough's appointment to the Federal Reserve Bank in 1996 was the culmination of more than two decades in banking. Born in Chicago in 1934, McDonough's childhood was marred by tragedy when his parents (first generation Irish from Roscommon and Mayo) died within a year of each other. McDonough joined the US Navy in 1956 and, four years later, armed with the scholarship he had dreamed of, he went to college and earned a master's degree in economics from Georgetown University. Following a six-year stint at the US State Department, McDonough joined the First National Bank of Chicago in 1967 and remained there for 22 years. On his retirement from the bank in 1989, he was vice-chairman of the board and a director of the bank holding company. He joined the Federal Reserve Bank in 1992 and was appointed chief executive in 1993 and president in 1996. McDonough is passionate about his Irish heritage and a great admirer of the Irish economic boom. 'As a son of the Diaspora, I am fascinated that successful Irish people are now moving back to Ireland,' he says. McDonough's influence and interests stretch far beyond the world of banking—he serves on the boards of the New

Kathleen Anne McGrath

York Philharmonic Orchestra, the New York Academy of Science, the Council on Foreign Relations and he chairs the Economic Club of New York.

JOHN McGAHERN

It has been said of John McGahern that anyone interested in reaching an understanding of the heart of Ireland need look no further than McGahern's stories. Novels such as *The Barracks* and the award-winning *Amongst Women*, short story collections such as *Nightlines* and *The Collected Stories*, and television and radio plays such as *Swallows* and *The Power of Darkness* span

almost 30 years and capture the evolution of modern Irish society. McGahern was born in Dublin in 1934, studied at University College Dublin and worked for a time as a primary school teacher and later university lecturer in the UK and the US. McGahern has been acclaimed all over the world—he is a recipient of the Chevalier de l'Ordre des Arts et des lettres, the Prix Etrangere Ecureuil, the American Irish Foundation Award, An Comhairle Elaíon Award and he holds honorary degrees from Trinity College Dublin, University College Dublin and Université de Poitiers. Now in his sixties, McGahern has been described as the literary bridge between old and new Ireland.

KATHLEEN ANNE McGRATH

Forget Hollywood interpretations of female naval officers. Commander Kathleen Anne McGrath is the real thing. In 1998 McGrath took command of the USS Jarrett, the most recent highlight of a glittering career in the US Navy. McGrath was born in Columbus, Ohio, the daughter of James and Martha McGrath, and attended California State University. Commissioned through Officer Candidate School in 1980, McGrath complete a tour in Yokosuka, Japan, and attended Surface Warfare Officer's School before serving on the USS Prairie for three years as Deck Division Officer and First Lieutenant. In 1987 she earned a master of Arts degree from Stanford and attended Department Head School at Surface Warfare Officer's School. As Operations Officer on the USS Concord, McGrath was involved with Operation Sharp Edge and Desert Shield. In 1993, she took command of the rescue and salvage ship, USS Recovery. Just five years later, she took command of the USS Jarrett. McGrath has been awarded the three Meritorious Service Medals, three Navy and Marine Corps Commendation Medals, a Navy and Marine Corps Achievements medal and various campaign and service ribbons. When not on the high seas, McGrath lives in San Diego, California, with her husband Gregory Brandon, himself a former Naval officer, and their two children.

Judy McGrath

JUDY McGRATH

MTV has revolutionised youth and music programming around the world. Split second images, cutting edge graphics, trendy young presenters, and a highly intelligent branding and marketing strategy has made MTV a cultural phenomenon. And, as President of the MTV Group, Judy McGrath can claim much of the credit. Under her direction MTV has grown from a maverick cable channel to a global brand— the phrase 'MTV generation' has entered popular vocabulary as a catch-all term for the style and attitudes of an entire generation of young people. McGrath's grandparents were born in Ireland—the McGraths came from Armagh, and

her maternal grandparents, the Hardings, were born in the west of Ireland. McGrath started out with an English degree from Cedar Crest College in Allentown, Pennsylvania, a flair for words and a head full of bright ideas. Stints as copy chief at *Glamour* magazine, senior writer at *Mademoiselle* magazine, and copywriter for national advertising led up to her fateful move to Warner Amex Satellite Entertainment Company, MTV Network's predecessor company, in 1981. The new environment provided the scope she needed and programmes like *Devo Goes Hawaiian* and *One Night Stand with Journey* established her as a rising star. Promotions to editorial director, executive vice-president,

creative director, co-president and finally president followed in rapid succession. Earlier this year the MTV Music Awards, presented by Ronan Keating, brought Dublin to a standstill as rock stars, models, actors, sports personalities and their countless hangers-on jockeyed for headlines. McGrath says her abiding principle is to respect the young adults who tune in to the network and she is fully aware of the power she harnesses. Award-winning campaigns to heighten political awareness (*Choose or Lose*) and tolerance (*Free Your Mind*) have expanded MTV's brief. McGrath lives in New York with her husband, Mike Corbett, whose family hails from Counties Mayo and Galway.

KIERAN MCGOWAN

Kieran McGowan is widely regarded as one of the prime architects of the Celtic Tiger. As managing director and then chief executive of the Industrial Development Authority (IDA), is credited with bringing net annual job creation from less than 1,000 in 1991 to more than 10,000 in 1997. His methods—targeting the emerging hi-tech industries and companies that would suit Ireland's resources and capacities, investing in education and training and, of course, his infamous 'boy scouts to subversives' system, which aimed to turn diligent and obedient Irish managers of multinational plants into razor-sharp corporate politicians, who would progressively win more power, influence and security for the operations in the Republic—have been spectacularly successful and are copied the world over by small countries determined to move ahead. Dublin-born McGowan started out in pensions while studying part-time at UCD and moved to the IDA in 1966, becoming managing director 24 years later. He retired as chief executive of the IDA in 1998 and is now chairman of the Irish Management Institute. McGowan also holds positions on the Trade and Business Development Body of the Irish North-South Ministerial Council and was Commissioner General for Ireland at EXPO 2000 in Hanover this year. When the economic history of Ireland is written, McGowan will surely feature among the greats.

ALASTAIR MCGUCKIAN

From the farmlands of Ulster to the deserts of Saudi Arabia to the stage of the Cork Opera House, Alastair McGuckian's journey has been a fantastical one. Born in 1936, McGuckian studied agriculture and worked on the family farm in County Antrim, where he developed systems of livestock farming that improved efficiency. In 1968, he formalised his theories into a standard package for farmers interested in improving the efficiency of their livestock enterprises and founded Masstock Systems Ltd with his brother Paddy. Since then, the family business (his son Ciaran and nephews Patrick and Eoin now work

Kieran McGowan

Alastair McGuckian

for the company) has diversified into research and agri-chemicals and has established divisions in Saudi Arabia, China, the US, Africa, Russia and Romania. At the age of 54, while on business to Saudi Arabia, McGuckian decided to write a musical. 'We could not move in or out of Saudi Arabia during the Gulf War, so I decided to put my free time to good use and *Ha'penny Bridge* was born', he says. *Ha'penny Bridge* premiered at the Cork Opera House earlier this year and tells the story of the love between an Irishwoman and an Englishman against the backdrop of the Civil War. 'I'd describe it as a musical extravaganza,' McGuckian says. 'I think it's a show for people who like musicals. It's not an opera, it's not straight theatre—it's a full exciting piece of entertainment, with drama, laughter, music, and romance.'

MARK MCGWIRE

Sixty and sixty-one are lucky numbers for Mark McGwire, the famed Saint Louis Cardinals baseball player. He broke Babe Ruth's record of 60 home runs and calmly passed Roger Maris' 61 homes in 1997, becoming baseball's home run king. McGwire's two home run balls now sit in the Baseball Hall of Fame, and yet he continues to astonish the crowds, with a 70-home-run record by the end of 1998. Off the field, McGwire has been a strong advocate on behalf of abused

children and a source of inspiration for all. He started a foundation which funds child abuse centers in St. Louis, Missouri, and Los Angeles, California, and has given $3 million of his own money to the cause. The 6-foot-5-inch red-haired Californian, who has yet to trace his Irish roots, is also the father of a 12-year-old son, Matthew. It was at a similar age as his son is now that McGwire had his first opportunity up at bat. Even back then, he hit a home run, recalls a former little league teammate Dan Magee. 'McGwire hit it into the next field,' Magee recalls in amazement.'

VINCENT K. MCMAHON

Studio head, creative director, producer, writer, promoter, marketer, showman—for the past 20 years Vincent McMahon has been the driving force behind the phenomenon that is World Wrestling Federation. Make no mistake about it, the World Wrestling Federation is a phenomenon—every week 20 million Americans join countless millions in more than 120 countries around the world as they tune in to WWF events. Wrestling is in McMahon's blood. He was reared by his mother and a series of step-fathers but did not meet his birth father, wrestling promoter Vincent J. McMahon, until he was 12 years old. 'I idolised him instantly,' McMahon says. His passion for wrestling was awakened during trips with

Vincent K. McMahon

his father to matches at Madison Square Garden. McMahon married his high school sweetheart, Linda Edwards, and went to college, but he continued to pester his father for a chance to prove himself. The chance came in 1971 when McMahon was 26 years old. He promoted his first wrestling match in Bangor, Maine. The event was a resounding success and McMahon joined his father's business in 1972. Ten years later, he bought the company from his father. And proceeded to turn the traditional wrestling industry on its head. McMahon introduced story lines, flamboyant costumes, characters and rock music and the WWF soon moved from fringe Saturday morning television to mainstream entertainment. Then in 1985, McMahon pulled off another marketing coup—he introduced the pay-per-view format to WWF and it worked. In April this year, more than 800,000 fans purchased the WWF's premier event, Wrestlemania, making it the most watched non-boxing event in pay-per-view history. In 1999 *WWF Smackdown!* debuted on UPN, immediately becoming the network's highest rated programme. In February this year, he announced the formation of XFL, a new professional football league jointly owned by NBC. Twenty-nine years after he joined his father's business, McMahon's sports empire (conservative estimates put its value at just short of one billion dollars) is still a family business—McMahon's wife Linda is CEO, their son Shane is president of WWF New Media and their daughter Stephanie is an account executive in the New York office. And, like all Irish families, at the end of a hard working day, the McMahons like nothing better than to kick up their heels and party.

J. P. MCMANUS

J. P. McManus is a legend in racing and gambling circles. Nicknamed 'The Sundance Kid' in the 1970s due to his bravado and successes at the racecourses and in the gambling rooms of Europe, McManus today is a phenomenally successful Geneva-based financier and bloodstock breeder. As with all the best legends, his life was not always so glamorous. McManus was born in Dublin in 1951, but grew up in Limerick and

reputedly started gambling at the age of nine. He joined his father's plant hire business when he left school and launched his bookmaking business when he was just 20 years old. However, he quickly realised that he preferred gambling to bookmaking, and stories of £100,000 bets at Cheltenham were soon making the rounds. His string of winning horses include *Cill Dara*, *Laura's Beau*, *Danny Connors* and *Istabraq*, the three-time winner of the Champion Hurdle at Cheltenham—'It's a joy to own a horse like him,' McManus says. Golf is another passion. The J. P. McManus International ProAm attracts the biggest names in professional golf (Tiger Woods is a personal friend)

and amateurs happy to pay £40,000 per team for the privilege of playing with the stars. All expenses are paid by McManus, so all the money raised goes to charity. Earlier this year, McManus was revealed as the 'mystery benefactor' who had donated £50 million to the proposed national sports stadium. Despite lavish homes in Geneva and Limerick (McManus is a tax exile), his private jet, prized race horses, and estimated wealth of £400 million, McManus is described by friends as a down-to earth Irish man, an image he is happy to perpetuate: 'When I go out on a Saturday night it's with the same people I went out with over 20 years ago.'

J. P. McManus

DAVID McWILLIAMS

Although many believe the Celtic Tiger sprang upon us with little or no warning, there were those who predicted its coming. One of the economic prophets was David McWilliams. In 1994 at the age of 27, he predicted the Irish economy would grow 'at least three times faster than the European average, with the enviable combination of Asian growth rates and European inflation until the end of the decade'. At the time, the Irish economy was characterised by emigration and unemployment and with Europe in a recession, the outlook did not seem rosy. Yet, the forecast was spot on, and par for the course for this dynamic young economist. Born in 1966, McWilliams studied economics at Trinity College Dublin and the College of Europe in Bruges. 'Ireland seemed to be in such a mess in the 1980s. I wanted to understand why we appeared to be getting things so wrong,' he replies when asked what attracted him to economics. He joined the Central Bank of Ireland in 1989, and four years later was recruited by the Union Bank of Switzerland. He was appointed director with responsibility for the bank's global investment strategy and all its European economic forecasts, becoming the youngest ever director at UBS. While compiling in-depth reports on European economies for UBS, he made his now famous six-year forecast for Ireland. McWilliams returned to Ireland in 1999 and married his partner Sian in County Galway. He set up Iconic Ltd, an investment company that trades out of New York and offers economic and strategic advice to international clients and added a couple of new strings to his bow—as a presenter of TV3's flagship current affairs programme, *Agenda*, and a columnist on *The Sunday Business Post*. The past year has been dominated by the arrival of the couple's daughter, Lucy. So what does this 34-year-old economic maverick predict next? Never one to toe the Establishment line, McWilliams believes that unless the Government acts decisively on inflation, the economy is now in serious danger of overheating. Again, local commentators are sceptical. McWilliams claims that Ireland could face a short, sharp period of recession in the next four or five years. But, when this froth is blown off the economy, it is likely to recover strongly and quickly.

SPIKE MILLIGAN

'I woke up this morning and I was still alive, so I am pretty cheerful,' he declared on his 79th birthday. Spike Milligan must, therefore, have felt positively chirpy when he celebrated his 82nd birthday earlier this year. Irrepressible, irreverent and revered around the world as one of the originators of modern comedy, he was the comic genius behind *The Goon Show* and the inspiration for *Monty Python*. Born in India in 1918, Milligan's father was an Irish NCO in the British Raj and the family lived there until his father retired from the military and they moved to England. Milligan joined the British Army at the outbreak of World War II, where he served in the Royal Artillery through the North African and Italian campaigns and was hospitalised for shell shock. Although he has suffered more than ten mental breakdowns and has been diagnosed with manic depression, Milligan has never stopped working—film roles, television appearances, and of course the books and collections of poetry that have delighted children and adults alike: 'Said a tiny Ant/To the Elephant/"Mind how you tread in this clearing!"/But alas! Cruel fate!/She was crushed by the weight/Of an Elephant, hard of hearing'. His favourite book is *The Looney*, first published in 1987. 'That was the funniest book ever written by

George Mitchell

anyone,' he says. 'It was full of wonderful Irish whimsy.' Milligan has six children: Laura, Sean and Sile with his first wife, June; a daughter, Jane, with his second wife, Paddy, a daughter with a Canadian journalist, and a son, James. He dismisses charges that he was something of a Casanova in his youth. 'I never made a play for any particular woman; they would make a play for me. I was a contented bachelor; I just did what I was told. I am a peaceloving man, but I always seem to have turbulent women in my life.' These days, Milligan busies himself with galvanising support for environmental issues and vegetarianism—'I'm Irish, I love potatoes. It's a wonder they didn't call me Spud Milligan in the army.'

GEORGE MITCHELL

If the contributions made by George Mitchell to Northern Ireland were summed up in one sentence, it would be in the words of Sinn Féin leader Gerry Adams: 'Senator Mitchell's role was indispensable to the success of the negotiations process and to the securing of the Good Friday Agreement.' As independent chairman of the peace negotiations in Northern Ireland from 1996 to 1998, the former US senator from Waterbury, Maine, effectively and patiently brought the disputing parties to the table. Week after week, month after month, one would require the patience of a saint to endure the rantings of Ian Paisley and his colleagues, who regard compromise as surrender. But Mitchell cajoled and supported all the parties to cross the great divide. He pushed for the decommissioning of paramilitary weapons and helped achieve the historic 1998 Good Friday Agreement, which was overwhelmingly endorsed by the voters of Ireland, North and South. At the end of it all, says Mitchell, the treaty was 'by far the longest and most difficult task I've undertaken'. Before his appointment in Northern Ireland, Mitchell served 14 years in the US Senate. There he was equally praised as 'the most respected member' of the Senate by a bipartisan group of senior congressional aides. During his last six years, until 1995, he served as Majority Leader. Mitchell, 67, has also authored four books, the last of which, *Senator George*

Mitchell—Making Peace, speaks to Northern Ireland. As for the peace broker's own Irish heritage, his grandfather came to the US from Ireland at the end of the 19th century. Although the county of origin is unknown, Mitchell can be sure he is welcome in Ireland anytime.

PADDY MOLONEY

Little did Paddy Moloney realise when he founded The Chieftains in 1962, that the band would still be going strong in 2000. Their music has spawned any number of mix and match 'trad' groups, but The Chieftains are the undisputed

Erin Moriarty

kings of the genre, as attested by their incredible output of 36 critically acclaimed albums in 38 years. They have played for presidents and kings, not to mention their millions of fans around the world. One high point soars above all others, says Paddy—playing on the Great Wall of China in 1983. Dublin-born Moloney dates his love of music back to his summer holidays in his grandmother's home in County Laois where singing and set dancing comprised the nightly entertainment. A pivotal figure in the rejuvenation of traditional Irish music in the 1960s, Moloney has remained at the epicentre of the music scene since then—a keeper of the flame, certainly,

Spike Milligan

but one who is not afraid to add to the mix through collaborations with people such as Van Morrison and Sting. Moloney, now 62, continues to tour and release records with The Chieftains (reviews of their latest offering, *Water from the Well*, refer to the sheer power of their music in full flight). Moloney lives in County Wicklow with his wife Rita and their two sons, Aonghus and Padraig, and daughter, Aedin.

TOM MORAN

The CEO of an $8 billion-plus company might be expected to roll up to work in a chauffeur-driven limousine. Not Tom Moran, President and CEO of Mutual of America—a Harley Davidson is more his style. This genial insurance giant is applauded for his tireless charity work—Concern Worldwide and the American Cancer Foundation are just some of the charities with which he is involved— and for his dedication to the peace process in the North of Ireland, from where his maternal grandmother and paternal great-great grandfather hail. Moran serves on the Board of the National Committee on American Foreign Policy, the body that first invited Gerry Adams to speak in the US. Moran is New York born and bred. He grew up in Staten Island and studied mathematics at Manhattan College (he marches with his alma mater in the St. Patrick's Day Parade every year) and joined the pension underwriting department at Mutual of America in 1975, as, he laughingly recalls, the 'paper clipper'. The 'paper clipper' moved up through the ranks, gaining invaluable and varied management experience, and was appointed President and CEO in 1994. Moran lives in New York with his wife Joan and is a leading Irish American—the Calvary Medal and The Ellis Island Medal of Honour are just two of the awards presented to this genial insurance giant.

ERIN MORIARTY

As the news correspondent for the CBS television show, *48 Hours*, Erin Moriarty has tackled some of the most controversial issues in the US over the past ten years, whether it be teenagers facing the death penalty, battered women or abortion.

The importance of her work has been recognised time and again—Moriarty has received nine Emmy Awards and the Outstanding Consumer Media Service Award. Born in the Mid West to parents from County Cork, Moriarty trained to be a lawyer at Ohio State University, before switching to journalism. In 1983, she joined WMAQ-TV Chicago and the television bug bit. Three years later she moved to CBS News as a consumer correspondent on *This Morning* and *Evening News With Dan Rather* and then joined *48 Hours*. She lives in New York with her husband and, later this year, they hope to travel to Ireland with her twin sister Shellah for a Moriarty clan reunion.

VAN MORRISON

World class musicians may appear to be ten a penny in Ireland at the moment, but none can clam the status of Van the Man, a star of the old school who has been on the road in one way or another for the best part of 40 years. His importance to Irish culture was officially recognised last year when he was honoured as the first inductee to the Irish Hall of Fame. Notoriously reticent, he summed up the experience thus: 'A lot of people I knew showed up. It was good.' His music cannot be neatly filed under rock 'n' roll, or jazz, or pop— and that's just how he likes it. When the Belfast Blues Appreciation Society sought to erect a

Van Morrison

plaque on the wall of the house where he was born in 1945, he tried to block the move, citing invasion of privacy, and when a national newspaper referred to him as a rock star, he complained that the term was 'not only amusing but ridiculous'. Whether he likes it or not, Van Morrison is a musical icon and a national treasure.

DANIEL PATRICK MOYNIHAN

Senator Daniel Patrick Moynihan is undoubtedly the quintessential New Yorker, erudite, opinionated, and elegant in an Ivy League professorial sort of way. His impeccable Irish roots coat him with a patina of blarney most intellectuals never achieve. It has made him the nation's most courageous liberal politician. If there is anyone in the US who carries the torch that still flickers from the New Frontier administration of John Fitzgerald Kennedy, it is Moynihan. During his almost 25 years in the US Senate he formed a remarkable partnership with Massachusetts Senator Edward M. Kennedy. Together they championed legislation affecting the nation's poorest citizens, as well as issues affecting Ireland. Moynihan's political acumen and allegiances go back to the early 1950s when he was a member of Averell Harriman's New York campaign. It was here in the brawl and bluster of New York state politics that he developed his real political muscle. Moynihan enjoyed a prominent position of influence on the Governor's inner staff. Later, his brain power and tempestuous defence of the poor, in the tradition of Franklin Delano Roosevelt, made him a significant player in the administrations of Presidents Kennedy, Johnson, Nixon and Ford. The quality of his thought and voice gave him power that crossed both political parties. The author of more than 18 books, he is a man as at home in the rarefied halls of Harvard University as on the sidewalks of New York. Choosing not to run for a fifth term in 2000, Moynihan left the Senate when his term expired in 2000. The US media compared him with the great Thomas Jefferson, the ultimate accolade for an US politician. It's a long way from a saloon keeper's family in Hell's Kitchen to the Senate, but this distinguished Irish American, a renaissance man in the truest sense, has made the journey in style.

Daniel Patrick Moynihan

LIAM MULVIHILL

As Director General of the GAA since 1979, Liam Mulvihill has presided over an extraordinary period of growth and change within Gaelic games. And he is the first to ring the changes: 'As the country has grown up, so, too, has the GAA,' he says. 'There is a new confidence in the Irish population, a pride in being Irish. In many ways the GAA reflects that mood and Gaelic games have thrived on that confidence'. Gaelic games have also thrived under the leadership of this 54-year-old from Longford. His family were ardent GAA supporters and Mulvihill naturally moved from playing (he won a Leinster and All-Ireland medal in college Gaelic football) to managing when he joined the GAA Central Council in his twenties. Mulvihill is particularly proud of the £140 million redevelopment of Croke Park, the GAA flagship stadium. And he recognises the need for the GAA to reflect the continuing drift from rural to urban and commuter living in Irish society as well as the renewed interest in Gaelic games in the North of Ireland, where players and supporters traditionally fell under suspicion from certain quarters because of their association with the GAA. In 1999, Mulvihill's daughter, Daráine, contracted meningitis, and Mulvihill professed himself amazed at the kindness and support shown to him and his wife, Máire. 'The support we received was an enormous source of strength for the whole family. Daráine has handicaps to overcome, but together we will do it. That is the most important thing in life for us now.'

Liam Mulvihill

MARTIN NAUGHTON

Dundalk-born Martin Naughton is one of the most successful business-men in Ireland and around the world. An engineer by profession, he was educated in Ireland and at Southampton University, where he studied mechanical and production engineering. In 1973, Naughton founded Glen Electric and developed a range of convection heaters. Strategic acquisitions and clever marketing increased the scope of the business and the Glen Dimplex Group today (of which he is chairman) has an annual turnover of £650 million and employs 2,000 people in Ireland with another 4,000 employed in Northern Ireland, UK, Canada, and France. However, Naughton's interests extend far beyond the indus-try he now dominates. The acquisition of six rundown Georgian houses opposite Government Buildings was an imaginative—some said fool-hardy—investment. But Naughton and his part-ners believed that Dublin deserved a world-class hotel. And that is what they got—The Merrion Hotel rivals the best in the world and is the place to see and be seen in Dublin and has attracted rave reviews from travel magazines around the world. Naughton was an early supporter of French chef Patrick Guillbaud and his restaurant at the hotel is the only Michelin two star estab-lishment in Ireland. Naughton is an influential trustee of the University of Notre Dame and was instrumental in attracting a Notre Dame campus to Ireland. He is also a valued member of the Council of State which advises the president. Naughton and his wife Carmel, Chairman of the National Gallery of Ireland, are ardent collectors of the Irish paintings that adorn the walls of their home, Stackallen House in County Meath, which they have restored to its former glory. Naughton's combination of business acumen, negotiating skills, and down-to-earth charm rendered him the obvious candidate as the first Chairman of the cross-border trade and development body and he is often called upon to speak to visiting digni-taries keen to learn the secrets of the Celtic Tiger success story.

LIAM NEESON

Dignity and poise are the words most often used to describe Liam Neeson's simmering presence on film screens. The former teenage boxing champ and trainee teacher from Ballymena, County Antrim, has come a long way since he arrived in Hollywood and slept on a couch at his agent's home, promising himself that if he didn't make it before the money ran out, he would go back to his old haunts in London. Luckily for us, supporting roles in films *Excalibur* and *Suspect* came his way before his pockets emptied. His breakthrough leading role came in 1990 in Darkman and in 1993 he made his Broadway debut in Eugene O'Neill's drama *Anna Christie*. The play was a pivotal moment in his life—he subsequently married his co-star Natasha Richardson, and he so impressed one member of the audience that he was offered a role in a new film. The guy in the audience none other than Stephen Spielberg and the film was *Schindler's List*. Neeson was nominated for an Oscar, a Golden

Globe and BAFTA Award in the best leading actor category, and he became a superstar. Neeson is justifiably proud of the film and counts it, with *Michael Collins*, as his finest work. 'They were both stories that touched people's lives and needed to be told and shared,' he says. When he jokingly told the press that he was going to quit the film business after his popular stint as Jedi Master Qui-Gon Jinn in *Star Wars: The Phantom Menace*, he was surprised they took him so seriously. 'Everyone and their mother called my agent to see if it was true. I have no intention of retiring, but I do want to peel away, like an onion, all the layers that I am not interested in and get to the real meat that will make the hair on the back of my neck stand up.' The hairs on the back of his neck may have stood up recently for an entirely different reason, when he was involved in a motor bike accident in New York, where he lives with his wife and children. But Neeson is already back at work scripting his long-awaited film about the adventures of a guy he grew up with in Northern Ireland. He says of his upcoming film, 'It's very delicate, very hilarious, and at the same time incredibly tragic, too, as only the Irish seem to be able to do.'

OWEN NOLAN

What hurling is to Ireland, and baseball is to the US, so hockey is to Canada. Children across the provinces grow up playing the game on frozen ponds across the country, dreaming of one day playing professionally in the National Hockey League. Owen Nolan came to that dream a little later than most. Born in Belfast, he moved to Canada with his family and didn't start playing hockey until his early teenage years. But once he did, natural athletic talent and a fierce competitiveness made him a force to be reckoned with. His skills were recognized in 1990, when he was selected as the first overall pick in the NHL Draft by the Quebec Nordiques. Today, with over 640 NHL games under his belt, Nolan has established himself as one of the league's leading offensive threats, having scored over 250 goals in his career. The 28-year old Nolan headed west to California in October 1995 when the San Jose Sharks acquired him. He was recently named the

2000 Seagate Technology Sharks Player of the Year. Nolan's performance last season earned him a spot in the 2000 NHL All-Star Game. His star shone brightly in international play when he represented Canada at the 1997 World Championships in Finland, scoring four goals and adding three assists as he helped his team win the gold medal. Irish by birth, raised in Canada, and now living in California, it's fitting that Nolan was named the fifth team captain in San Jose Shark's history in 1998. With team mates hailing from Sweden, Russia, the US, and Germany, Nolan will be using a little Irish charm and a lot of determination in the quest for the Stanley Cup.

PEGGY NOONAN

We knew her words long before her face became familiar. Her syntax and lyrical vocabulary made Ronald Reagan dance in our ears. Peggy Noonan gave 'the Great Communicator' the gilded poetic imagery of conservative constancy. Her vocal brushstrokes had already tinged Dan Rather with linguistic elegance during a stint at CBS. But it will be her White House years, 1984 to 1986, as Special Assistant to the President, that will mark her great contribution to US politics. In the West Wing she was both sensible and scintillating, transferring her remarkable political intuition into the Reagan teleprompter. It was

Martin Naughton

magic. The native New Yorker then became George H. Bush's Chief Speech writer during the 1988 Presidential Campaign. Since then she has gone on to write and reflect on US politics in such prestigious journals as *Time*, *Newsweek*, *The New York Times*, *The Washington Post*, *Forbes*, *Mirabella*, *Harpers Bazaar* and *The Washington Monthly*. She has also managed to squeeze out best-selling books such as *Simply Speaking*, *How to Communicate Your Ideas with Style and Grace* and *What I Saw at the Revolution*, *A Political Life in Reagan Era New York*. Noonan's gift with words should come as no surprise considering the depth of her Irish roots in the

mystical soil of County Donegal. 'Ireland spooks me a little, in a way that I enjoy. The Irish are the great individualists of Europe. They're all so different. And frequently eccentric,' she laughs. Noonan continues to be highly regarded by the intelligentsia of Upper East Side New York. If George Bush Jr. ascends to power, it is likely that Noonan will be invited to play a part in the new Compassionate Conservative regime.

GRAHAM NORTON

Graham Norton may have followed in the footsteps of Terry Wogan to become only the second Irish

person to host a prime time chat show on British television. But the similarities end there. His show, *So Graham Norton*, which he describes as 'kitsch and tell' is a weekly rollercoster ride of camp irreverence and gentle celebrity baiting that has made Norton a household name. Raised in Bandon, County Cork, Norton studied English and French at University College Cork, worked for year in the US ('I loved it; I could do whatever I liked over there'), and was accepted at the London Central School of Speech and Drama where he made a startling discovery: 'It suddenly dawned on me that I was a very camp person!' Appearances at the Edinburgh Festival and on the stand-up comedy circuit culminated in the moment when Norton exploded onto our television screens and our consciousness as the manic Irish dancing, folksong-singing youth priest in the award-winning comedy, *Father Ted*. His late night quiz show *Carnal Knowledge* followed and Norton went on to win a British Comedy Award for his work on *The Jack Docherty Show*. 'I've always had a desperate need to show off,' says Norton. 'When I was at school and working in restaurants, I was very loud and annoying. I'm lucky because now it's my job!'

Peggy Noonan

 AIDAN O'BRIEN
He scored his first winner on his first day as a trainer when *Wandering Thoughts* won at Tralee on 7 June 1993, and he has dominated Irish jumps racing ever since. Still only 31-years-old, Aidan O'Brien has been declared a prodigy and compared to Vincent O'Brien (no relation), the greatest Irish trainer of all time. Sir Alex Ferguson, the great manager of Manchester United and a self-confessed perfectionist himself, declared he stood in awe before O'Brien's attention to detail and warm relationship with every member of his staff. Born into a farming family in County Wexford, O'Brien really made the breakthrough in 1997, winning the first three Irish classics, with *Classic Park* and *Desert King*, and a second National Stakes, with *King of Kings*. That same year, he trained his first flat winner in Britain (*Harbour Master* in the Coventry Stakes at Royal Ascot) and the following year his

Graham Norton

first runner, *Shahtoush*, won on his first visit to Epsom. This year, the O'Brien-trained *Istabraq* lifted Irish spirits around the world by winning the Champion Hurdle at Cheltenham for the third time. Married to the former model and champion trainer Anne-Marie Crowley, O'Brien keeps a low profile away from the race track and trains his flat horses in Ballydoyle at the former base of Vincent O'Brien. Without doubt the most dynamic trainer in the country, the trainer and voice of Irish racing, Ted Walsh, said of him: 'He's got bundles of energy plus that great enthusiasm you associate with being young. He's quiet, unassuming and easy to like. You'd have to be proud that Ireland could produce such a talent.'

CONAN O'BRIEN

The Simpsons' creator Matt Groening said of Conan O'Brien when he worked as a writer and producer on that hit show: 'If he can make a bunch of bitter, self-hating comedy writers laugh, then I'm sure he'll have no trouble making the rest of America laugh'. And he has. *Late Night With Conan O'Brien* is now in its seventh year and has overcome initially disastrous reviews to become one of NBC's top ratings winners. In 1997, the network realised it had a star on its hands (*The Washington Post* dubbed him 'the most intelligent of the late-night comics') and O'Brien secured a five-year contract, reputedly to the sum of millions of dollars. Born in Brookline,

Massachusetts, in 1963, O'Brien attended Harvard University where he studied American history and literature when he wasn't busy as editor of the *Harvard Lampoon*. After graduation stints as a comedy writer on *Saturday Night Live* and *The Simpsons* brought moderate success and led up to 26 April 1993, when he was named host of NBC's new late night talk show. O'Brien's ancestors fled Counties Waterford and Kerry during the Famine and O'Brien visited Ireland in 1996, a trip that offered him an insight into his Irish identity. 'I've inherited a wide face, a love of heavy foods, and a sense of humour,' he said, with a flicker of a smile.

DAVID O'BRIEN

David O'Brien, part of the renowned racing family and son of legendary trainer Vincent O'Brien, has achieved acclaim in not one but in two very different arenas. As part of the family tradition he followed in his father's footsteps as a horse trainer and even trained the 1984 Epsom Derby winner, *Secreto*. In 1989, he quit training altogether, taking to farming the land instead. This didn't quite satisfy his restless spirit and in the early 1990s, inspired by his love of wine, he hit on the plan of buying a winery. He found his dream location at Château Vignelaure in Provence and in 1994 he joined forces with well-known wine producer Hugh Ryman. The challenge facing the partnership was to restore both the house and vineyard to its former glory. Since 1995 his tremendous efforts have paid off and Chateau Vignelaure is attracting worldwide attention. His new-found success as a wine producer still owes something to his old career. He comments wryly on the challenges of wine making: 'If you can survive the terrible disappointments in horse racing you can survive anything.'

DENIS O'BRIEN

'As long as there is a risk involved, Denis loves it,' say friends of 42-year-old Irish entrepreneur Denis O'Brien. No doubt the rewards are welcome, too. Earlier this year, O'Brien netted a reported $250 million from the sale of Esat Telecom to

Aidan O'Brien

British Telecom—Esat was sold for $2.5 billion, well above the $1.1 billion target. Setting up Esat in 1991 was a major achievement for O'Brien, who had to fight hard to break into a market that was not then deregulated and he has been praised for the tenacious way he loosened the grip of the state monopoly, Eircom (then Telecom Éireann), on the telecommunications market. No doubt O'Brien learned a thing or two when he worked as Tony Ryan's personal assistant at Guinness Peat Aviation, where Ryan surrounded himself with the most dynamic business minds in the country. O'Brien also proved adept at securing hard-to-get licenses—in 1989 he won a licence

for his radio station, 98FM, and in 1996, he defeated heavy international competition to win Ireland's second mobile telephone operating licence. Although he claims to intend to retire in two years and spend more time with his young family, O'Brien is already working on new projects, principally in the energy sector, where he is a major shareholder in ePower, a new company that observers say will pose a significant threat to current operators. 'I am so motivated,' O'Brien says. 'The best part of my day is jumping out of bed and going to work.' The tidy profit from the sale of Esat has also allowed him to indulge his second great passion—golf. Earlier this year

O'Brien secured a 9.2 percent stake (at a cost of more than $2 million) in PGA European Tour Courses, the London-listed company that operates golf courses in Britain and continental Europe. This follows his $28 million purchase in 1998 of the Quinta do Lago leisure complex on the Portuguese Algarve. Shrewd, dynamic and courageous, O'Brien is probably the outstanding entrepreneur of his generation.

EDNA O'BRIEN

In an essay on James Joyce the Irish novelist Frank Tuohy wrote that while Joyce's *Portrait of an Artist as a Young Man* and *Dubliners* were the first novels to document the Irish Roman Catholic and shine light on his surroundings, 'the world of Nora Barnacle had to wait for the fiction of Edna O'Brien'. This comparison with Nora Barnacle was based on their similar upbringings. Both women suffered under the care of violent fathers, turning to their mothers for comfort, and both had their first experiences with the outside world in convent schools. O'Brien was born in Tuamgraney, County Clare, in 1930 and was educated at the Convent of Mercy in Loughrea, and at the Pharmaceutical College in Dublin. It was her experiences at the Convent of Mercy that would provide O'Brien with the material upon which many of her books are based, in particular *The Country Girls*, *The Lonely Girl* and *Girls in their Married Bliss*. *The Country Girls*, probably her most famous book, was written in 1959 during her first month in exile in London, and was subsequently made into a film. Love in all its facets, both good and bad, is the principal theme of most of O'Brien's novels, highlighting the plight of women trapped in disastrous relationships—her own marriage to Ernest Gebler, with whom she had two sons, was dissolved in 1964. The men in O'Brien's novels are usually devious and brutal in nature and it is this element, combined with the other autobiographical elements in her work, that have intrigued her readership. Noted for her simple style and powerful characterisation, O'Brien has also written several works of non-fiction and has firmly established herself among the finest Irish writers.

Denis O'Brien

Edna O'Brien

PETER O'BRIEN

'I want to change the world into a John Lavery painting,' declares 47-year-old designer Peter O'Brien. And why not? O'Brien dates his obsession with glamour to his childhood in Dublin, stolen afternoons spent watching Hollywood musicals like *My Fair Lady*, and his Aunt Sissy who loved to dress up for dances at the Dublin Musical Society. O'Brien's signature style is very chic and tremendously popular. Although born in London, O'Brien's family moved back to Dublin when he was a toddler. O'Brien's talent for drawing was obvious from an early age, but he left school at 15 and worked as a window dresser, before sending some of his sketches of ballgowns to Eve Pollard, then a Fleet Street editor. She encouraged him to pursue a career in fashion and, emboldened, O'Brien compiled a portfolio

and talked his way into St. Martins College of Art in London. After college, he completed a post-graduate course in New York and then moved to Dior in Paris in 1981. 'I was a dogsbody,' he recalls. 'I had this fantastic notion that it was all sketches and cheek kissing, but it was very disciplined, which I didn't expect.' From Dior, O'Brien moved to Givenchy, then Chloe and then on to Rochas. Earlier this year, after 19 years in Paris couture houses, O'Brien presented his first show under his own name, with many of his designs inspired by Ireland. 'I love the sea around Dun Laoghaire and I dream of having a house in Killiney,' he says. But home for the moment is Paris, where O'Brien is widely regarded as one of the few genuinely charming and self-effacing designers in what is a notoriously competitive industry.

STEPHEN O'BRIEN

To maintain the City of London's status as one of the most developed cities in the world seems like a task that would make even the most astute of businessmen recoil in fear, yet as Chief Executive of both London First and its subsidiary London First Centre, Stephen O'Brien has taken charge of this awesome responsibility. As Chief Executive it is O'Brien's job to engage business in promoting and developing London's infrastructure and resources so that it may lead the league of world cities in this century. To even consider tackling such a Herculean task would be unthinkable without a wealth of experience. There is no question that 54-year-old O'Brien eminently qualifies for the position. From 1983 to 1992 O'Brien was the Chief Executive of Business in the Community, an organization that helps to create working

Peter O'Brien

Baroness O'Cathain

partnerships between British companies and the public sector, voluntary organisations and trade unions on a number of social and economic issues. Prior to this, O'Brien was Chairman of Charles Fulton Holdings and Chairman of the Foreign Exchange and Currency Deposit Brokers Association. O'Brien has a highly developed social conscience and finds time among his demanding career commitments to pursue his involvement in other community activities— among many worthy causes, O'Brien was a Co-Founder of Cranstoun, an organisation that administers rehabilitation houses for former drug addicts and he served as Vice-Chairman and Trustee of the Church Urban Fund. The list of charitable

works goes on and on. Small wonder then that O'Brien was awarded the CBE in 1987, in recognition of his sterling work in business and society. O'Brien has been married twice and has four children and three stepchildren.

BARONESS O'CATHAIN

Baroness O'Cathain has the kind of resumé that leaves you breathless just reading it. The term 'high achiever' simply doesn't do justice to what she has packed into her life. Detta O'Cathain was born in Cork in 1938, her father was from Belfast and her mother from Warwickshire. The family moved to Dublin when she was four. After a

conventional education at the Loreto Convent Rathfarnham and Laurel Hill in Limerick, she took a degree in University College Dublin. In 1966, she married William Bishop and left Ireland. Subsequently she studied Finance for Non-Managers at the London Business School and was awarded a place on the Advanced Management Programme at the Harvard Business faculty. In the course of her brilliant executive business career she has worked variously as an economist, corporate planner, economic adviser and marketing director in most of the major arenas of British industrial life. She has acted in the capacity of economic adviser to Rootes Motors/Chrysler, Carrington Viyella and British Leyland. She was a Managing Director of the Milk Marketing Board and at the Barbican Centre. She has also held non-executive directorships with Tesco, Channel Four, and Midland Bank amongst others. In the early 1990s she went to the House of Lords, spending from 1991 to 1995 on the cross bench. With her business acumen and enormous range of financial expertise she has been a great asset to the many select committees she sat on, dealing with monetary policy, energy, EU structural funds, trade and external relations. A self-confessed workaholic ('I work my socks off,' she admits.) the idea of retiring is anaethema to her, although she does cherish a romantic dream of owning a cottage in Connemara where she could take long walks, read books and watch wildlife. An avid gardener whenever she is at her home in Sussex, she swims a half a mile most days and, in quiet moments, enjoys studying the Bible. She visits friends in Ireland several times a year and still retains an emotional attachment to Ireland and appreciates the influence of her Irish background. 'Everybody here tells me I'm very Irish,' she says. 'I'm not afraid to speak my mind, I'm upfront, open and not at all reserved.'

JOHN O'CONOR

'The maestro with the Irish accent', 'Beethoven with a brogue'. Concert pianist John O'Conor has been called many things in his time. But one thing's for sure, whether performing, teaching or organising O'Conor strides like a Colossus over

John O'Conor

Ireland's musical landscape. A world class concert pianist, his dazzling virtuosity has been a source of pleasure to millions for decades. The first Irish pianist to achieve major international acclaim, his masterful and poetic renditions of the classics of the piano repertoire have brought him the adulation of music lovers worldwide. He has guested with the world's greatest orchestras as well as collaborating with every leading conductor. Born in Dublin, where he still makes his home, his love of music developed at an early age, somewhat against the odds. 'My father was tone deaf and my mother turned musical just once a year on Christmas Day.' They gave him music lessons, he says 'in an attempt to see if I was good at anything'. His parents only viewed his music as a pastime and he had to struggle to show them he intended to make it a career. Despite the many obstacles, in 1973 he was awarded First Prize in

the International Beethoven competition and crowned this achievement by winning first prize in the Bosendorfer piano competition. He has the distinction of being the only Irish pianist ever to have won both of these prestigious prizes. A tireless champion of Irish composer John Field, he has single handedly been responsible for re-awakening interest in Field's concertos. His work with the Royal Irish Academy of Music has transformed it into a busy music conservatory with more than 2,000 pupils and a well-deserved reputation for excellence. O'Conor is also the Chairman of the Dublin International Piano Competition, an increasingly important competition that attracts talented young concert pianists and a prestigious judging panel. The piano has been good to O'Conor, both professionally and personally—he met his wife, Mary, when she came to him for piano lessons nearly thirty years ago.

Patrick O'Connell

The Inn at Little Washington, some 70 miles west of Washington, DC, lies deep in the heart of the Virginian countryside. But that doesn't deter Washington high rollers from making the journey to what has become one of the most famous restaurants and hotels in the US. Owned by chef Patrick O'Connell and Reinhardt Lynch, The Inn is a haven of fine food, superb wine (the wine cellar boasts 15,000 bottles), four-poster beds and comfy armchairs and has recently clocked up its fifth five-star Mobile Guide Award. O'Connell is understandably proud of his achievements. A native of Washington, DC, O'Connell launched his career in the restaurant trade with an after-school job in a neighbourhood eatery and financed his drama studies by working as a waiter. Then he realised, he says, that the living theatre of the restaurant was more compelling than the traditional stage. So he taught himself to cook, and the rest is Virginian folklore. O'Connell is acclaimed as one of the top chefs in the US and The Inn has attracted rave reviews from the *The New York Times* and is rated top in all categories by *Zagat's*. True foodies can even book a table in the state-of-the-art kitchen, so they can watch the action unfold around them. Not surprisingly, the Inn has kept O'Connell extremely busy since it opened, and he hasn't visited the County Mayo home of his maternal grandparents in a couple of years—a state of affairs he plans to address very soon. Incidentally, O'Connell tells us his grandmother shares the surname Hoban with the architect who built the White House, whose senior officials now regularly make the 140-mile round trip to savour his culinary masterpieces.

KEVIN O'CONNOR

In the space of just five years DoubleClick Inc has grown from two people in a basement to a global corporation employing more than 2,000 people in 23 countries. Co-Founder and Chairman Kevin O'Connor cannot quite conceal his sense of wonder at the rapid success of this supplier of Internet advertising for corporate marketeers and web sites. 'I get to do what I love, which is building stuff and innovating. The fact that I get paid for it is even better,' he says. Fresh out of the University of Michigan with a degree in electrical engineering in 1983, O'Connor co-founded ICC, a software company that developed products to address PC connectivity in Ohio. Looking for new challenges, O'Connor tested the computer networking waters with the creation of Remote LAN Node in 1991. The following year, ICC was sold to another software company, DCA, where O'Connor served as Chief Technology Officer and Vice-President of research until 1995. It was time for a change. O'Connor quit his job and began to focus on developing a business on the Internet, and in 1995, DoubleClick was born, the first network on the Web that set the standard for the network model of advertising on the Internet. In 1998 the company went public in an offering that

dazzled Wall Street analysts and shot O'Connor into the pantheon of new-media millionaires. O'Connor's ancestors left Ireland in the 19th century and moved to Canada before settling in Michigan. In 1994 O'Connor and his wife Nancy visited Ireland for the first time. The trip made an indelible impression: 'Every time I hear Irish music I get goose bumps,' O'Connor says. The O'Connors have two sons and live in New York.

SINÉAD O'CONNOR

Her achingly beautiful music has pierced our souls and her strident outbursts have given us piercing headaches. Sinéad O'Connor was the archetypal wild child. Born in Dublin in 1966, she responded to a childhood marred by divorce with increasingly bad behaviour that resulted in her expulsion from school and bouts of shoplifting. Luckily, she found solace in music and began studying voice and piano at the Dublin College of Music and gigging around the country. In 1987 she released her debut album *The Lion and the Cobra* to critical acclaim. Commercial success came with the 1990 release of *I Do Not Want What I Haven't Got*. Then events took a turn for the worse. Her tirades were seized upon by a scandal-greedy media—she supported the IRA, she hated U2, she would not perform if the *Star Spangled Banner* was played before any of her concerts, she refused to accept the four Grammy nominations she received for *I Do Not Want What I Haven't Got*. Then she tore up a photo of Pope John Paul II and roared 'Fight the real enemy!' during a live performance on *Saturday Night Live*. Understandably she went a little quiet after that stunt, studying opera in Dublin, appearing in a production of *Hamlet*, and touring with the WOMAD Festival. Last year, her revelation that she had been ordained as a priest by a Tridentine bishop and should now be known as Mother Bernadette Mary proved she still had the ability to shock an apparently Sinéad-immune public. This year, she went back to what she does best—make music. O'Connor's new album (the first for six years) was released this year to widespread critical acclaim. Aptly titled *Faith and Courage*, it

was described by *Rolling Stone* as 'the Sinéad album you've been wanting for years'. O'Connor is now a mother of two and claims to have toned down her outbursts. 'I'm 33 years old now,' she said, 'so I'm slightly less confrontational, obviously. I'm more confident in what I'm saying now. When we're younger, we're not so sure what we're on about, so we almost have to be defensive. As you grow older, you learn how to communicate in ways that are not threatening.' Fine sentiments, but we're not holding our breath.

DION O'CUINNEAGAIN

Rugby players are not often renowned for their gazelle-like qualities on the pitch, but Dion O'Cuinneagain is a noteworthy exception. The 27-year-old came to Irish rugby attention by rather a circuitous route. His father, Conall, was born in Ireland but emigrated to South Africa when he and his new bride, Vivien, fell in love with the country while there on their honeymoon. O'Cuinneagain's athletic abilities began to shine when he was a school boy in Cape Town—he made the South Africa Schools rugby team for two consecutive years in 1989 and 1990 and won a silver and bronze medal in the 400m and 110m hurdles at the South African Championship. While at the university, he made the South African Sevens Team, captaining the Springboks Sevens team for

Patrick O'Connell

Sinead O'Connor

three, and made more than 70 appearances for Western Province. The Irish rugby management's realisation that someone with a name like O'Cuinneagain must have Irish blood coincided with O'Cuinneagain's ambition to play in the World Cup. 'I moved to Manchester Sale Rugby Club in November 1997 to try to win a place in the Irish Test Team and and I won my first cap for Ireland in April 1998. Ironically I won my first two caps for Ireland against South Africa. Both games were quite emotional for me, especially in the singing of national anthems. But the only thing that matters to me now is playing for Ireland, all previous allegiances are in the past.' O'Cuinneagain eventually took over the captaincy from Paddy Johns and led Ireland in the World Cup. 'It was a dream come true,' he says. O'Cuinneagain recently played at club level for Ballymena in Northern Ireland and at provincial level for Ulster, where he continued to impress on the field. His coach at Ballymena, Andre Bester, declared him 'the most outstanding number eight in Irish rugby'. This is a view not held by all. In recent times injuries have seen him drop out of the Irish side and he has returned to finish his medical studies in South Africa. But don't rule him out—he is likely to be a force in Irish rugby again.

CHRIS O'DONNELL

At the tender age of 12, Chris O'Donnell had already packed some acting experience under his belt. He was the boy behind the counter in the McDonald's commercial who served Michael Jordan his meal. Since then, this Irish American boy from Chicago has come a long way. He secured his first Hollywood role at age 17, as Jessica Lange's eldest son in *Men Don't Leave*. Then two years later, in 1992, in his breakthrough role as the wholesome prep-school kid hired to guide a blind Al Pacino in *Scent of a Woman*, O'Donnell earned a Golden Globe nomination for Best Supporting Actor and the Chicago Film Critics Award for Most Promising Actor of the Year. If that weren't enough, three years later he went from being 'The Last Boy Scout from Tinseltown' (a name he was given for his goody-

Kevin O'Connor

two-shoes roles—to becoming a heart throb in the eyes of young women around the world. His role as Robin in *Batman Forever* in 1995 and *Batman and Robin* in 1997 heralded his arrival as a star and elevated him to iconic status at home. 'I've got nine nephews and nieces who freak out when they see Robin,' says O'Donnell. Despite his early fame, the 30-year-old actor is content to lead a fairly regular, low-profile life. O'Donnell is married to his longtime girlfriend, Carolina Fentress, and still lives in his native Chicago. With more then a dozen film and television movies already completed, the sky is the limit for this clean cut heart throb.

DANIEL O'DONNELL

Blessed with the appeal of both a heartthrob and the boy next door, singer Daniel O'Donnell confounds even the most cynical of critics with his sincerity and extraordinary rapport with people. With CD and video sales that top the five million mark, it's not just his warmth that attracts such a loyal following, it's his star quality. Born in the village of Kincasslagh in 1961, this shy Donegal lad has come a long way from the days when he helped out in his local store and sang at socials in the parish hall. Little did he know then that his marvellous singing voice would bring him to such prestigious venues as New York's Carnegie Hall

and the Sydney Opera House. He has performed for presidents and kings, won numerous awards and is a continuing force in the country music scene. Not that success came immediately or easily. As a youngster Daniel guested with his sister Margo and her country and western band. When O'Donnell formed his own group, he often had to drive the tour van himself and was even at the point of giving up his most cherished ambition when he ended up in debt. However his perseverance paid off and since signing a record deal with Ritz Records sixteen years ago, he has graduated with honours to the league of superstardom. His favourite place on earth is the stage and he can't hide his genuine affection for people. And Donegal is still definitely home.

ROSIE O'DONNELL

Newsweek magazine has dubbed her the 'Queen of Nice' and this tough-talking New Yorker has proved it is still possible to produce a hit daytime chat show without resorting to the contrived stunts and questionable ethics of some of her competitors. Rosie O'Donnell was born in the US in 1962, but spent several months in her father's native Donegal when she was ten years old following the death of her mother, Roseanna—a tragedy she has called the defining moment of her life. Humour offered a refuge from a difficult adolescence, and O'Donnell decided to try to make it as a stand up comedian. Forays into the movie business (*A League of their Own*, *Sleepless in Seattle*, and *Beautiful Girls*) brought her to national attention and O'Donnell is now established as the public's favourite host of the Tony Awards. In 1995 O'Donnell adopted her son Parker and decided to concentrate on television work so she could spend more time with him. Her daytime chat show debuted in 1996 and has earned her two Emmy Awards. Since then, O'Donnell has adopted two more children (Chelsea Belle and Blake Christopher) and established the For All Kids Foundation, which distributes money to children's charities. She produces her award-winning show from the NBC building at Rockefeller Center in New York and keeps a close eye on her children in the custom-built nursery next door to her office.

Daniel O'Donnell

CATHY O'DOWD

True grit, determination and a passionate love of the Great Outdoors are what inspire Cathy O'Dowd. The first woman in the world to climb Everest from both sides, she only took up climbing by accident. Born in Johannesburg in 1968, into a comfortable middle class home, she was aware of her Irish heritage from an early age, O'Dowd being a relatively uncommon surname in South Africa. After a conventional schooling she majored in history, classics and history of art at Wits University. It was the lure of romance that prompted her to join the climbing society where the object of her affections was a member. Then in November 1995 O'Dowd's life changed dramatically and

irrevocably when she answered an advertisement for the first South African expedition to Everest. Chosen out of 200 women applicants, O'Dowd joined the expedition as an apprentice and following in the footsteps of Edmund Hillery and Tenzing Norgay set out for the world's most daunting summit. It was a baptism of fire as the trip coincided with the 'killer storm' of 1996 that killed five climbers. Undeterred, O'Dowd and her companions pressed on and, despite her novice status, she reached the summit on the 26 May 1996. 'That was a magical moment, standing on the highest point on the planet, so high you could see the curve of the earth', recalls O'Dowd. She was hooked. Since then her absolute passion

for climbing has driven her to return to Everest several times. As she herself admits: 'To climb to the top once is the feat of a lifetime. To try a second time on a harder route seems a bit odd. To fail and then try a third time you need to be a little crazy.' However O'Dowd's particular brand of craziness has pushed her to conquer other disciplines as well. She has written two books on her experiences, and also runs a new media company based on publishing with adventure themes and travels the world lecturing on her experiences. Clearly the spirit of adventure that drove her Irish great-grandparents to strike out for Cape Town in the 1890s is alive and well in Cathy O'Dowd. As she puts it: 'There is, I think, a thread that connects so many of the citizens of the world back to their Irish roots. Perhaps all we share is a yearning for adventure, a gift of the gab, and a sense of humour. But it does seem to be enough to allow us to make a disproportionate impact in the countries to which fate led us.'

NIALL O'DOWD

In 1995, *The London Observer* newspaper described publisher Niall O'Dowd as being 'at the very hub of Clinton's secret diplomacy between the White House and the government in Dublin and Sinn Féin in Belfast.' Whether they meant it as high praise or outraged criticism matters little to the founder publisher of *Irish America* magazine and the *Irish Voice* newspaper. No one can deny the enormous role that O'Dowd played in bringing about what many believed to be impossible, breaking the deadlock in the decades-old Irish Troubles. When Sinn Féin leader Gerry Adams arrived at the White House for an historic meeting with President Clinton, O'Dowd, a man of extravagant Irish political connections, was the conduit for peace. The founder of the Irish American peace delegation that helped to bring about the 1994 IRA ceasefire, O'Dowd has been a tireless champion of the issues affecting the Irish ever since his arrival in the US. With the founding of his weekly *Irish Voice* newspaper, the first new Irish weekly in 60 years, O'Dowd committed himself to acting as a voice for new Irish immigrants in the US. His articulate and

tireless defence of undocumented Irish in the US led to the legalization of tens of thousands living there. With his continued support the subsequent passage of the Donnelly and Morrison visas reshaped the conditions of Irish immigration in the US. O'Dowd's voice continues to be bold, bright, and indisputably Green.

BRIAN O'DRISCOLL

'He's probably the best centre in the Northern Hemisphere'. This was London Irish Coach Dick Best's appraisal of Brian O'Driscoll, the young Irish International rugby star. It was O'Driscoll's performance against France in the Six Nations Championship in March this year, during which he scored three tries that earned him the international acclaim he now enjoys. After a succession of disappointing performances prior to the game against France, Irish team manager Warren Gatland decided to introduce young blood in to the team, and it was this decision that provided O'Driscoll with the perfect showcase to exhibit his skills. O'Driscoll was born in Dublin in 1979 and began his sporting career at the age of eight when he played Gaelic football for his national school. At ten years of age he was playing soccer for a local team and for Clontarf at the Community Games. Brian first began playing rugby (at first on the wing and then at out-half) at Willow Park and Blackrock College—schools that are synonymous with glory in rugby. He changed to play centre for Leinster Schools, and all his subsequent performances have been in this position. Modest and media-shy, O'Driscoll is reluctant to engage in discussions about his private life, but does admit that he has been known to partake in some 'serious unwinding' with his team mates after an important game. When not involved in rugby, O'Driscoll enjoys a few rounds of golf at the Royal Dublin Golf Club, where he is a member. With his IRFU contract coming to an end and the interest shown in him by many English and French clubs, there is much speculation about O'Driscoll's next career move. Whatever the outcome, it is certain that O'Driscoll will continue to make an impact on the international rugby scene for the foreseeable future.

ARDAL O'HANLON

As the gormless but lovable Father Dougal in the hit television comedy, *Father Ted*, Ardal O'Hanlon found himself catapulted to fame. Comedy awards, sell-out tours, and film roles followed in rapid succession and established O'Hanlon as one of the great comic talents of the 1990s. Then, in the late 1990s, he took a leap into the unknown and wrote his first novel, *The Talk of the Town*, a brilliantly observed tale of a 19-year-old's frustrations and dreams set in a small Irish town. 'It was a huge gamble,' O'Hanlon admits. 'You risk ridicule and opprobrium, because people object to comics writing books. But I suppose I always wanted to write, long before I got sidetracked into comedy. And, more than anything else, I think I needed a break from performing—for a start because it's quite nerve-wracking, and adrenalin-soaked, and it's quite a wearing lifestyle. And I needed a break from the ludicrously high profile that something like *Father Ted* gives you.' *The Talk of the Town* was a surprise best seller in Ireland and the UK and was released in the US (under the title, *Knick Knack Paddy Whack*) earlier this year. So what is next for this multi-talented man from Carrickmacross? O'Hanlon is working on his second novel and hopes to move back to Ireland 'somewhere like Carrickmacross' to raise his three-year-old daughter, Emily. Beyond that, he says, he is 'almost bereft of ambition. I've done most things I wanted to do and loads more I never dreamed of. I'm as bemused by the whole thing as anybody.'

DAVID O'LEARY

When he was forced to retire as a professional football player in 1995, David O'Leary said at the time, 'It is a big blow to be told you can no longer play. But I take with me some wonderful memories and have no idea what I will do now.' What he has done is transform himself into the highest paid manager in the English Premiership—in August this year O'Leary signed a new six-year contract at Leeds United, reported to be worth approximately £12 million to him. Dublin-born O'Leary made his debut for Arsenal in 1975 and went on to notch up 722 league and

Brian O'Driscoll

Ardal O'Hanlon

cup appearances for the Gunners in 18 years before joining Leeds United in 1993, where he played only 12 matches before an Achille's tendon injury ended his playing career. He stayed on at Elland Road as George Graham's assistant and, when Graham moved to Spurs, he acted as caretaker manager, bringing in youngsters from the Youth Team, changing tactics and setting out to play open and exciting football. He wasn't the club's first choice as manager, a fact splashed daily across the British tabloids, but O'Leary played his cards deftly—his Arsenal and international room-mate for many seasons, Niall Quinn, said, 'Just because David doesn't sound or act aggressively should not hide the fact that he has a wonderful presence. Nobody will get the better of David O'Leary in mind games.' Clearly not, as he became Leeds United's 19th manager, and the first from the Republic of Ireland. 'I want to build an empire at Elland Road,' O'Leary said, and he has certainly laid the foundations—in 1998/99 Leeds finished fourth in the League and qualified for Europe; in 1999/2000, the club finished third in the League and won through to the semi-final of the UEFA Cup. Alex Ferguson has declared him the best young manager in the country and a potential manager at Old Trafford, and Celtic offered him the post of manager at Parkhead earlier this year. But O'Leary and his family are happy living in Harrogate and his sensitivity has endeared him

to Leeds fans—his tight-lipped fury at the controversial decision to go ahead with the UEFA Cup semi-final first leg in Istanbul this year despite the death of two Leeds fans and his decision to drive straight from the airport to the spontaneous shrine erected at the gates of the ground on his return home impressed many. His new deal with Leeds will take him up to 2006—a perfect time to take over the management of the Republic of Ireland team, for which he earned more than 60 caps during his playing career. 'I'd love to manage my country— that would be the proudest moment of my life. But the bottom line is that for international management you need the experience of 15 years involvement with a club at the highest level. So hopefully by the time I'm 50 somebody will take pity and give me a chance.' O'Leary will be 48 years old in 2006. Close enough.

MICHAEL O'LEARY

As Chief Executive of Ryanair since 1994, Westmeath-born Michael O'Leary is credited with transforming the no-frills airline into a major player on the aviation scene. He has been well rewarded for his sterling efforts. The successful flotation of the company in 1997 reportedly netted him £17 million from selling part of his shareholding—his remaining stake is reputed to be close to £70 million. Not a bad record for this 39-year-old business studies graduate of Trinity College Dublin. O'Leary worked for accountants Stokes Kennedy Crowley before joining Ryanair as Chief Operations Officer in 1991. He was made a Director of Ryanair Ltd in 1988 and appointed Chief Executive of Ryanair Holdings in 1997. O'Leary likes to present an informal image, often photographed in jeans and open-necked shirts, and enjoying nothing better than a game of football or rugby. But the unorthodox image belies a steely determination to protect the interests of Ryanair, and employees and competitors alike regard him as a tough negotiator and daunting adversary. One would expect nothing less from a protege of Dr. Tony Ryan, one of the sharpest business brains in Ireland.

TONY O'MALLEY

It has been said that along with Jack B. Yeats, Tony O'Malley has been the leading figure of Irish 20th century Irish art. But unlike Yeats, O'Malley was a latecomer to the world of art. Working in the bank for the first part of his life O'Malley eventually retired in his fifties for health reasons. Looking more like a man of 67 than one of 87 it is hard to believe that O'Malley has been close to death three times in his life—once in his twenties as a result of tuberculosis, then from a heart attack when he was 46, and finally in his fifties when his toe became gangrenous and the doctors gave him a year to live. Thankfully he is still with us and going strong. It was while convalescing in a sanatorium in Kilkenny in the 1950s that O'Malley's interest in art developed and he honed his skills by sketching patients and staff. On his retirement from the bank in 1958 O'Malley decided to move to St. Ives in Cornwall to pursue his painting. While there he met his future wife, Jane Harris, a Canadian who had moved to Cornwall for the same reasons. The couple visited Jane's sister in the Bahamas every winter from 1974 to 1987 and during these sojourns O'Malley completed some of his most important work. His abstract style and use of vivid colours so impressed Seamus Heaney that the poet commented that O'Malley paints the words he writes. The O'Malleys moved back to Ireland ten years ago and now live in County Kilkenny, O'Malley's birthplace. A recent retrospective of O'Malley's in the prestigious Philips Gallery in Washington, DC was a great success. O'Malley must allow himself a flicker of a smile when he reflects on a time when he was so shy about his artistic endeavours that he hid them under his bed.

MARTIN O'MALLEY

Martin O'Malley will remember 2 November, 1999, for the rest of his life. On that day he became the youngest person ever-elected Mayor of Baltimore. And he did it with an almost unheard of 91 percent of the vote. Today, using his campaign themes of accountability, change and reform, O'Malley has set out to improve public safety, education, and economic development

Michael O'Leary

dollars for peace and reconciliation projects; as a director of the Irish Georgian Society, she works tirelessly to raise funds to protect Ireland's architectural heritage; and as a director of the Ashford Hotel in County Mayo, she has been closely involved with a book charting the history of the estate. Throughout it all she remains calm and as impeccably groomed as one would expect of a former model. AIF President Loretta Brennan Glucksman is among many dazzled by this dynamic woman: 'Sheila is thoroughly organised and efficient, and she has a wonderful business mind that enables her to cut through clutter.' O'Malley has immersed herself in Irish culture since her Belfast-born mother, Noreen O'Toole, insisted she visit Ireland during a backpacking trip around Europe. She has visited Ireland almost every year since then. 'Being Irish is a major part of my identity', O'Malley says, 'I feel grounded in a very atavistic way when I am in Ireland.'

throughout a city of more than 640,000 residents. Prior to his election as Mayor, O'Malley served on the Baltimore City Council from 1991 to 1999, and as an Assistant State's Attorney for the City of Baltimore from 1988 to 1990. A native of Rockville, Maryland, he attended Gonzaga High School in Washington, DC, and graduated in 1985 from Catholic University and later from the University of Maryland's School of Law. After winning election to a third District City Council seat in 1991, the Mayor rapidly rose through the ranks. O'Malley and his wife, Katie Curran, have two daughters, Grace and Tara, and a son, William. At Baltimore's Loyola College commencement ceremonies this past May, 37-year old O'Malley spoke to the class of 2000 and touched on his Irish heritage. 'Today I have the job, the challenging and honourable job, of Mayor of Baltimore City. Before this job I was a father and a lawyer and a mediocre folk singer in a rock 'n' roll Irish band. Before those jobs I had other jobs, as I am sure all you have had. But after this job and before all of those, I was and will be Martin, son of Thomas, son of William son of Martin, a poor exiled Irish speaking farmer, whose people had endured 700 years of political, religious, and economic oppression. Jobs are not who we are, they are just the things we do while answering a higher calling.'

Tony O'Malley

SHEILA O'MALLEY

Her workload would stun many self-proclaimed stressed out executives into silence if not reduce them to tears. As President of Rockfleet Media, Sheila O'Malley's empire covers three newspapers in New Jersey and three television stations in Maine, Wisconsin, and Northern Michigan; as a member of the Board of Directors of the American Ireland Fund, she also serves as co-chairperson of the annual dinner, which has raised millions of

THOMAS O'NEILL

As CEO of PriceWaterhouseCoopers LLP, Thomas O'Neill directs the world's largest professional services organisation and more than 150,000 employees in 150 countries. His ancestors hail from County Antrim, but O'Neill is a fluent French speaker from Quebec, Canada. O'Neill studied commerce at Queens University in Kingston, Ontario, and joined the audit staff at the Toronto division of Price Waterhouse in 1967. He steadily moved up through the management ranks, serving for a time in the Brussels office, until he was appointed Chairman and CEO of the Price Waterhouse Canada in 1996 and CEO of PriceWaterhouseCoopers LLP Canada in 1998. Earlier this year he was named CEO of the global organisation. Extremely influential in Canadian business, O'Neill has been a member of the Business Council on National Issues since 1996 and was a member of the Queens School of Business Advisory Council for three years. He has lectured at the University of Toronto and is Vice-Chair of the Board of Governors at Queens University. O'Neill lives in Toronto with his wife Susan, and when he has time, he likes to play tennis and golf and indulge his love of Shakespeare.

ANTHONY J. F. O'REILLY

The closing weeks of 1999 brought two accolades for Dr. A. J. F. O'Reilly—he was named Irish Person of the Year in the ESB/Rehab People of the Year Awards and he was identified as Ireland's Wealthiest Man. One cannot help but wonder which accolade brought him most satisfaction. Born in 1936, O'Reilly trained as a lawyer and enjoyed a celebrated career as a rugby international, but it is as Ireland's most charismatic and successful businessman that O'Reilly is perhaps best known. As the Chief Executive Officer of Heinz Corporation for close on 20 years, he was the driving force behind Heinz's astonishing success—when O'Reilly stepped down from the day-to-day running of the corporation in 1998, its value had soared from $900 million to $23 billion. News this year of his decision to take a more hands-on approach as Executive Chairman of Independent News and Media, his Dublin-based media empire with interests in the UK, Australia and South Africa, sent the company's share prices soaring. A major shareholder in Waterford Wedgewood, O'Reilly also recently acquired the luxury table top company Rosenthal, prompting observers to ponder the good Doctor's plans for dominance of the luxury goods market. O'Reilly's Midas touch extends beyond the realms of business. In 1976 he cofounded The Ireland Funds with Pittsburgh businessman Dan Rooney and called on people of Irish descent around the world to promote the Fund's goals of 'Peace, Culture and Charity' in Ireland. Today, the American Ireland Fund (created when The Ireland Fund and the American Irish Foundation merged in 1987) hosts 60 events annually in 39 cities around the world and has raised in excess of $100 million for projects promoting peace and reconciliation in Ireland. O'Reilly has been a tireless persuader for things Irish for the past 40 years, whether at a business conference in the City of London, a drinks party in Washington or a rugby dinner in Sydney. This handsome and impeccably groomed Dubliner is the ultimate networker and an outstanding host, with an enviable ability to recall names at will. His friends and contacts stretch around the world through his tenure at Heinz,

Sheila O'Malley

his chairmanship of the Food Manufacturers' Association of America and his myriad other interests. A spectacularly good after dinner speaker, articulate and often inspirational, O'Reilly has the added advantage of being an excellent mimic. Indeed one distinguished Irish politician suggested that the goodwill that O'Reilly has generated for Ireland has far outshone the activities of politicians and many who are paid to promote the country. O'Reilly has also involved himself with promoting education in Ireland—the O'Reilly Hall was a significant addition to the Belfield campus of his old university and he funded the erection of a building at Trinity College Dublin in honour of his parents. When The

Ireland Fund announced the launch of a $100 million fundraising campaign for its charitable projects, O'Reilly kickstarted the project with a personal donation of $5 million. Married to Chryss Goulandris, the Greek shipping heiress, the O'Reillys have homes in Dublin, Kildare, Pittsburgh and Deauville and are noted for the lavish and stylish parties that attract the great and the good (and the Duchess of York). The news this past May that O'Reilly has added Monet's *Le Portail (Soleil)* (at a cost of $24 million) to his collection at his Castle Martin estate in Kildare should help to ensure that an invitation to an O'Reilly party remains the hottest ticket in town.

Terry O'Neill

DOLORES O'RIORDAIN

The spark is back in Dolores O'Riordain's eyes—whether that's due to a two-year break from the music scene, the birth of her son Taylor, or the phenomenal success of The Cranberries 'comeback' album and world tour is anybody's guess. Born in County Limerick in 1971, Dolores O'Riordain joined The Cranberries in 1990 and blasted on to the international stage in 1993. The world was soon captivated by the petite singer with the distinctive voice. However, a punishing schedule took its toll on her health while her frequent outbursts (earning her the dubious accolade 'The Mouth of the Shannon') made headlines around the world, further fuelling the frenzied media interest in her life. A halt was called in 1996. Now this new millennium sees a new Dolores O'Riordain—refreshed, revitalised and absolutely resolute in her determination to protect her family life and have as stable a lifestyle as possible, even when touring. Now living in a small town in County Limerick, O'Riordain travels to sold-out gigs by private jet, 'sings her song', as she puts it, takes her bows, and returns home to make her son's breakfast, stroll around their farm, and go for a pint in the local pub with her husband and friends. O'Riordain is happy at last. 'It was great to sample what gigantic fame is like,' she admits, 'but I never want to be that famous again'.

SONIA O'SULLIVAN

Fleet of foot and sweet of temper, Sonia of the laughing eyes, has captured the hearts of sports fans everywhere. The County Cork athlete has put Irish athletics on the map ever since she burst on to the sports scene. Basically, Sonia was born to run. Born in Cobh, County Cork, in 1969, Sonia's father worked with the Irish navy and was a keen sportsman. Whether it was games in the school yard or running home from Mass, Sonia has always played to win. This competitive edge gives a Jekyll and Hyde aspect to her personality. Off track she is sunny tempered, a real charmer. In a race it's a case of the killer instinct. She applies herself with feverish intensity to everything she tackles. She secured her first Irish title at fifteen and two years later won a scholarship to Villanova University Pennsylvania, the famous athletic academy that has nurtured some of Ireland's finest sporting talent. Her early career was marred by false starts and setbacks, but she gritted her teeth and persevered. She won the World Student Games 1500 meters in 1991, was European Champion in 1994 and World Champion in 1995. Controversy and bad health dogged her performance at the 1996 Atlanta Olympics and dashed O'Sullivan's hopes for that elusive gold medal. But, she recovered her form and 1998 was a bumper year as she notched up a world's best over two miles, was European Champion in the 5,000 and 10,000 meters as well as becoming World Cross Country Champion in the 8k and 4k competitions. O'Sullivan was radiant following the birth of her daughter Ciara, describing it as the best thing to ever happen to her. Word is she's fighting fit and coming to top form just in time for the Sydney Olympics.

PETER O'TOOLE

Peter O'Toole is one of the finest stage and screen actors of the 20th and 21st centuries. His fame as an actor is equalled only by his notoriety as a one time hellraiser and womaniser. Nominated seven times for an Oscar and the recipient of numerous accolades for his theatre performances O'Toole's career has at times been overlooked by the media who prefer to focus on his hellraising antics rather than on his achievements as a thespian. Born in

County Galway in 1932, O'Toole spent his boyhood in Yorkshire, England, where he worked as an apprentice journalist with the *Yorkshire Evening News*. Between 1951 and 1953 he served with the Royal Navy, after which he attended RADA. It was there that he befriended Richard Harris, Alan Bates and Albert Finney, in whose company he gained his reputation as a hellraiser. As well as working for the Old Vic Theatre Company and the Royal Court, O'Toole was also a member of the Abbey Theatre Company. But it was his performance as T. E. Lawrence in David Lean's film *Lawrence of Arabia* that established him as an international star. Other milestones include *The Lion in Winter*, *Goodbye Mr. Chips*, *The Ruling Class* and *The Stunt Man* all of which earned him Oscar nominations. When asked whether he was disappointed that he never received an Oscar, he declared: 'It's an honour to be nominated. That I didn't win the prize is OK.

I'm not dead yet.' Now aged 71, O'Toole continues to act—recently co-starring with Ben Affleck in the Dean Koontz thriller, *Phantoms*—and as a professional cricket coach. Although O'Toole lives in London with his son Lorcun, he is a frequent visitor to his native land. Reflecting on the great literary tradition of Ireland, O'Toole remarked that 'this country may be the most primitive part of Europe, but it's also the most literate. One of those juxtapositions that creation serves up so nicely.'

L. JAY OLIVA

There are some New Yorkers who believe that New York University President Dr. L. Jay Oliva should reformulate his family name to 'O'Liva', so demonstrative are his maternal Irish roots. Proud of both his Irish and Italian heritage, he approaches both groups with erudition and understanding. But make no mistake. This Russian scholar knows the back country twists and turns of a Limerick road. He can appreciate the shades of difference and nuance among Irish pubs while shirting the cobbles of old Dublin lanes. The 14th President of NYU, which is the fifth largest employer in New York, is first and foremost a man of the world, which of course comes in handy at the very heart of New York life amid the urban campus of Greenwich Village. Holding an honourary doctorate from University College Dublin, Oliva has helped to make NYU's Irish studies programme one of the finest in the nation. Ground zero of all things Irish at NYU is Glucksman's Ireland House, a stately early 19th century New York City mansion at the end of Fifth Avenue on the edge of Washington Square. Inspired and donated by Oliva's great friends, former Wall Street buccaneer Lew and American Ireland Fund President Loretta Brennan Glucksman, it is a treasured addition to the local Village landscape of affluent, savvy, artsy learning. Oliva delights in the busy buzz around Ireland House, 'perpetual motion' is his description. He has been its intellectual architect and champion, and has helped to place Irish studies there on a real front burner in New York. Oliva is a quintessential Irish American New Yorker who is excited to bring what is best about the Irish to the greatest city in the world.

Anthony J. F. O'Reilly

Martin O'Neill

Dolores O'Riordain

Sonia O'Sullivan

L. Jay Oliva

OLIVER PEYTON

Irish-born Oliver Peyton has reinvented the concept of eating out in England over the past five years. Born in Swinford, County Mayo, in 1962 and educated at Summerhill College in County Sligo, Peyton runs an empire of six restaurants and 800 staff. He is the original Good Time Charlie. The son of a labourer-turned-entrepreneur, Peyton defines his childhood as cosseted. After winning a scholarship to study textiles at Leicester Polytechnic, he discovered he preferred business to artier pursuits and entered the drinks industry, spearheading the sale of designer beers in trendy nightclubs. In 1987 he cut a deal to import Absolut Vodka into the UK from Sweden and as a marketing ploy upped the vodka's strength from 37.5% to 40% which boosted the drink's iconic status. Transforming the basement of the old Regent Palace Hotel, Piccadilly, into an Art Deco shrine, he opened the Atlantic Bar and Grill in 1994. Since then he's added five more eateries to his list and has his sights set on opening a gentleman's club. A renowned hedonist he's cut down on the partying but is still a phenomenally driven character—his skill at working a room has been compared to an art form. Loyal to his family, his sisters Caitriona, Siobhan and Marie all work with him and Peyton is a regular visitor to Ireland. Family lore has it that his great-grandmother saw a vision of the Blessed Virgin Mary at Knock. His relatives even sold holy water to pilgrims. In his own way, Peyton, too, is continuing a tradition of peddling dreams to people.

GREGORY PECK

P Gregory Peck is quite simply a movie legend. Born in LaJolla in California in 1916, his career has spanned more than 50 films over as many years. A pre-med student before switching to acting, Peck's breakthrough role came in 1944, with *Keys of the Kingdom*, for which he received the first of his four Oscar nominations—he eventually took the award home in 1962 for his role as Atticus Finch in *To Kill a Mockingbird*. Peck holds Ireland dear (one of his ancestors was the patriot Thomas Ashe), and he and his wife Veronique are frequent visitors to his father's native Kerry. 'Being Irish touches my heart', he says, 'because of the strong ties with my father and grandmother'. His tireless support of the film school he helped to found at University College Dublin was recognised earlier this year when the National University of Ireland awarded him an honorary degree of Doctor of Literature on his 84th birthday. True to form, when Peck was awarded the prestigious Marian Anderson Award, which honours individuals for their humanitarian efforts, he donated part of his award to the Film Studies Programme at University College Dublin. Peck lives with his wife in Beverley Hills, California, and occasionally takes his hugely successful one-man show, an anecdotal evening of stories and film clips, to theatres around the country.

REGIS PHILBIN

To say Regis Philbin is the hottest personality on US television is an understatement. The man is on fire. As host of the wildly popular *Who Wants to Be A Millionaire* Philbin can be seen almost every night quizzing contestants on their tenuous path to a million dollar grand prize. He continues to host the *Live With Regis and Kathie Lee* talk show, seen every weekday morning across the country. Even his 'millionaire' wardrobe started a fashion trend in men's clothes. And at age 66, after more than 30 years in the television business, he shows no signs of slowing down. A proud graduate of the

University of Notre Dame (which bestowed upon him a honorary doctor of law degree), Philbin started his career hosted a television show in San Diego, before moving on to jobs in Los Angeles, St. Louis and back to Los Angeles, where he took over duties at *A.M. Los Angeles*. In 1983, Philbin returned to his native Manhattan and created *The Morning Show* on WABC-TV. Philbin is currently writing his second book, *Who Wants To Be Me?* His first literary effort, *I'm Only One Man*, became a best seller when published in 1995. Philbin and his wife Joy live in Manhattan and Connecticut, and travel frequently to Ireland. And there's no doubt what his answer would be when asked how he feels about his Irish heritage. Proud. Just as his Irish ancestors would be of what he has accomplished. Jimmy Neary, the well-known New York restaurateur is a long-time friend and host to Regis Philbin (who dubbed Neary New York's favourite leprauchan), and he maintains that Philbin is immensely proud of his Irish roots.

VINCE POWER

What would summer in London be without The Fleadh in Finsbury Park? Launched in 1990 and held there every year since then, The Fleadh was the brainchild of one man—Vince Power. Originally conceived as a showcase for the best of Irish music, The Fleadh is now synonymous with summer days and great music and has crossed the Atlantic to enthral audiences in Chicago, San Francisco, Boston and New York. But The Fleadh is only part of the story that is Vince Power's £40 million Mean Fiddler empire. Born in Tramore, County Waterford, 16-year-old Power fled poverty and the study of the artificial insemination of live-stock for the bright lights of London. By the early 1980s, Power had built up a successful furniture business, but when he opened his first Mean Fiddler bar in Harlesden, north London, he realised where his heart lay. Today, more than 20 Mean Fiddler bars and live music venues play host to established artists such as Eric Clapton and Christy Moore as well as showcase up-and-coming acts—The Pogues, Oasis and Radiohead are just some of the bands who have cut their teeth at Mean Fiddler venues.

Oliver Peyton

And still that is not the whole story. There is the Reading Festival (occupying pride of place in Power's eyes), the Phoenix, Creamfields and Homelands—festivals enshrined as rites of passage for thousands of teenagers. Power may live in England, but home to the 50-year-old father of eight, will always be County Waterford. 'I'm very grateful to have had the opportunity in England to do what I've done. But I still consider myself to be very, very Irish.' In August this year, Power and his business partners bought Celtworld in his home town of Tramore, a £4 million 'mythology' centre backed by Bord Fáilte and the EU that flopped in 1992 after only three years in business. Power plans to develop the centre into a major concert and club venue for the area. Not bad for Tramore's favourite prodigal son.

PHILIP PURCELL

As Chairman and CEO of Morgan Stanley Dean Witter & Co., since 1997, Philip Purcell heads one of the most powerful financial services companies in the world, with more than 15,000 employees in offices around the world. Born in Utah, Purcell is a graduate of the University of Notre Dame, holds a master's degree in business administration from the University of Chicago and a master of science degree from the London School of Economics. Purcell has held senior management positions at some of the most

influential companies in the world—he was Managing Director of the Chicago office of McKinsey & Co., Senior Vice-President at Sears, and as chairman of Dean Witter Discover, he led the company to eight straight years of earnings growth and guided the successful launch of the Discover credit card in the mid-1980s. A former Director and Vice-Chairman of the New York Stock Exchange, Purcell was elected to the Board of Directors of American Airlines and its parent, AMR Corporation, earlier this year. Donald J. Carty, chairman and CEO of American and AMR said on his appointment 'Philip Purcell is widely respected on Wall Street and broadly experienced in business. His insights and acumen will be invaluable to our Board.'

AIDAN QUINN

With a childhood spent in both Rockford, Illinois, and his parents' hometown of Birr in County Offaly, it's no surprise that actor Aidan Quinn jumps at the chance to work in Ireland. Films such as *The Playboys* (1992) and *Michael Collins* (1996) were shot there, but perhaps the one closest to his heart was *This is My Father*, a 1999 collaborative effort with his brothers Paul (writer and director) and Declan (cinematographer). The 41-year-old made his film debut in 1984 starring in *Reckless*, and got a major break with *Desperately Seeking Susan* a year later. He has gone on to work with Brad Pitt and Anthony Hopkins (*Legends of the Fall*), Johnny Depp (*Benny and Joon*) Meryl Streep (*Music From the Heart*), and recently portrayed Paul McCartney in a television movie. Married to actress Lorraine Bracco, Quinn lives with his wife and two children near Manhattan. But Ireland is always on his mind, and Quinn is confident that with the creativity being fostered in Ireland and by Irish-American artists today, there will be more roles for him in the future that involve the Emerald Isle. 'As film-makers, most of us got into this business from a love of storytelling and there's just so many tremendous stories to be heard in every family's history that are unique and quite dramatic. I would think that the high number of good films coming out of Ireland would continue.'

Gregory Peck

Vince Power

JAMES QUINN

In 1998 James E. Quinn was appointed to the high-ranking position of Vice-Chairman of Tiffany and Co., the internationally renowned jeweller and speciality retailer. As Vice-Chairman, Quinn's responsibilities involve managing retail, corporate and direct marketing sales worldwide. Born in New York in 1952, Quinn attended Hofstra University where he received a bachelor's degree in communications and later Pace University where he received a master's degree in business administration. His involvement in other business and civic organisations exemplifies the regard in which he is held by the business community. Serving on the Board of Directors of BNY Hamilton Funds, Mutual of America Capital Management and the Fifth Avenue Business Improvement District, Quinn is also Trustee of the Museum of the City of New York and the Montclair Art Museum. Immensely proud of his Irish roots (his paternal grandparents hail from Dublin and Mullingar, and his maternal grandparents came from Kerry) he visits Ireland a couple of times a year and serves on the advisory committee of the North American Advisory Board for University College Dublin. Currently residing in New Jersey with his wife Diane and their two children, Brendan and Jenna, Quinn relaxes by playing golf and coaching children's sports programmes.

FERGAL QUINN

Fergal Quinn is one of the most important business figures in Ireland today. As Chief Executive of Superquinn, one of the largest foodstore chains in the country, Quinn's hands-on approach has endeared him to many of his customers—it is not unusual to see Quinn behind the cash register in one of Superquinn's branches. Quinn attended University College Dublin where he attained a degree in commerce. He got his first taste for business while working in his family's Red Island Holiday Camp in Skerries, County Dublin. Although Superquinn was a valuable asset for the Irish economy—more than 3,000 people are employed by Superquinn-Quinn felt he had more

to offer to his country and in 1993 he became a member of the Seanad. A man with a strong social conscience, Fergal has been active in a number of important institutions—he has been Governor of the Dublin Skin and Cancer Hospital since 1972 and Chairman of An Post, to name but two. His contribution to Irish Society has earned him various accolades not least being an Honorary Doctor of Laws award from NCEA, an Honorary Doctor of Laws award from Trinity College and a Papal Knighthood in 1994. Quinn is married to Denise and they have three sons and two daughters. Quinn says he likes to unwind by sitting on a river bank hoping to catch a fish. Far from the sound of a cash register.

STEPHEN QUINN

It was the 1960s and London was swinging and everybody's style bible was *Nova* magazine, where publisher Stephen Quinn started his illustrious career in journalism. Born in Kilkenny, Quinn took ship for England at the age of 18 and has lived there ever since. Currently Publishing Director of *Vogue*, one of the plum jobs in the English media, he has been at the forefront of creating some of the most stylish and radical magazines of the last twenty years. Joining upper crust style bible *Harpers & Queen* in 1976, during his term of office as Publisher, he broke all records on circulation and profits. Harbouring ambition to produce an intelligent glossy for men—'a magazine that would sit comfortably and confidently on the coffee tables of the well bred and well fed'—

Quinn joined forces with Condé Nast and in November 1998, *GQ* was born. Its hallmarks are sophisticated images married to the very best of writing and today it is market leader in its sector and boasts a circulation of 130,000. Quinn's inexorable ascent up the media ladder eventually brought him in 1991 to *Vogue*, Condé Nast's flagship publication and arbiter of high fashion since the 1920s. From his elegant offices in Hanover Square Quinn presides over a publishing empire that still sets the pace with fashion aficionados and style gurus alike. Quinn's hectic schedule leaves little time for relaxation, but he takes a keen interest in politics and current affairs and enjoys the theatre and visits to the cinema. Quinn still loves to return to Ireland for holidays *en famille*. An abiding affection for the land of his birth inspired him to co-found the Ireland Fund of Great Britain, a charity dedicated to promoting peace and reconciliation as well as helping the less fortunate members of the Irish community in the UK. It still gives him a kick that a humble Kilkenny man has netted one of the most prestigious and glamorous jobs in English publishing.

STEPHEN REA

R Neil Jordan's 1990 film, *The Crying Game*, won Stephen Rea an Oscar nomination and he was hailed as a new star in the Hollywood firmament. But Rea was no overnight sensation; he was already an acclaimed stage actor before he made the transition to film. Rea was born in Belfast in 1947, but prefers not to talk about growing up there ('Belfast was bleak, very bleak,' he says). Although he was an avid cinema-goer, he didn't set foot in a theatre until he acted in one, when he studied at the Abbey Theatre School in Dublin. He moved to London and performed at the Royal Court and the National Theatre. In 1980 he heard that the Belfast Arts Council had funds available to invest in arts projects, 'So I went to Brian Friel and asked him for a play that we would tour together. I'd only met him once, but he said yes and the play happened to be *Translations*, which is a very great play'. And that was the beginning of the Field Day Theatre Company. Field Day toured for ten years and Rea

Philip Purcell

appeared in all but one of the plays. Around 1990, he says, he lost the energy to tour: 'I had a family and I decided that if my interest in acting had been originally stirred by going to the movies, it was time I did some more movies'. So he did. Films like *Interview with a Vampire*, *Michael Collins*, and most recently, *The End of the Affair* have established Rea as a great character actor and his partnership with Neil Jordan is regarded as one of the great actor/director pairings in cinema. Earlier this year, Rea directed and starred in an adaptation of *The Plough and the Stars* in Dublin. The play was a sell-out, although critics were divided about Rea's modern interpretation.

RONALD REAGAN

From humble beginnings in a small Illinois town, Ronald Reagan, through sheer will, incomparable communication skills, and more than a dash of Irish charm, rose to become the most powerful man in the world as President of the United States from 1980 to 1988. The charismatic former actor, who appeared in over 50 films, first attracted notice on the national political scene when he served as governor of California from 1966 to 1974. But it was as President that Reagan became known as the Great Communicator, in large part for renewing a sense of optimism among Americans during the early 1980s. His sense of

Stephen Quinn

'During the 1990s, LA reached the lowest point in history. We were in the midst of the worst recession to hit our region; riots tore at our moral fabric; and confidence hit rock bottom.' But the second generation Irish man from Flushing, New York, has more than brought Los Angeles back to life. The local economy is on an upswing and crime is down almost 50 percent since 1995. 'Angelenos have been my partners in achieving tremendous success for their city,' said Riordan. While he promised to make the City of Angels 'the capital city of the 21st century' during his first term, upon being sworn in for his second in 1997, said Riordan, 'I took an oath to join Angelenos in turning Los Angeles around. Together, we have done just that.'

patriotism and democracy shone brightly when he challenged then Soviet leader Mikhail Gorbachev to tear down the Berlin Wall, a wish that became a reality in 1989. A much-publicized trip to Ireland during his Presidency strengthened his connection to the land of his ancestors. Reagan's great-grandfather, Michael Reagan, was born in 1829 in Ballyporeen, County Tipperary. The President visited the small town himself, bringing an international spotlight to Ireland during his stay. Today the former President, who lives in California with his beloved wife Nancy, faces the daily challenges brought on by Alzheimer's with the same dignity and grace that was displayed in a letter he wrote to the American public announcing his affliction. Despite living in the sunset of his life, Ronald Reagan remains for many a strong symbol of the US standing tall, at its strongest and proudest, a man who took great joy in serving the people of the country he loved so much.

RICHARD RIORDAN

Richard Riordan was sworn into office as Mayor of Los Angeles in 1993, shortly after the 1992 Los Angeles Riots, and was faced, only a year later, with the 1994 Northridge Earthquake. Anyone in their right mind may have thrown in the towel rather than face the enormous task of reviving the city. Even Riordan was later quoted as saying,

MARY ROBINSON

With her call to Irish women to rock the country not the cradle, Mary Robinson swept into power in 1990 on a surge of popularity that lasted for the duration of her seven-year term as President. Born in Ballina, County Mayo, in 1944, Robinson's gender was as much a topic of debate during the campaign as was her profile as a liberal lawyer—one of her critics infamously asked who was looking after her three children while she was campaigning for the presidency. Unprepared to succumb to the lethargy that seemed to afflict many of her presidential predecessors, Robinson battled for a modern and open presidency. Her sharp intelligence, steely determination and formidable legal skills—she was the youngest

Fergal Quinn

ever Reid Professor of Constitutional Law at Trinity College Dublin—made confrontation with the political figures of the day inevitable. This undoubtedly endeared her to the public at large and Irish women in particular, as did her work with the disadvantaged in Irish society and around the world—Robinson was the first head of state to visit Somalia following the crisis there in 1992 and Rwanda in the aftermath of the genocide in 1994. Reports suggest that she continues to battle in her current role as Commissioner of Human Rights at the United Nations—not only against famine, disease and abuses of human rights but also against UN bureaucracy and lack of funding. There have been successes. Robinson was the first High Commissioner to visit China, securing an agreement that should lead to a wide-ranging programme for the improvement of human rights there. Her visit to Mexico in late 1999 may have almost caused a government-wide 'nervous breakdown', according to one Mexican newspaper, but the government has nevertheless agreed to tighten up legislation related to the UN Convention against Torture. Lawyer, president, feminist icon, UN commissioner, Robinson remains a powerful force for change.

KEVIN ROCHE

Kevin Roche has been the recipient of virtually every architectural prize going. He learned his craft under Mies van Rohe, one of the most influential figures in 20th century design. Born in Dublin, he spent his childhood in Cork where his father was general manager at Mitchelstown Creameries. After studying architecture at University College Dublin he worked with renowned Irish architect Michael Scott on a number of projects. The late 1940s saw him moving to Chicago and that crucial stint as van Roche's pupil. In 1949 he embarked on one of his first major undertakings—the design of the United Nations headquarters in New York. Then he joined the prestigious offices of Eero Saarinen, which gave him the opportunity to work with Saarinen on all of his important projects from 1950 to 1961— the period when Saarinen garnered a reputation as one of most influential up and coming architects

in the US. In a career spanning more than forty years Roche has designed some of the most seminal buildings in the American cityscape. His list of credits include eight museums, thirty-eight corporate headquarters, theatres and centres for the performing arts. He has been the prime mover in the evolution of the Metropolitan Museum of Modern Art and as well as installing several of the new art collections, Roche has designed all of the new wings at the Museum. Its not just in the States that his artistic genius has made an impact. Roche currently has work in progress in Singapore, Japan, Malaysia, India and China. His recent return to Ireland, to create the ambitious Dublin Docklands Development, generated a good deal of controversy. But no matter. Whatever he's turned his hand to in the last forty years, Roche's work has always made people sit up and take notice.

DAN ROONEY

In 1964, Daniel M. Rooney watched as his father, the late Arthur J. Rooney, was inducted into the Professional Football Hall of Fame for his contributions as founder and owner of the Pittsburgh Steelers football team. Whatever dreams the younger Rooney may have had at that time, it's doubtful that this oldest of five boys would have imagined following in his father's footsteps. Yet this past summer, 36 years later, the younger Rooney, president of the Steelers since 1975, was inducted into the very same Hall of Fame for continuing the high standards and tradition instilled into the Steelers' organization by his father, not to mention being a central figure in National Football League operations for over 25 years. Now in his 45th year in the organization, and 25th as president, Rooney is one of the most active NFL owners and one of Pittsburgh's most involved executives in civic affairs. Among his community activities, Rooney is a Board Member for The United Way of America, The American Diabetes Association, The Pittsburgh History and Landmarks Foundation, University of Pittsburgh Medical Center, and the Mentoring Partnership of Southwestern Pennsylvania. Pride in his Irish heritage is evident in his strong commitment to The American Ireland Fund, which he helped

co-found in 1976 with Dr. Anthony J. F. O'Reilly, former President, Chairman and Chief Executive Officer of Heinz Company. With a trinity of goals—Peace, Culture and Charity—the two started The Ireland Fund to appeal for support for Ireland and its people from all Americans, but especially those of Irish descent. On St. Patrick's Day 1987, The Ireland Fund and the American Irish Foundation merged at a White House ceremony to form The American Ireland Fund and became the nation's, and the world's, largest private organization funding constructive change throughout Ireland, north and south. As President of the Steelers, the 68-year-old Rooney has seen his team win 14 division titles, five conference championships and four Super Bowls. He is a member of several NFL committees, including the board of directors for the NFL Trust Fund, NFL Films and the Scheduling Committee. He is also currently a member of the eight-person Management Council Executive Committee, the Hall of Fame Committee, and the NFL Properties Executive Committee. Rooney, who graduated from Duquesne University in 1955 with a bachelor of arts degree in accounting, lives in his native Pittsburgh with his wife, Patricia. They have nine children—Art, Patricia, Kathleen (deceased), Rita, Dan, Mary Duffy, John, Jim and Joan. Maintaining a tradition of excellence and running any business smoothly is tough enough, let alone one founded by your father in the often harsh media spotlight that comes with a professional sports franchise. Yet Dan Rooney has risen to the challenge with a professional career honoured with a Hall of Fame induction, and a lifetime of giving that would make his Irish ancestors proud.

KEVIN RYAN

When Kevin Patrick Ryan took the job of Chief Financial Officer of a company called DoubleClick in 1996, there were just 20 employees and minimal revenue. Today, thanks in large part to his contributions, the company has grown into a publicly traded industry leader, with over 2,000 employees in 23 countries. Named DoubleClick's Chief Executive Officer this past July, Ryan brings more than 15 years of business

Mary Robinson

MEG RYAN

Dubbed as America's Sweetheart for her whimsical, girl-next-door characterisations on the big screen, Meg Ryan is one of the biggest stars in Hollywood. Born Margaret Mary Emily Anne Hyra in Connecticut in 1961, she took her mother's maiden name (the Ryans hail from County Mayo) when she helped her secure a Screen Actors Guild card. Ryan had a strict Catholic upbringing and was a popular student at high school where she was voted 'cutest' girl in 1979. While studying journalism at NYU she began her acting career when she won a part in the television soap drama *As The World Turns*. She made her film debut in 1981 in *Rich and Famous* but it was her role alongside Billy Crystal in the 1989 romantic comedy, *When Harry Met Sally*, and in particular the fake orgasm in the deli scene, that established her as a household name. Despite her more gritty and down-to-earth roles in the movies *Promised Land* and *When a Man Loves a Woman*—in which Ryan played an alcoholic mother of two—her biggest box-office successes have been for her innocent screwball characters in films such as *Sleepless in Seattle*. It seems the movie-going public prefers to see Ryan in feel-good roles with happy endings. Ryan's marriage to actor Dennis Quaid had been until recently the stuff of which fairytales are

and financial experience to his role of overseeing day-to-day operations and the overall direction of the company. As a leading innovator of Internet advertising solutions and with an established record of product development in launching media, technology and data products, DoubleClick is the largest company in New York's growing Silicon Alley. Under Ryan's leadership, 1999 revenue grew 128% over the previous year. In fact, the *Silicon Alley Reporter* and *@NY* named DoubleClick, the New York Company of the Year. Prior to joining DoubleClick, Ryan was Senior Vice-President of business and finance at United Media, a licensing and syndication company. There, he launched the Dilbert Zone, the most popular and profitable comic strip site on the web. Ryan also worked for Euro Disney in France, and as an investment banker with Prudential Investment in the US and the UK. He earned his undergraduate degree in economics from Yale University and his masters of business administration from INSEAD in France. While Ryan spent almost 15 years abroad living in Paris, Geneva, Rome and London, Ireland is a favourite destination, and not solely because it is home to DoubleClick's international HQ. 'My father is 100 percent Irish', he says, 'even though he is fourth generation.' His brothers are named Sean Davey Ryan and Conor Kennedy Ryan, so it's no wonder that the technology capital of Europe receives frequent visits from this member of the Internet elite.

Richard Riordan

made—the couple married on Valentine's Day in 1991 and had a son, Jack Henry in 1992. So it came as something of a shock to the media and moviegoers alike when rumours that Ryan had been having an affair with *Gladiator* star Russell Crowe came to light and Quaid filed for divorce. Like so many actors Ryan can reflect on major roles she has turned down—she was offered the leading roles in the blockbusters *Silence of the Lambs* and *Pretty Woman*—but with her name high on the list of the most bankable actresses in Hollywood and her own production company, Prufork Pictures, those missed opportunities are but momentary distractions for a woman whose career is as vibrant as ever.

TONY RYAN

Regarded by many in the business world as possessing the greatest entrepreneurial mind in Ireland, Dr. Tony Ryan has experienced some triumphant highs and some devastating lows in his long career. Born in County Tipperary in 1936, Ryan was educated by the Christian Brothers in Thurles, before joining Aer Lingus as a station manager at Heathrow Airport. Ryan quickly saw the potential in aircraft leasing and founded Guinness Peat Aviation in 1975 with an initial investment of only $50,000. He based the fledgling company in Shannon and surrounded himself with the best business minds he could find— Former Taoiseach Garrett Fitzgerald and former Chancellor of the Exchequer Nigel Lawson provided the gravitas, and Denis O'Brien and Michael O'Leary the drive. The combination worked. Guinness Peat Aviation quickly became the talk of Wall Street and the City of London—at its peak the company was worth $4 billion and had more aircraft on its books than the entire British Airways fleet. The disastrous flotation of Guinness Peat Aviation brought the company to its knees, with debts of more than $200 million and Ryan's personal finances under tremendous pressure. But Ryan recovered from the debacle. The Ryanair Group, which he founded against furious opposition from Aer Lingus, is now the most successful low-cost airline in Europe and its successful flotation in 1997 generated some

Dan Rooney

£64 million for the Ryan family. Now Chairman of Irelandia Investments and Tipperary Crystal and Director of Ryanair, Ryan demands excellence from all who work with him, including his three sons, Declan, Cathal and Shane, who own stakes in Ryanair. Described by colleagues as 10 percent hard-nosed businessman and 90 percent Medici prince, Ryan's restoration of Lyons Demesne in County Kildare was a project of which the Medicis would have been proud—more than one hundred of the finest craftsmen in Europe toiled on the house and the result has astounded those lucky enough to be invited to one of Ryan's legendary dinner parties. Earlier this year, his sons announced that they were funding the

Dr Tony Ryan Academy for Entrepreneurship in west Dublin 'to effect our father's lifelong desire to extend creative opportunity for ambitious young people'. Described as a boot camp for business people with ideas who want to acquire the necessary management skills, the state-of-the-art campus offers intensive courses designed by the Entrepreneurship Centre at the Massachusetts Institute of Technology (MIT) and is aimed at entrepreneurs who want to acquire the management skills needed to implement their ideas. Ryan was delighted by the initiative and assured the press that the programmes would be 'radical and unconventional'. He would have been forgiven for adding, 'Just like me'.

SEAN SCULLY

In the words of one art critic: 'Scully is a landscape artist, but his landscape is the built environment of the modern city. Just think of the street-plan of New York, of the façades of the modernist skyscrapers, or the way light falls on the city's brownstone buildings.' Home for artist Sean Scully is certainly New York—he became an American citizen in 1983, but it took some time to get there. Born in Dublin in 1945 and raised in London, where he attended the local convent school, Scully took evening classes at the Central School of Art and went on to Newcastle University. He travelled to Morocco in 1969 where he was bowled over by the work of the local weavers and their use of bright colour (to this day he remains judicious in his own use of colour). In the early 1970s, he moved to the USA and attended graduate school at Harvard University (courtesy of a John Knox fellowship), and returned to London to hold his first solo exhibition at the Rowan Gallery—the show sold out. In 1975, Scully settled in New York, teaching at Princeton University and exhibiting regularly. Scully has a clear style, described as 'a crescendo whose momentum cannot be repressed', and he has been hailed as a pivotal figure in post-War abstract painting. Apart from continual exhibitions of new work in the US and Europe (including Ireland, where he always makes a point of exhibiting), major retrospectives of both his larger paintings and his work on paper have toured extensively—a major retrospective of his work at the Irish Museum of Modern Art was phenomenally successful. Scully lives in New York with his wife, the painter Catherine Lee.

ROBERT SHEEHAN

It seems as though the entire world is fascinated by lawyers—high-profile court cases like the O. J. Simpson trial and prime time television programmes like *Ally McBeal* have captured the public's imagination, with millions of viewers tuning in to watch cross-examinations and closing arguments. For 56-year-old Robert Sheehan, however, law offices and courts are part of his

Kevin Ryan

daily routine. As Executive Partner of Skadden, Arps, Slate, Meagher, and Flom, Sheehan leads the largest—and, some claim, by far the most profitable law firm in the US. Born and raised in New York, Sheehan earned an economics degree from Boston College and a law degree from the University of Pennsylvania. When he joined Skadden, Arps in 1969, the law firm employed only 25 lawyers; today, more than 1,500 lawyers operate from 22 offices worldwide and the law firm is high on the list of any young law graduate eager to make their mark in New York—not surprising considering the starting salary is a cool $100,000. Sheehan took a leave of absence in 1970 to work as a special consul to Representative Elizabeth Hiltzman while she was a member of the judiciary committee considering the impeachment of former President Nixon. He returned to the Times Square office of Skadden, Arps in 1976 and became a partner there in 1978, focusing on the banking and financial sector and acting for some of the multinationals and private investors across the US. Sheehan is regarded as a brilliant lawyer and motivator of people. Sheehan's family hails from County Westmeath, and Sheehan visited Ireland this past June with his wife, Beth and their children, Lily, Rob, and Will. A passionate golfer, Sheehan declared the Old Head of Kinsale golf course 'the best in the world' and he is already planning future trips to Ireland.

Robert Sheehan

MICHAEL SMURFIT

In this era of e-commerce whiz kids and overnight multi-millionaires, Michael Smurfit is from the old school of business. Born in 1936, he joined his family's Dublin-based and moderately successful corrugated box manufacturing business at the age of 19, became a director when he was 30, and Chairman and Chief Executive when he was 41. Under his steady and dedicated hand, Jefferson Smurfit Group has become a powerful international packaging corporation. HIs business acumen was brought to bear on Telecom Éireann, which he chaired. Astounded at the ten-year plan presented to him, Smurfit declared that to follow it would be to condemn Ireland to the third division in the technological industry. He rewrote the plan and helped to set in its place the infrastructure that has made the current hi-tech explosion in Irish industry possible. Always with an eye to the future, he established the Smurfit Business School, which has trained some of the brightest lights in Irish business. Although still hugely influential in business and politics, in recent years Smurfit has learned to relax a little—he enjoys the company of his family (six children from his two marriages) and the more material prizes from a lifetime in business—golf tournaments at his lavish K Club in County Kildare, an impressive art collection, a state-of-the art boat (named *The Lady McGee*, after his Belfast-born mother) and homes in New York, Paris, and Monte Carlo.

Meg Ryan

Sean Scully

SUSAN SPENCE

As Co-Founder and Executive Chairman of the SoftCo Group, 40-year-old Dubliner Susan Spence has been in the vanguard of e-commerce development in Ireland over the past decade. She took her first step in the computer industry in 1981, and quickly advanced to senior management positions with major international corporations such as Hewlett Packard and McDonnell Douglas, until in 1990 she realised a long-held ambition and founded SoftCo with her business partner Jim Coffey. Spence's company pioneered the development of information management and e-business technologies and solutions and is now a market leader (with an annual growth rate of 45%), redefining how worldwide business is being conducted. Spence is as excited today about SoftCo as she was ten years ago: 'We employ 200 people, have offices throughout Europe, Asia and the US, and we are heading into the most exciting period of our expansion. I want those people who have been part of SoftCo's development to share in even greater prosperity, as the company expands.'

As the mother of young twins ('without doubt my greatest achievement'), Spence also wants to prioritise time with her family and 'get to more football matches!'

KATHLEEN SULLIVAN

When 44-year-old Kathleen Sullivan was appointed Dean of Stanford Law School last year (the first female dean in Stanford's history), she might have been forgiven a moment or two of self-congratulation. But she didn't dare. Her Irish grandmother's admonition that she should never 'let her head get swelled up' was too deeply ingrained. Those around her, however, fought a battle of superlatives when they spoke of this no-nonsense lawyer. Her mentor Professor Lawrence Tribe described her as 'dazzlingly good and brilliantly quick'; Stanford President Gerhard Casper declared her 'an outstanding teacher and scholar, an active lawyer and a public intellectual'; the *National Law Journal* ranked her one of the fifty most influential women lawyers in the US;

and *The Washington Post*, *The New York Times* and *USA Today* pinpointed her as a future appointee to the Supreme Court. Sullivan dates her interest in the law to the dark days of the 1970s when the events at Watergate unfolded on her parents' television set in an Irish Catholic community in Queens, New York, where she grew up with her two younger siblings. 'It was a brief moment when lawyers were the heroes and it was the first time that it occurred to me that women could be lawyers', she says. So Sullivan studied constitutional law at Harvard, graduated summa cum laude, began teaching law there at 29, earned her tenure at 33, and was appointed the first Stanley Morrison Professor of Law at Stanford at the age of 41. During the course of this rapid ascent, Sullivan gained an enviable reputation as a litigator (she argued two cases in the Supreme Court), published numerous articles in leading law reviews, and was elected to the American Academy of Arts and Sciences in 1986. As one of the most influential constitutional lawyers of her generation, Sullivan's views on judicial matters are sought by everyone from US senators who are drafting legislation to national newspapers and television programmes who want to present complex legal matters in lay man language, a cause close to Sullivan's heart. 'Law is a social practice, not some kind of secret priesthood. If you can't translate law into terms that non-lawyers can understand then we're not doing all we could to make law succeed,' she says. Sullivan insists that teaching has always been the absolute centre of her career—for her, shaping the next generation of lawyers in the classrooms of Stanford is more exciting than any high-profile court case or lofty appointment. Her students speak of her wit and the 'life altering' effect of her classes. Sullivan is unmarried and lives on the Stanford campus. She is obviously aware that she is tipped for the Supreme Court, a post she describes as a dream job. But, for the next five years at least, she is charged with leading Stanford Law School, its 600 students, and its $26 million budget. 'Who could resist teaching at a world class law school in paradise?', she replies when asked about her reasons for staying at Stanford. Sullivan is exactly where she wants to be. For the moment.

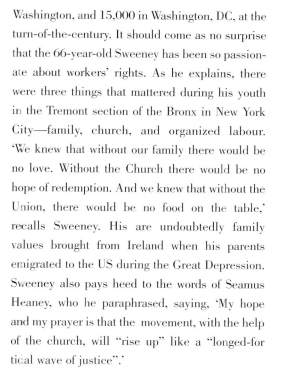

Michael Smurfit

Washington, and 15,000 in Washington, DC, at the turn-of-the-century. It should come as no surprise that the 66-year-old Sweeney has been so passionate about workers' rights. As he explains, there were three things that mattered during his youth in the Tremont section of the Bronx in New York City—family, church, and organized labour. 'We knew that without our family there would be no love. Without the Church there would be no hope of redemption. And we knew that without the Union, there would be no food on the table,' recalls Sweeney. His are undoubtedly family values brought from Ireland when his parents emigrated to the US during the Great Depression. Sweeney also pays heed to the words of Seamus Heaney, who he paraphrased, saying, 'My hope and my prayer is that the movement, with the help of the church, will "rise up" like a "longed-for tical wave of justice".'

DANA TASCHNER

Dana Taschner's grandfather arrived in Boston from Ireland and rode a buckboard across the country in search of gold. The San Diego-based lawyer still maintains a few slabs of gold from his grandfather's days and a sense of adventure that contributed to him being named the Solo Practitioner of the Year by the American Bar Association. As a solo practitioner for the past ten years, Taschner has been a champion of the underdog. In a 1993 case that made law, Taschner represented the children of a woman who had been killed by her husband, a police officer. His successful prosecution of the case was later cited in support of an amendment signed into law by President Clinton prohibiting police officers convicted of domestic violence crimes from carrying weapons. In his most recent case, the 40-year-old lawyer is battling the LAPD in the largest police corruption scandal in the country. Taschner began his law career with Baker & McKenzie, the world's largest law firm. Taschner's interest in the law is equalled by his love for Ireland. He and his wife, Cheri, visited Ireland recently to have one of their three children christened at University Church in Dublin. Going back to Ireland, says Taschner, 'was a dream come true'.

Susan Spence

JOHN SWEENEY

If there is anyone who speaks to the concerns of working class families in the US, it has to be John Sweeney. As president of the country's largest labour organization, the AFL-CIO, he has provided a strong voice to more than 13 million workers. Sweeney came in as president in 1995, promising to politicise workers' rights, and since then he has led a particularly fierce battle against President Clinton's efforts to bring China into the World Trade Organization. Sweeney helped raise the awareness of the globalization of workers' rights to an unprecedented level in history, and galvanised workers, students, and other groups who demonstrated 30,000-strong in Seattle,

John Sweeney

won two consecutive majority governments as Premier since 1996, most recently in the provincial general election of February 1999. His political career dates back 20 years when Tobin was elected to the House of Commons in 1980 as Member of Parliament for Humber-St.Barbe-Baie Verte. Tobin was also appointed Parliamentary Secretary to the Minister of Fisheries and Oceans. He won re-election to Parliament in 1984, 1988 and 1993, and served as Minister of Fisheries and Oceans from 1993 to 1996. Tobin, who studied at Memorial University of Newfoundland, is married to Jodean Smith of Happy Valley-Goose Bay, Labrador. They have three children, Heather Elizabeth, Adam Vincent and John Joseph.

KATHLEEN KENNEDY TOWNSEND

It is somehow fitting that Kathleen Kennedy Townsend's birthday falls on 4 July, Independence Day in the US, because she is part of a family intertwined with the history of the US in the 20th century. Townsend is the eldest child of the late Senator and US Attorney General Robert F. Kennedy and Mrs. Ethel Kennedy. And she has followed in her father's footsteps with a career in public service. The 49 year old has served as Maryland's first female lieutenant governor since 1995. Prior to that, she served as Deputy Assistant Attorney General in the US Department of Justice. Townsend is a *cum laude* graduate of Harvard University and a graduate of the University of New Mexico Law School. She and her husband David, a college professor, have four daughters. The Democrat has led initiatives in her state to target crime and at-risk neighbourhoods by creating new partnerships between citizens, police, the business and religious communities and public agencies. Recently, there were rumours circulating around Washington, DC, and in senior political circles to the effect that Kennedy would run as Al Gore's vice-president on the Democrat ticket. Although that didn't come to fruition for this campaign, Kennedy certainly has a long way to go in her political career and future presidential tickets should not be ruled out.

BRIAN TOBIN

Brian Tobin was born and raised in the western Newfoundland community of Stephenville, part of a Canadian district whose residents are heavily dependent on seasonal employment in fisheries and forestry. Today, as the sixth Premier of Newfoundland and Labrador, Tobin has an intimate understanding of the importance of those traditional industries. But he has also worked on maximizing other emerging sectors, such as information technology and offshore petroleum, and the efforts of his government have led to a stunning economic turnaround for his native province. In 1998 and again in 1999, Newfoundland and Labrador led all of Canada

in Gross Domestic Product growth, and is predicted by leading financial forecasters to do so for a third time in 2000. Hibernia, Canada's largest offshore oil discovery is in full production and work is progressing on other sites already in various stages of planning development. By 2004, it is expected that Newfoundland and Labrador will produce almost 40 percent of the nation's light crude oil. Newfoundland and Labrador's information technology sector accounts for over half a billion dollars worth of business annually, and the province's diversified fishery exceeds the half billion dollar mark each year. Clearly quite a job has been done by the 46-year old former journalist. In fact, Tobin has

Dana Taschner

THOMAS J. TRACY

Thomas J. Tracy is a highly successful Californian industrialist who is immensely proud of his Irish heritage. A third generation Irish American on both sides of his family, his ancestors hailed from Counties Carlow and Mayo. Educated by two renowned religious orders—the Benedictines and the Jesuits—he graduated in 1961 with a degree in economics. Today he is President and Chief Executive Officer of Genuine Parts Distribution. A larger than life character, he has passionately championed a host of worthy causes throughout his life. For his dedication to the Catholic Church both in Ireland and in the US, he was declared a Papal Knight of the Holy Sepulchre in 1996. But it is a measure of the breadth of the man that he is much more than just a generous donor to Church charities. His affinity with justice is the spur behind his commitment to peace and reconciliation in Northern Ireland. A regular visitor to the Province, he is always superbly briefed and has a determination to see both sides of the story that is invaluable in reconciliation work. No wonder then, that he has the rare distinction, as a staunch Catholic, of being described by an English newspaper as a Unionist sympathiser. Among the twenty-eight Irish-related organisations he supports are Co-Operation North, the Northern Ireland Partnership, the Irish-American Cultural Institute, and Northern Ireland Industrial Development. In recognition of his immense contribution to Irish American relations in 1996, he was accorded the prestigious American Ireland Fund award for Distinguished leadership. Another accolade followed in 1999 when University College Cork bestowed on him a degree of Doctor of Laws *honoris causa*. Perhaps what best encapsulates Thomas Tracy's attitude to Ireland are the simple words he had inscribed on a commemorative gift to the Taoiseach—'From those who left to those who stayed'. Tracy and his wife, Erma Jean, have four daughters and a son.

PHILIP TREACY

When Philip Treacy was five years old he said he wanted to sew. His parents batted not an eyelid and said, 'if that's what you want then fine'. Now Irish-born milliner Philip Treacy has been in the front ranks of *avant garde* hat design for over a decade. From his boutique in London's Elizabeth Street he continues to produce hats that are masterpieces of exotic flights of fancy and invention. Manhattan socialites adore his creations and supermodels love him so they display his wares

Thomas J. Tracy (centre)

free of charge. Seldom parted from his pooch, Mr Pig, Treacy inspires unwarranted warmth and affection in the bitchy world of haute couture. The son of a baker, and born in Ahascragh, County Galway, he comes from a family of seven brothers and one sister. He displayed an early talent for art that eventually earned him a scholarship to London's Royal Academy of Art. While still a student, Treacy was commissioned by couturier Victor Edelstein to design hats for his collection, an unprecedented accolade. Treacy graduated in 1990 with a first class honours degree. He had already made an impression on fashion giants Rifat Ozbek and John Galliano, and it wasn't long before he had his own studio in Belgravia and an increasing band of loyal devotees including Lady Isabella Blow. Since he presented his first collection in 1993 he has been the darling of the fashion crowd, working with luminaries such as Karl Lagerfeld, Thierry Mugler, and the late Gianni Versace.

DAVID TRIMBLE

For some, the abiding memory may be of an Orange sash-clad David Trimble as he marched down the Garvaghy Road, side by side and step by step with the notorious Ian Paisley. But there can be little doubt that the First Minister of the Northern Ireland Assembly provided courageous leadership during the complex negotiations that culminated in the Good Friday Agreement. His role is a difficult one, and his leadership of the Ulster Unionist Party often teeters on a knife edge, but Trimble is a man of substance. He saw the future of Unionism when his more recalcitrant colleagues saw only the glories of a distant past. And he took the step forward. His political courage has not gone unnoticed—Trimble has been feted at Whitehall and the White House, he enjoys unprecedented support from the Irish government, and he was awarded the Nobel Peace Prize in 1998. Now 56 years old, Trimble continues to drag his party kicking and screaming into devolved government and a new future. Decommissioning and the implementation of the Patten Report are obstacles to his progress, but this pragmatic Unionist will undoubtedly continue to face down his critics and take one step at a time.

U2

'I don't want to be in a band unless it's the best band in the world,' says Bono. And U2 is the best band in the world. Without doubt. Beyond question. Acclaimed and worshipped the world over, it is nevertheless to their home town of Dublin that you must look to understand the phenomenon that is U2. For it is there they truly hold court. 'Dublin is important to all of us,' says Larry Mullen Jr. 'It gave us a break. This is where it all happened.' And it is happening still. Bono, Larry, The Edge, and Adam Clayton still live in Dublin, they record many of their albums there, they own a hip hotel and a trendy nightclub. They are, to all intents and purposes, the uncrowned kings of the city. When the biggest names in music converged on Dublin earlier this year for the MTV Awards, the loudest applause and longest ovation were reserved for the four eccentric-looking characters sitting quietly in the front row. That same week the widely held view of U2 as rock royalty was reinforced when all four band members were granted the Freedom of the City of Dublin—Bono and The Edge immediately exercised their newly granted right to graze sheep on St. Stephen's Green. Formed in 1978 when Larry pinned an ad on the bulletin board in Dublin's Mount Temple High School, U2 have

David Trimble

been at the top of the game for more than 20 years. The music may have evolved from the stadium rock of *Boy* and *War* to the multimedia extravaganza of *Zoo TV* and *Pop Mart*, but the U2 'sound' remains immediately recognisable. This is in no small part due to the distinctive voice of Bono, frontman extraordinaire and latterly political lobbyist to the power brokers of the West. Bono's involvement over the past couple of years with Jubilee 2000, an campaign that calls for the abolishment of Third World debt, has taken him to the White House, Downing Street, and the Vatican. But this year sees a return to the music and the long-awaited release of their new album, recorded in Dublin. 'It's the sound of four guys playing in a room, rediscovering what they're good at,' says Bono. 'It has fire and it has spunk. That should put loads of people off.' Somehow we doubt that.

EDWARD WALSH

Edward Walsh truly qualifies for the epithet 'Renaissance Man'. Born in 1939, this native of Cork and founding president of the University of Limerick is also a registered silversmith and author of over fifty publications. A chartered engineer by profession, and a key figure in the Irish academic world, he has brought his visionary approach to bear on a broad range of cultural and academic institutions at home and abroad. When Limerick became the location for the first new university to be established in the Republic of Ireland he was its first president—a post he held for twenty-eight years in total. Originally a graduate of the National University of Ireland he also received a masters degree and a doctorate from Iowa State University in the field of nuclear and electrical engineering and has honorary doctorates from no fewer than four different universities. He is currently involved in steering a new flagship informatics project for Ireland as well as holding the chair of the Irish Council for Science Technology and Innovation. He has been convinced that the way forward for Irish society is to create a highly educated science and technology literate elite. To that end he has presided over many advisory boards and at last in the year 2000 he sees much of his work coming to fruition. He developed the concept of the National Digital Park, which will be a nerve centre for cutting-edge technological developments. Walsh regards Seán Lemass as one of the unsung heroes of Irish society, for his visionary attempts in the 1960s to transform Ireland into a legitimate manufacturing base. In many ways Lemass is Walsh's antecedent because he, too, is passionately concerned that if Ireland does not produce a science-literate population we could be in trouble in years ahead. Walsh's vision and his dream is to add value to what we offer multinationals whilst also creating our own entirely indigenous industries.

JAMES WALSH

Congressman James Walsh has had more than a touch of Irish in him ever since his earlier days in the Tipperary Hill section of Syracuse, New York, which was named in honour of the Irish who helped build the Erie Canal, and where America's only green traffic light sits above the red. The second generation Irish American followed the political footsteps of his father, who served in Congress from 1972 to 1978. As a congressman, he chairs the Friends of Ireland Congressional Committee, a bipartisan group of congressional representatives who closely follow events in Ireland. Walsh has led several delegations to

Brian Tobin

Northern Ireland. He joined President Clinton's historic first-time trip in 1995, and was a member of the distinguished delegation that accompanied the president to Ireland in 1998 following the Good Friday Agreement. The New York congressman also serves as chairman of the US–Irish Interparliamentary Group, which communicates with the Republic of Ireland's parliament on issues of mutual concern. To add to this, Walsh is also responsible for the 1998 Walsh Agreement, which allows citizens of Northern Ireland to live and work in the US for five years. The 53-year-old politician has been honoured by so many for his work, from the Ancient Order of Hibernians to the American Ireland Fund, but for Walsh, whose grandfather, Michael Joseph Walsh, was forced from County Tipperary by poverty and despair, 'It is a rare opportunity to return something to my grandparent's homeland.'

LOUIS WALSH

While young girls the world over swoon before posters of pop bands Westlife or Boyzone, it is likely that none of them has heard of Michael Louis Walsh, the brains behind the bands and a man with a remarkable ability to brand and export the charms of fresh-faced, fame-seeking Irish teenagers. In 1992, observing the nascent success of UK boy band, Take That, Walsh determined to reproduce the winning formula and, after auditioning 150 boys—many of them not even musicians—he selected the Boyzone line-up. From its first success in 1994, the band went from strength to strength, outliving Take That, and going on to become the world's top performing boy band. Teen quintet, Westlife, formed by Walsh in partnership with Boyzone singer, Ronan Keating, in 1998 has been equally successful. This year its record, *Fool Again*, took the band into the Guinness Book of Records for achieving five successive Number One entries in the UK pop charts with its first five singles. One of nine children (seven boys and two girls), Walsh was born in 1956 and grew up in Galway. He hated school, though he did manage to complete his schooling before running away to Dublin, where he slept on his eldest sister's floor and dreamt of showbusiness, stoking his burning

desire to work in the music industry. 'It's all I've ever been interested in, since I was a kid. There was nothing else,' he says. At 17, he went to work at Tommy Hayden's theatrical agency in Dublin. 'He had all the big Irish bands and DJs and I made the tea,' Walsh remembers. Constantly on the lookout for talent, Walsh is widening his net, promoting Samantha Mumba, whom he describes as an Irish Janet Jackson. Managing the fairer sex is not, however, new to Walsh, who discovered girl band B*witched in the early 1990s, although he sold them on before they really hit the big time. Walsh lives in Dublin, a city he loves. He remains resolutely single. No children, no pets. 'I'm just into the music,' he laughs.

PATRICK WALSH

Dr. Patrick Walsh has literally been on the cutting edge of medicine for 25 years. As professor and director of the renowned James Buchanan Brady Urological Institute in Maryland, he has revolutionized modern techniques for removing a cancerous prostate. By discovering the location of tiny nerves that were previously damaged unknowingly during surgery, Walsh has made it possible to cure prostate cancer with surgery and preserve sexual function in most men. The result of his 25-year-long crusade to cure prostate cancer has not gone unnoticed. In 1996, Walsh received the Charles Kettering Medal for his 'Most Outstanding Recent Contribution to the Diagnosis or Treatment

Edward Walsh

Vivien Walsh

Louis Walsh

sourced from around the world. Meath-born Walsh launched her first collection in 1992 and is now acclaimed as Ireland's leading costume jeweller. Initially inspired by her grandmother's antique French jewellery, these days Walsh's inspiration comes from sources as diverse as modern architecture and the colours of a Tuscany sunset. Described as a very clever buyer with a great eye, Walsh has introduced several exciting new labels to Ireland—the work of Australian duo, Scanlon & Theodore is only available in Europe at Vivien Walsh and Harvey Nichols in London. Walsh has been in the fashion business for many years and has seen trends and designers come and go. When asked about her greatest achievement to date, Walsh laughs, 'Still being here. I've been in and out of business, and in is infinitely better'.

JAMES DEWEY WATSON

Irish genes, the gift of Irish-born maternal grandparents, are no laughing matter to James Dewey Watson. They have taken him where no man has gone before. At the same time, those genes have made him the *enfant terrible* of modern science, a precocious genius who sometimes forgets to tie his shoe laces. For this 1962 Nobel laureate, genetics is the blueprint of life. Watson, who doubles his Celtic genes with the addition of Scottish ancestry, mingled with an English descent from his father, was only 34 years old when he received the Nobel Prize in Medicine for his part in the discovery of deoxyribonucleic acid—better known as DNA. A Chicago native, Watson demonstrated rare, prodigy-like abilities when he enrolled at the prestigious University of Chicago at the age of 15. There he developed a refined taste for the classics and bird watching, while majoring in zoology. He graduated at the age of 19 in 1947, and was accepted for graduate school at Indiana University, where he earned his PhD in zoology and developed his growing fascination for the study of genetics, due in no small part to his love for bird watching. In 1950, at the famous Cavendish Laboratories, Watson met his most famous colleagues in the study of genetics, Francis Crick and Maurice Wilkins, with whom he would share the Nobel Prize. In their work, they

of Cancer'. Beyond awards, he has also treated such luminaries as King Baudouin of Belgium and is the man television networks call for the latest developments in prostate research. Unimpressed by material success, Walsh, who could be a star draw at the grand dinners and great social events connected to American cancer charities, prefers instead to work from an unpretentious office and drive a five-year-old saloon car. Absolutely dedicated to the art of healing, Walsh is a third generation Irish-American proud to follow in the footsteps of two other giants in surgery—Irishmen Sir Peter Freyer, who performed the first open prostatectomy in the world, and Terrance Millin, the developer of the retropubic approach.

Says Walsh, 'I credit my Irish heritage for giving me the wisdom and skill in making these discoveries.' From a humble family in Akron, Ohio, the 61-year-old doctor has come a long way.

VIVIEN WALSH

Vivien Walsh may keep a low profile, but to the fashion cognoscenti, she is one of the most influential women in Ireland. Jewellery designer, boutique owner and an ambassador for talented Irish designers and craftspeople, her boutique in the centre of Dublin is a virtual treasure trove of her exquisite jewellery and a range of exclusive clothing, shoes and accessories that she has

Patrick Walsh

continues, and both she and her husband are confidantes of Prince Charles. Weston's office in Canada is a vice-regal position. She serves as a Constitutional officer of government, entrusted with responsibility for the smooth functioning of the Constitution and the democratic will of the people. Under Canada's Constitution, Weston appoints the province's Premier and approves all decisions of the provincial Cabinet. From her residence in Toronto, Canada's largest and most English city, Weston executes her duties with an impeccable grace—as befits a former model—that has endeared her to Ontario's citizens. She is married to Galen Weston, Chairman of George Weston Limited, a company that controls the Dublin-based fashion centre, Brown Thomas Limited. Intensely stylish and regularly named on Canada's Best Dressed List, Weston's impeccable fashion sense has inspired women across Canada, and Brown Thomas' preeminent status in Irish fashion circles owes a debt to her stylish influence. The Westons have two grown children, Alannah and Galen Jr. With a Irish love for all things green, Weston is the author of *In a Canadian Garden* and *At Home In Canada*. She is also a passionate supporter of countless cultural and youth programmes. Observers say Weston is having a powerful impact on the quality of life of Ontario residents, and enjoys record levels of popularity among Canadian people.

proposed that the DNA molecule is shaped like a double helix, an entity resembling a slightly twisted ladder with phosphate and sugar deoxyribe fashioning the rails; and of a pair of nitrogen-containing nucleotides creating the rungs. Their discovery unveiled the very origins of life itself, carrying science into the murky and messy primordial world. For Watson, the great leap for humanity in our lifetime hasn't been the exploration of space, but the explosive world of genetics. As befits a man who is at the very epicentre of genetic advances, he is particularly proud of his Irish roots.

HILARY WESTON

Since January 1997, Dublin-born Hilary Weston has been Ontario's second female to hold the prestigious office of Lieutenant-Governor. Born Hilary Frayne, her Irish origins provide her with a refined and historic sense of diplomacy as the Crown's representative in the Canadian Province, with all the pomp and pageantry that goes with it. Among the responsibilities associated with the post is that of welcoming the Queen and other members of the Royal Family on official visits. Weston's English home is at Belvedere, famous as the house from where the previous Prince of Wales made his abdication broadcast. The link with the English Royal family

Hilary Weston

WESTLIFE

Boyzone first earned Ireland its reputation as master producers of teen pop, a genre previously dominated by British and American outfits. Their international success was phenomenal and it seemed that their achievements could not be surpassed, but surpassed they were and by none other than five fellow Irishmen. Westlife made pop chart history by becoming the first group to have five singles enter the British charts at Number One. And there is at least one member of Boyzone who is quite happy to see their lengthy reign as the number one boy band usurped by Westlife. Ronan Keating co-manages this pop sensation with Boyzone manager, Louis Walsh. Westlife members Kian Egan, Mark Feehily and Shane Filan all hail from County Sligo and the quintet is completed by Dubliners Bryan Fadden and Nicky Byrne. The group's recent recording with Mariah Carey, the most popular female singer in the US, is indicative of their degree of success across the Atlantic. In the UK the group managed to achieve the much sought after Christmas Number One in 1999 with their heartfelt rendition of the 1970s hits *I Have a Dream/Seasons in the Sun*, knocking Sir Cliff Richard from the top of the charts. Though adored by millions of teenage girls around the world, only Nicky is romantically attached—his girlfriend is none other than Georgina Ahern, daughter of An Taoiseach Bertie Ahern. Recently Westlife were honoured with the Freedom of the Borough award from Sligo Corporation in recognition of their international success. Given the group's clean-cut image and usually harmless antics it seemed somewhat out of character for them to become embroiled in controversy when they helped to launch the Royal British Legion's annual drive for fundraising on Poppy Day, an event that was censured by Sinn Féin. Nonetheless, their records continue to sell in the millions, their posters adorn teenagers' bedroom walls around the world, and parents sigh with relief that these clean-cut pop idols have found favour with their children. Westlife's star is still in the ascent, and the future looks bright for this Irish pop sensation.

Westlife

Bill Whelan

BILL WHELAN

Bill Whelan is best known as the award-winning composer of *Riverdance*, but his musical career stretches far beyond that famous seven-minute intermission piece in the 1994 Eurovision Song Contest. Born in Limerick in 1950, Whelan grew up listening to everything from Irish music to opera to Elvis Presley. In the 1970s he began writing and arranging pieces for string quartets until he met Donal Lunny and became a member of Planxty, a relationship that culminated in *Timedance* in 1981—also, ironically, an intermission piece at a Eurovision Song Contest. In 1989 he was appointed composer to the W. B. Yeats International Theatre Festival at Dublin's

Abbey Theatre, and in 1992 his specially commissioned orchestral work, *The Seville Suite*, premiered in Seville as part of the celebrations for Ireland's National Day at Expo '92. Meanwhile, Whelan's compositional work in films met with great success—his credits include *Some Mother's Son*, *Dancing At Lughnasa*, and *Lamb*. Then came *Riverdance*. 'I thought that the more interesting the rhythm, the more interesting the dance. Perhaps Irish jigs and reels could be pushed into something that wasn't quite squared and straight'. How right he was. *Riverdance* became a worldwide phenomenon, Whelan was honoured with the 1997 Grammy Award for Best Musical Show Album, and the *Riverdance* CD went platinum in

the US, Ireland and Australia. Whelan shrugs off criticisms that the music of *Riverdance* is a jumble of different sounds and influences and that he has diluted the pure Irish sound. 'It's funny, because in the US I'm typecast as the Irish composer and in Ireland, I'm typecast as the non-Irish composer. I can only be honest about what I do and I'm still madly interested in what Irish music can deliver to us as Irish people.' Whelan's next project is a musical exploration of Spain and South America. Toes are tapping already.

KEITH WOOD

Keith Wood is the heart and soul of Irish rugby, the captain who strikes fear into the heart of opponents as he charges at them and through them in game after game. As he says, 'I don't actually want to be running into contact all the time, but if I totally throw down my game and play in an X, Y and Z sort of way, then I'm not really Keith Wood any more. I'm not playing the way I want to play.' Even South African coach Nick Mallett admitted Wood is the best hooker in the world. Born in 1972, Wood followed in the footsteps of his father, Gordon, who played for Ireland and the 1959 Lions, and won his first cap for the senior squad in 1994. Wood was named captain of the Irish side in 1996 and led the team for nine tests until their defeat at Twickenham in 1998. Wood also took on the captaincy of London Harlequins during this period, and he now admits 'I'd have to hold up my hand and admit I had too much on my plate.' His much-publicised dispute with the IRFU only added to the pressures on him. But he's back— stronger than ever, captaining the Irish squad since last year, and finally ending a string of defeats with victory over Scotland in the Six Nations Championship in February this year. Lansdowne Road is a magical place for him. 'I find it very difficult to explain to people how much I love Lansdowne Road. The first time I played there I remember pulling on my jersey in the dressing-room and thinking "no-one can ever take this away from me".' The feeling is reciprocated, the ovations he receives from the crowd at Lansdowne have been known to bring a blush to the cheeks of this big man.

The Clash of the Ash

BY TOM HUMPHRIES

Kilkenny's Henry Shefflin in action

History will record that of all the misfortunes to have befallen the downtrodden Irish, none was as dangerous or debilitating as the tidal wave of wealth that mercilessly struck the nation in the late 20th century.

Our brave little island, accustomed as it was to famine, plague, pestilence, war and accordion music was suddenly attacked by a virus to which it had no antibodies—success. Wealth and the threat of full employment gnawed pitilessly away at the national self-image. We grew smug and fat and allowed our memories grow short. One truth emerged—if there is one thing more tedious than a little island nation lachrymosely lamenting all its troubles, well, it's a little island nation imagining itself to be the centre of the universe. Solemnly we decided that having a Planet Hollywood franchise in town meant that we were officially twinned with Tinseltown. We had a duty to be tacky. The phenomenon of second-rate celebrities drinking in our pubs was taken as an international endorsement of our incredible lovability. We felt no need to apologize for Riverdance. Forgetful of our own diaspora we came over all Aryan when considering the possibility of allowing immigrants to share our good fortune. People who thought they knew Ireland found that they couldn't locate the heart of the place anymore. They recognized the phony baloney of medieval banquets and they knew about Easter Revolutions and pub opening hours. They were immune to blarney. They knew the back road into Thurles and where to get a good soft pint of Guinness after they've taken it. They saw past the postcard visions of freckled red heads loading creels of turf onto the backs of donkeys. They knew about information technology, for God's sake. They don't know Ireland though. Not anymore.

It's easy to forgive them. It doesn't take much to miss out on the pulse of a country on the make, just a knack for looking the wrong way at the right time, just a wrongheaded thought that sport is too much seriousness in pursuit of too much trivia. To know this country you have to know the sounds, the smells and the feel of hurling, the unique, shining game of stick and ball that is one of the jewels of our living culture. Miss it and you know nothing of Ireland today, nothing of Ireland past. Imagine this. Imagine the classroom in which we vegetated during the overcast 1970s. High windows. Chalk dust in the air. The Virgin Mary teetering high in one corner. De Valera on the other wall watching her like a hawk. Acne everywhere. Therein presided a teacher of the

Irish language who hailed from County Clare. He was never the most phlegmatic of men and his traffic light red complexion purchased him the most imaginative of schoolboy nicknames, Redser. Irony like pasta had yet to reach Ireland in the 1970s. Anyway Redser suffered from the seasonal affective disorder that was part and parcel of being a devotee of Clare hurling. Clare's hurling seasons were like Woody Allen films—they seldom ended happily and often took tragic-comic turns. We were the fall guys. From spring onwards Redser's moods oscillated with the fortunes of the Clare hurling team. Oscillated? By late May he was suicidal verging on homicidal. It was a tough time for Clare, their nascent side never quite made the breakthrough. Whatever pains they suffered were nought as compared to the travails we went through one hundred miles away in northside Dublin, however. Clare's specialty at the time was the league and through the spring as they reached two finals in succession Redser's mood would brighten and our lives would be easier. Clare brimmed with potential and every morning we stood with Redser and offered prayers that they might thrive at last. Naturally they would find a way not to thrive. They hurled below themselves to spite us, they invented ever more ingenious ways to fail, they became celebrated for their creativity in securing defeat. Typically they would lose a league final in May just in time to give our summer examinations the tingle of anticipation that

must have preceded the Spanish Inquisition. We knew three things. One: we yearned to see Clare succeed. Two: they would never succeed. Three: hurling mattered. What's the point of this? Well, hurling is substance. It is continuity. I think of Clare, I think of Redser, all those years when Clare yearned to express itself as a hurling county, all those Sunday afternoons when we either journeyed to see them beaten or heard news of their demise come crackling over a car radio.

It matters. In a changing, depreciating world hurling holds its value like nothing else. When all else fails in Ireland, when we are cursed by peace and prosperity and left to survey our own numbing vacuity, hurling will save us from being an idiot culture. You have to have grown up with a Redser or been dragged to Munster finals by hurling men or to have stumbled somehow on the arcane glories of the game to know the sense of place, the sense of community and the sense of passion that hurling engenders. You have to recognise the game as a manufacturer of myths and legends, a supply line of heroes. Yes. Hurling will teach you all you want to know about the sore history of this island. And take your breath away while doing it.

Listen. Ireland isn't Celtic Tiger wealth and a decade-long discussion about house prices. Ireland is a last second point by Ciaran Carey, a haymaking clearance by Brian Lohan, a quick as a fish turn by Joe Deane, a bony-fingered catch by Joe Rabbitte. It's all those moments when you

James O'Connor from Clare

Kilkenny's Henry Shefflin and Fergal Ryan of Cork

catch us with our guard down, with the traditional caution gone and the old dour mask laid on the floor. Times when our hats fly through the air. In a country made dark by bad religion and bloody invasions and lousy politics the pure sport of hurling has been our fiesta, our Mardi Gras, our carnival. And when finally we got rich and handled it with the class of the Beverly Hillbillies it was hurling that flourished and stood as an affirmation of all that could be culturally special about Ireland.

There is so much more to hurling than that which meets the eye and, by the way, what meets the eye is truly sensational and glorious. Hurling isn't merely a patch of grass, two goalposts and thirty players in search of a ball. The game is the most common expression of our hunger for poetry, the truest expression of Ireland's wild beauty. Hurling is art wrapped up in sport. Hurling's rhythm is measured out in perfect arcs, the pentameter of honest play. A ball dropping from the sky into a swirling thicket of arms and hurleys. A length of ash flashing on a scurrying ground ball. An overhead pull exploding the air as it meets with the sliotar and makes all heads turn and all jaws drop. Two sticks and two shoulders converging like thunder clouds. Sawdust in the square boys! The abrupt punctuation mark of a score. Celebration. Ya boy ya! It goes beyond that again, though. Its elemental and untameable nature distinguishes the game and tethers it to our hearts.

Sure, hurling is tracksuits and training and sweat and practice, but to watch and to play is to join arms with a line of ancestors who disappear over the horizon at that point where history becomes myth. Hurling percolates through the community and leaves its mark even on those who disdain the game as a relic of a peasant past. There is no purer strain of bigotry in Irish sport than that which resides in the hearts of those who cannot abide the game. Their animus is an expression of the tensions of change, the need to force Ireland to be something different. Something at more homogenous ease in a world of franchises and mega-mergers. Hurling is defiant.

You need to know certain things, facts that underpin our little civilization. Men and teams have defined geography and vice versa. If Tipperary hadn't got hurling we would think of a different sort of place when the name was mentioned. The character of Kilkenny people is written in the way they play the game. We didn't know the grain of Clare until their hurling blossomed late in the century and redefined the place for us. You need to develop the reflexes. Try word association tests. Cloyne? First thought: Christy Ring. Gowran? First thought: D J Carey. Tullaroan? First thought: Lory Meagher. And so on through The Faythe and Buffers Alley and Maddens Terrace and Ballyhale and Bullaun and Ballygunner and a thousand other spots that have the sanctity of grottoes because of the hurlers who sprung from there.

And know that the geography made the hurlers. Delve through the sociological history of the country and you will find the explanations for how certain counties play the game, how the styles evolved. Which areas enjoyed the patronage of landlords, which hewed the game out of a rough version of hockey and which places especially in the north west saw the game die in their arms. History is the glue that holds the game together in these times.

These days to know the minutae of the game is to know about rights deals and sponsorships and under the table payments to managers, yet the playing of championships is a sort of sacred duty one of those things that we have never let go out of fashion. The preamble to the formal history of hurling is legend. The stuff we all learned in the classroom. Tain Bo Culaigne from the 9th century: Setanta was pucking his ball in the air (silver ball, bronze hurley), minding his own business when he was confronted by the slavering hound of one Cullain. We know that Setanta in the mood could have soloed past the hound with a large meatball on the bas of his hurley and wearing a couple of lambchops as shinguards. Instead he went for the big play and planted the sliotar at considerable speed down the hound's gullit. From then on Setanta would be Cullain's hound or Cu Chullain. The game of hurling existed as a reference point in our history from even before then. Mentioned in heroic literature and bardic texts from the

Clare's Stephen McNamara and Cathal Moore of Galway

8th century (the first sportswriting!), depicted on high crosses in Monasterboice and Kells from the 10th century, it is a recurring motif of history, an extended metaphor for heroism right through the ages until such time as the game became formalized in 1884 when one Michael Cusack organized his Metropolitans (no less!) to play Killimor in Ballinasloe on Easter Sunday for the prize of a ten sovereign silver trophy. Afterwards the teams raced each other for free beer. And the hurley itself is an emblem of aspiration and heroism. Weeping men carrying hurley sticks at the funeral of Charles Stewart Parnell. Rebels training with hurley sticks on their shoulders instead of guns. Coffins lowered into the earth with the occupant's club jersey and favourite hurley making the long journey with him. The game deserves a wider audience but history has penned it in. Ireland has colonized no place so its sport is its own. It's the world's loss.

There is no more difficult way to hit a ball with a stick. The golfer, pampered and swaddled from birth to death, begins by placing his aerodynamic little sphere helpfully atop a plastic tee. Thereafter he calls upon the services of various custom-made implements with which to fashion his progress towards the green. A story, which is too good to be apocrophyl, illustrates the point nicely. Christy Ring of Cloyne, the greatest player ever to have wielded a hurley, the Babe Ruth of the game was introduced to golf one afternoon by

a friend who was eager to see how the great man's skills would translate. They stood on the first tee and Ring absorbed the rules. 'This area of short grass here which stretches away in front of us, that's the fairway, Christy, and the idea for now is to hit the ball into the idle of the fairway about 150 yards ahead of us. Straight on up, boy.' So Ring takes out a big old wood, surveys it for a second and without so much as a practice swipe propels the ball 150 yards down the fairway and stalks after it. 'Now,' says the friend, gathering his breath and handing Ring a skinny two iron, 'Do you see where that ring of very short grass is up there, with the flag in the middle? I want you to aim for there or thereabouts.' So Ring grabs the iron and pulls cleanly and the ball plops onto the green. The friend is apoplectic with excitement and they march towards the green and see Ring's ball just four feet from the hole. 'Christy,' he says grabbing the hurler's arm, 'Do you know what this means? You could score a birdie on your first hole of golf. The idea you see is to get the ball into this little hole where the flag is.' And Ring interrupts, vexed and exasperated. 'Arrah, in the name of all that's holy, boy, why didn't you tell me that and we standing at the start?'

What else? The baseball hitter copes with all manner of trickery, but apart from the pitcher's armaments the environment is friendly. The baseball hitter chooses his stance, cocks his bat, narrows his eyes and judges the pitches as they descend on him. A cricketer has it easier again. Padded like a piece of mailed china and fed tea and sandwiches like a chap in mourning, the worst he faces is a spin bowler with a bad mind. The ice hockey goon has skill and works with a racedriver's speed, but the puc in the main clings obligingly to the ice while the ice hockey stick has a blade broad enough to thresh the corn of an entire county with two sweeps. Tennis? Well, after dinner Mr Agassi, you will be using this old catgut racket and Mr Becker and perhaps Mr Sampras here will be shoulder charging you, getting out in front of you, doing their all to prevent you hitting that ball the way you want to.

The hurler is a different creature, living off skill and wit like no other animal alive today. The flight of the ball is rendered slightly imperfect by the thick seams that hold the sliotar together. You only get your choice of stance when you line up for the national anthem and never after that. At all other times the ball whips around in a frenzy and the hurler tames it with a variety of skills that he deploys with a surgeon's feathered touch. The smallest reflex move a hurler makes is so laden with skill and learning that words are inadequate to describe the fluid beauty. There are other beauties to the game, quieter pleasures that it takes time to absorb but which make the game an oasis of sanity in a world gone demented. For instance. The game is eternally, defiantly local. Your hero, your town's greatest hurler might deliver your

Paul Shelley of Tipperary and Dermot O'Sullivan of Cork

Brian Corcoran playing for Cork

milk, teach your kids, cut your meat, sell you insurance. That proximity never ceases to amaze. You can walk into Brian Whelahan's bar in Birr and buy a drink from him, into Anthony Daly's sportshop in Ennis and buy a jersey from him and so on. There is never more than one or two degrees of separation between an Irish person and a hurling star. The rivalries are at once passionate yet gentle. There is no segregation of fans, no chest bumping, no hype, no riots. How has this game survived? There are few distractions. No New York Yankee fan ever paid money to see George Steinbrenners ample girth gamboling in the South Bronx for a night, no Manchester United season ticket holder hankers after an afternoon watching

Mr Martin Edwards trying to juggle a football. Yet the owners of professional sports franchises around the world insist on inserting themselves conspicuously between the action and the audience. They hiss about the limits of the market, the needs of the stockholders and the need to trade assets for a profit. Hurling, ah, hurling is free of these vipers. They wouldn't dare trespass. Hurling knows that winning is good, losing is bad and losing to your next door neighbour is very bad. If there is meddling it is done by the abstemious aldermen who populate county boards and club committees up and down the country. They tend the game like deacons tending the parish. With due humility.

Humility is part of hurling's personality. The game never forgets its reverence for the past. The highest form of braggadocio ever seen on a hurling field was when some Tipperary players high fived each other in the late 1980s. It was an occasion of sin and we thought the game would never recover and still we aren't done talking about the intransigent arrogance of Tipp people. Remember how when Art Foley saved from Christy Ring in 1956? While the game raged on Ring walked in and shook Foley's hand. 'Tis far from high fives we were all reared.

The humility comes from time, place and temperament. When the spring evenings draw longer in hurling towns the young fellas will be

'Aerial Battle' involving Colin Lynch and James O'Connor of Clare and Brian Greene of Waterford

Frank Corcoran of Cork charges through the tackle of Paul Shelley of Tipperary

out on the greens and on the fields knocking a ball around. Conversation is filtered through the sound of practice and the appreciation of truths. Your elders were always your betters. There's always a hurler somewhere who'll skin you, who'll send you back to school. Listen up for the story of the day we played this crowd thirty-five years ago. You might learn something. Hurling never allows you to travel far from the earth. The stick, the hurley, the caman, call it what you will—the tool that rests so reassuringly in your palm is special. The

hurley, the implement of magic, is a personality on its own. Each one hewn from the root of an ash tree and made into something to be loved or loathed. Nothing insults the artist quicker than an unforgiving plank tossed into his hand. Every hurler searches for Excalibur, that wand with the sweet spot. When he finds that perfect cut of lightness and flexibility and grip he will anoint it with linseed oil to hold the qualities in. He will spare the stick the rough and ready risk of practice games. On the field they'll be pucking around and on the

sidelines and in the saloon bars those of us who envy and revere them will be talking about hurling. Just talking. Talk is the oxygen of the game, the way in which recondite truths are circulated. No fans are more knowledgeable than hurling fans. Those of us whose living depends on writing about the game often reflect that it is a good days work when a sports journalist writes something about hurling that would stand the scrutiny of a good pub conversation. After playing and watching, talk is the third pleasure of hurling. Leaning into a chat, wondering which of the kids will make it. Wisdom is conventional in these matters and odds are always long. A kid is too scrawny, too chicken, too one-sided, too lazy, too much like the brother. Either that or he is too little like the father, too fond of the jar, too fond of the books, too fond of the women, too fond of the horses, too full of everything except the right stuff. Hurling is not a game for optimists or spin doctors. It's too serious for that. About hurling we worry like a parent. Is it growing quickly enough, is it sturdy enough, is it free from bad influences? In lean times we fret about its popularity, in good times we question its quality. Yet hurling defies us every summer.

Hurling prevails and heroes keep on being born. When D J Carey was a pasty little ghost of a kid in Gowran, the women would stop him on the street and tell him to mind himself. He was too small to be hurling with the big fellas, he'd get hurt. Hurling prevailed though—his teachers in Kilkenny saw something else and because he lived so far away in Gowran they gave his mother a job in the school that she might ferry him with her. The kid they used to call Dodger became one of the greatest hurlers we have known. By rights we knew we shouldn't see his match again for a generation but even his greatness was paralleled by a kid from Birr. Brian Whelahan had hurling in

his family they way some people have trouble in theirs. He'd play on D J Carey in school games and they grew into men together and through the 1990s they were the best to be seen anywhere, the two icons at the front of a generation that played in their prime during the greatest era the game has known. What an unlikely pleasure.

Hurling people aren't optimists and it was assumed that the plastic world would devour the game. These were kids that we should have lost to television or video games or play stations or street corner culture. They should have grown up in a world where this game of theirs was dead and mourned only by their elders. Surprise. To those

Galway's David Forde under pressure from Paul Curran and Martin Maher of Tipperary

**Eddie Walsh of Kilkenny
and Barry Murphy of Cork**

who love the game the closing years of the 20th century brought nothing but high harvests. In the late 1980s we wondered seriously if the game mightn't dwindle and die before our eyes. Instead, it replenished itself. An enlightened sponsorship policy and the spread of hurling's gospel led to better championships and better attended games. The personalities and the rivalries grew larger every year and when we danced dizzily into the new millennium we saw fit to check ourselves and wonder if we weren't living through hurling's golden age right now. Every summer now throws up matches of perfect beauty. We are spoiled. If we don't get a handful of masterpieces we deem the season a dud. The rivalries have never been better and surprises never sweeter. In an Ireland driven crazy with money and greed, hurling stands for the best of ourselves. Ah, the plotlines. Tipperary in their pomp and arrogance treated the hurling peasantry of Clare to some hard times and some foot in the stomach oppression. Clare have repaid them with equal kindness. The counties had locked stares so hard by 1999 that Cork stole through the gap and won an All Ireland, which set the permutations deliciously askew again. What a time we have had of it. Summer Sundays out on

the road following the crowd to some pitch or other. The game has kept us sane. Wexford arose briefly and surprisingly, claiming an heroic All Ireland before subsiding again. Limerick sent out a heroic team that deserved more than the heartbreak it got. Until Cork finished the century off with an impudent title win we'd had an unprecedented lock out of the great aristocrats of the game. Kilkenny, Cork and Tipp starved as we savoured every new season. The story of Ireland can be read in hurling still. If you ignore the game you miss the soul of the country, the best it has to offer. You cannot paint a picture of Ireland without it. The boomtime has hit the country hard in the past half decade and how gladly and easily we could forget ourselves with the price of a makeover in our pockets. Our self-confidence is best reflected in the glorious renaissance of a simple game, however. Pitch to pitch, parish to parish, county to county, year by year. Hurling has been lifted up and polished again and as usual the players have responded. It is rarely that a sport aspires to be culture rather than a mere business but hurling has succeeded. It is a glory; in this neon era it is our Cistine Chapel. Where would we be without its grandeur?

Irish Art in the 20th Century

BY ROBERT O'BYRNE

When Sir Hugh Lane first began to formulate his ideas in 1904 for a Gallery of Modern Art in Dublin, he had very specific intentions in mind. At the time, he believed the visual arts had been neglected in Ireland and that the best way to encourage them was to create a gallery where the best examples of contemporary painting and sculpture might be seen. This is why, in 1908, he established the Municipal Gallery of Modern Art that now bears his name. However, Lane was wrong to imagine

that the Irish visual arts were in a deplorable condition. The main problem was that some of their best exponents at the time were scattered among England, France and Ireland itself. The history of Irish art over the past one hundred years has been the story of a culture developing sufficient confidence to stay at home and no longer feel the necessity to travel. Almost a century after Hugh Lane insisted on the importance of a distinctive Irish 'school' of art, it has finally come into being, though not necessarily as he would have

envisaged. In fact, the two artists responsible for originally inspiring Lane in his ambition were based in Dublin. Walter Osborne, who regrettably died from pneumonia at the age of only 44 in 1903, was the most successful painter of his generation, producing a mixture of society portraits and scenes of urban life. Like so many other artists of this period, he had spent time in both Belgium and France, particularly Brittany, and these works from the 1880s continue to have enormous appeal today. Back in Ireland from 1892

onwards, he showed regularly at the Royal
Hibernian Academy and was a founder member of
the Dublin Art Club. Although Osborne's elegiac
style of naturalism is immediately recognisable,
his work does sometimes suggest the influence of
Whistler. That might also be said of the other artist
whose pictures acted as a catalyst on Hugh Lane.
John Butler Yeats is better known today as the
father of Jack and William, but he had a long,
though never very satisfactory, career specialising
in portraiture. The quality of his work could never
be in question, but he was chronically undisci-
plined. His letters, selections of which have been
published, are highly amusing, not least for the
prevaricating character they unwittingly reveal.
By 1908, Yeats had moved to New York where he
was to remain until his death fourteen years later.
He was by no means the only Irish artist who left
his native country, never to return. Probably the
best-known today is Roderic O'Conor who, having
grown up in Roscommon and studied in Dublin,
settled in France where he became a close friend
of Gauguin. The latter's influence is sometimes
apparent in O'Conor's work, particularly his
nudes, but so, too, are elements of Van Gogh and
Monet, especially in the Irish artist's seascapes,
usually painted in savage shades of red. Roderic
O'Conor, who lived until 1940, had almost nothing
to do with Ireland but this was certainly not true of
two Irish artists who, although they enjoyed their
greatest commercial success in London, regularly
crossed back over the Irish Sea throughout their
lives. Both Sir John Lavery and Sir William Orpen
were enormously popular portraitists during the

early decades of the 20th century and their work in this genre was in constant demand. They also produced landscapes and interiors of great charm and beauty—perhaps because these were more personal, they can have a very special appeal.

Although younger than any of the artists mentioned so far, Harry Clarke should be included because, while he lived until 1931, his work essentially belongs to a pre-modernist Ireland and, as has been frequently noted, is almost a stylistic throwback to the 1890s. Clarke's genius lay in his technical skills as a stained glass artist because he was capable of overcoming enormous challenges to produce exquisite pieces that, for sheer virtuosity, have never been equalled. Like Osborne, he died young but left a substantial body of work behind him. From what has gone before, it might seem that art in Ireland was a male prerogative. Actually, the first half of the 20th century was notable for the number of extremely fine female artists working in this country. Almost without exception, their backgrounds were Protestant and Anglo-Irish and suggest a generation that, excluded from exercising their considerable energies in other fields, turned to art as a creative outlet. Sarah Purser might best be described as the original of the species, not least because thanks to a very long life (she was aged 95 when she died in 1943) she spanned two centuries. Purser was an extremely successful

Below, Peacocks, by Mildred Anne Butler; opposite (top), A Corner of the India Tea Room, by Sir John Lavery; opposite (bottom), Still Life with Fruit and a Jug by Roderic O'Conor

portrait painter, as was the much less known but just as able Sarah Cecilia Harrison. By comparison, lifelong friends and almost exact contemporaries Mildred Anne Butler and Rose Barton specialised in watercolour landscapes and urban scenes respectively. Whereas the former's inspiration was most commonly her Kilmurry home in County Kilkenny, the latter regularly turned to the streets of Dublin for her ideas. In post-Independence Ireland, another generation

of Irish women artists appeared. It is particularly interesting to note that they were often more ardent champions of the modernist movement than their conservative male counterparts. This group included Mary Swanzy—the oldest as well as longest living—who, thanks to time spent during the first decade of the century in Paris, was greatly influenced by post-Impressionism and Cubism. Far more explicit evidence of Cubism is visible in the art of Mainie Jellett whose abstract paintings created an enormous stir when first shown in 1920s Dublin following her return from France. While there, she had attended the same studios as another Irish woman, Evie Hone, who came to specialise in stained glass for which she received many commissions, the most famous being the great window of Eton College Chapel on which she worked in the years prior to her death in 1955.

By comparison with these adventurous women, the male artists who came to prominence in Ireland during the 1920s can seem a timid bunch. However, they were preoccupied with creating that dream of Hugh Lane—a distinctive Irish art. The most driven by this concern was Sean Keating, Orpen's favourite pupil and in many respects (at least with regard to his work) Ireland's nearest equivalent to Britain's Augustus John. Keating's work is a complex blend of social realism and symbolism, particularly in his large mural commissions from official institutions. He was a deeply patriotic man who sought to inspire the nation through his work. Paul Henry's motivation was far less overt, although during the years he spent on Achill Island, County Mayo, from 1910 onwards, he was anxious to portray the

Opposite page, Spectacular stained glass windows by Harry Clarke adorn the Catholic church in Cong, County Mayo; above, The Travellers, by Gerard Dillon

remorselessly hard life of Ireland's rural poor. But after the mid-1920s, he produced landscapes that, while by no means idealistic in character, possess a spirit of tranquillity, due primarily to the subdued colour palette he preferred. His wife Grace Henry was also a very fine artist whose reputation has always tended to be overshadowed by that of her better known husband. Meanwhile, the tradition of portraiture was maintained not just by Keating (whose work in this area can

sometimes be excessively bombastic) but by the unjustly neglected Patrick Tuohy. Another former student of Orpen, Tuohy was a slow worker, perhaps because he had been born with a disabled left hand. The relatively small number of examples of his work are prized by knowledgeable collectors, but the need to find commissions obliged him in 1927 to emigrate to the USA where he tragically committed suicide three years later at the age of 36. Among his most famous students

was Norah McGuinness. Originally from Derry, she was one of the next generation of Irish women artists who achieved renown, two others being the sisters Eva and Letitia Hamilton. All three share the same appealing quality of domesticity in their work. While unquestionably charming, the art of these women is less sophisticated than that of their predecessors. This is also true of a group of painters who achieved renown in the 1930s and who tended

The Road to Donegal, by Norah McGuinness

to specialise in portraying the Irish landscape, which had changed little over the preceding few centuries. Their canvasses therefore have value as historical records of a world that, in the post-Second World War years, would alter radically. Among the best known of these painters is Maurice MacGonigal who throughout his career constantly returned to Connemara for inspiration. Stylistically, he shares many characteristics with his friend Sean Keating, although MacGonigal's landscapes are far less inclined to dwell on the heroic. Nor do those of Belfast-born James Humbert Craig, whose images of Antrim and Connemara are in the tradition of earlier artists such as Nathaniel Hone and Dermod O'Brien.

Since the mid-18th century, landscape painting has been a constant feature of Irish art, thanks in part to the attachment this country's population has always felt with land ownership. Neither Craig nor fellow Ulsterman Frank McKelvey particularly romanticise the scenes they painted, but their work expresses a devotion to the subject matter that would be shared by most observers, both then and now. This explains why their work has never failed to attract a strong following. Less easy to explain is the appeal of Jack B. Yeats' expressionistic art, which, although so highly distinctive that it created no school of followers, has always been greatly admired by Irish collectors. The son of portraitist John B. Yeats, Jack's early work as an illustrator gave his pictures an instantaneous attraction. But his later paintings, especially from the 1940s onwards, with their dark tones and heavy impasto, are unquestionably challenging. While he never moved into abstraction, Yeats' approach

Child Alone (above) and Image of Samuel Beckett (opposite), by Louis Le Brocquy

to figurative art grew steadily looser and might have discouraged mass appeal. However, he remains the exception proving the otherwise established rule that Irish buyers are predominantly conservative in their tastes.

This was certainly shown in the post-War years when a new generation of Northern Irish artists began to emerge and, because they mostly eschewed landscape, had to struggle to win acceptance. A decade ago, this group was given the collective name of Irish figurists, to indicate that

the human form and condition were the primary concerns of their work. The three finest were George Campbell, Gerard Dillon and Daniel O'Neill, close friends who sometimes lived, worked and exhibited together. All of them had to take on other jobs in order to support their painting, which, inevitably, shares certain characteristics—not least a fondness for strong colour, simple, almost naive, forms and a keen interest in the depiction of the mundanities of life. No wonder, then, that they could not necessarily

presume on widespread appreciation of their efforts, although posthumously their art has become much prized. So, too, has that of another Northern Irish painter from the same period, John Luke, whose brightly-coloured, almost surreal paintings are today greatly admired. Meanwhile, abstraction was at last beginning to gain some attention thanks to the efforts of artists like Patrick Scott and Cecil King. Scott originally practised as an architect and the discipline he learnt is apparent in his work, where great beauty and

control are successfully combined. There is an easily traced line between his 'Bog' paintings of the early 1960s, in which tempera was allowed to soak directly into an unprimed surface, and the same artist's 'Gold' paintings of some twenty years later. A similar sense of steady evolution is also apparent in the art of Cecil King who, although his earliest pieces had a soft-edged romanticism, soon opted for the most minimal of abstract art in which the surface of the picture is unbroken save for one or two fine lines of contrasting colour. At the same time, figurative art, albeit of a more impressionistic kind than before, continued to enjoy popularity because it was championed by a group of painters who included Patrick Collins, Camille Souter and the English-born Barrie Cooke, all of whose work has remained in favour.

But the artist who has dominated art in Ireland for more than four decades is Louis Le Brocquy. His early work was based around the human form but might be described as post-Cubist in spirit. Later, the representational elements grew less overt and by the late 1960s Le Brocquy had started to paint the series of head portraits of famous Irish men such as Joyce and Beckett, for which he would receive international renown. During this same period, he also created a masterly series of illustrations for Thomas Kinsella's translation of the ancient Irish epic, *The Tain*. Le Brocquy's wife Anne Madden is equally well-known for work that tends to have a greater degree of abstraction than that of her husband.

It is a curious feature of 20th century Irish art that its finest practitioners have all tended to work in isolation from the more popular trends of the time; that is as true of Le Brocquy as it was of Jack

Levanto on the Italian Riviera, by Mary Swanzy

Yeats. But these artists also attract the greatest critical acclaim even during their lifetimes, as did the Northern Irish painter William Scott whose still lives have an irresistible authority deriving from the artist's close study of American abstract painters such as Mark Rothko. Scott's most beautiful studies are of pots and bowls set against backgrounds of luminous colour. This use of rich tones is also a defining characteristic of Tony O'Malley, particularly in the work he produced from the later 1980s onwards. These dazzling outbursts are unusual in Ireland, where the nature of the country's light naturally inclines artists towards more sombre shades. Inevitably, because Ireland has always been a country marked by emigration, a number of artists working in the second half of the 20th century were based elsewhere. Undoubtedly the most famous of all was Francis Bacon, who was born and raised in the greater Dublin area before moving at the age of 16 to various other cities, eventually settling in London. By the late 1940s, his 'Screaming Popes' series had brought him the fame he retained until his death in 1992. Much of Bacon's work is bleak in character and overwhelming in impact, reflecting the man's pessimistic outlook and forceful temperament. It was not until recent years that his Irish origins were fully acknowledged, but in 2000 the artist's London studio—complete with all its contents—was installed in Dublin's Hugh Lane Municipal Gallery of Modern Art. Another artist with Irish roots who only late in life gave these attention was the Australian Sir Sidney Nolan who also died in 1992 at the age of 75. His early work

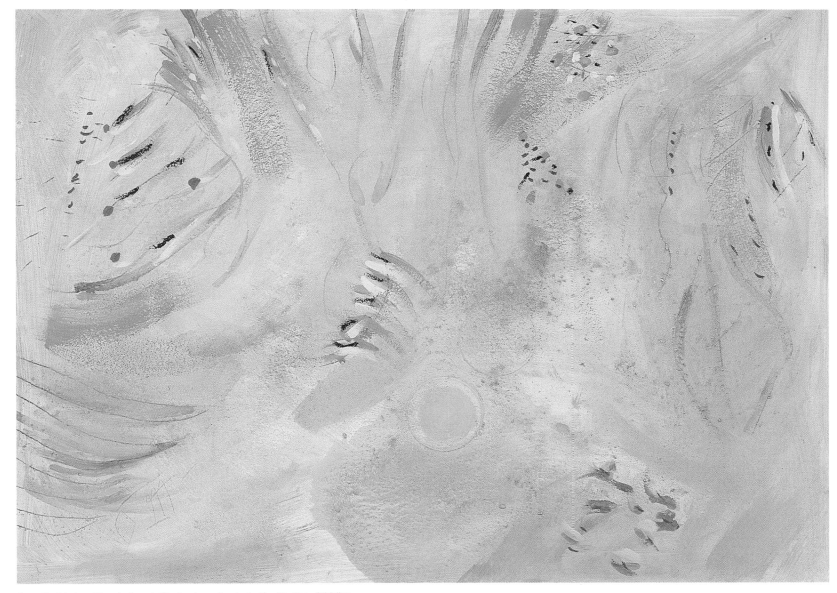

Opposite, Interior of Francis Bacon's Studio; above, Sun in the Pond by Tony O'Malley

in Australia was based around landscapes and by the mid-1950s he was being shown at the Venice Biennale. At his best, he is an energetic figurative painter, which became clear when a retrospective was devoted to this artist in Dublin in 1973. As a result of the attention paid to him in this country, he announced his intention to donate fifty-five paintings to Ireland but in the end only six were given during his lifetime. Sean Scully is the third painter who might have been expected to suffer neglect in his country of origin. However, this highly successful New York-based painter now shows regularly with a commercial Dublin gallery and was given a retrospective exhibition in the Irish Museum of Modern Art in 1996. Based around the interplay of different coloured stripes, Scully's frequently large paintings have the same mesmeric allure. As the 20th century closed, Irish art had become as dense and diverse, not to mention self-assured, as that of any other country. Traditional genres like landscape continue to have their admirers and advocates (Sean McSweeney, for example) as does figurative art of which the finest practitioners now include Hughie O'Donoghue, producing substantial canvases from his Kilkenny studio, and the prolific Michael Mulcahy. Abstract expressionism has its admirers, too, not least Milan-based Richard Gorman and Charles Tyrell. Many of the most imaginative artists working today and moving with ease between a diverse range of materials are women—Dorothy Cross, Kathy Prendergast, and Alice Maher. Today, there are only two constants in Irish art—that the old consistencies have gone and that these have been replaced by the sense of confidence that Hugh Lane aspired to encourage almost one hundred years ago.

Kick Up Your Heels

By John Kelly

E arlier this year, an Irish boy band called Westlife hit the Number One spot in the British charts. That used to be a big deal, but in Dublin, we now receive such news with quiet dignity. We no longer get overly excited about this kind of thing. In fact, these days, we are quite dulled to somehow predictable Irish successes. It is, after all, Westlife's fifth Number One in a row—an extraordinary commercial achievement that actually out-Beatles the Beatles and makes U2 look like a bunch of losers. The fact that you cannot find anyone under the age of twelve who actually likes Westlife is possibly beside the point.

The phenomenal success of Westlife certainly says something about the state of pop music, but this is hardly the place for me to rant in confusion. It also begs many questions as to why our allegedly soulful, spiritual and mystical Ireland is suddenly so very skilled at this type of enterprise. Never forget that we also have Boyzone and B*Witched to crow about—two equally incredible success stories inextricably linked with Westlife. Between them they have extended the national territory to cover the bedroom walls of every child in Europe and beyond. Whether you find anything to celebrate in this phenomenon depends entirely on your age, or your financial stake.

And then we have the 'Celtic' thing. How did all that happen? How did we get so stunningly adept at marketing that particular version of ourselves—one that is all about pop, pap and prancing paddies? Who for instance, apart from the man himself, could ever have foretold the coming of Flatley? Who in their wildest fantasies could ever have dreamed up The Corrs slinking around the planet in their black shifts? In the old days, they would have worn white blouses and long black skirts and sung *The Castle of Dromore*. They would have won medals at the Feis. Now, in full-throttle Ireland, they get to rule the world. These are indeed heady days.

To find the beginnings of this sort of thing, you have to go back a long way. You must travel backwards beyond The Corrs, beyond U2, beyond the Clancys, beyond John McCormick and park your time-machine in New York at the start of the last century. The old cylinder was being replaced by the flat disc and music was changing. Many new possibilities were emerging and, as markets were eagerly sought, music was frantically recorded to appeal to them. A specifically Irish market was spotted quite early on, and soon an assortment of New York labels like Emerald, Gaelic, and (of course) Celtic were devoting themselves to Irish music and what passed for it. This was that crucial moment when the music industry, that spoilt offspring of technology and marketing, first started leering at things Irish. And we leered back.

Inevitably the bigger companies moved in. They had spotted the success of those specialist labels and they set about turning what had previously been a mysterious niche into a much bigger deal. Columbia and Victor got involved and they, too, set about seriously targeting specific immigrant communities, including the Irish. It didn't take much market research to recognise that it was a community that had the music and the interest to sustain a concerted rush of Irish material and, as fast as the music came out, people snapped it up.

The Corrs

The Chieftains

Christy Moore

Sometimes they even sent it back to Ireland. And there it was—the beginnings of the 'Celtic' thing. It was the Americans who started it.

As the Irish abroad continued to reinvent the Ireland they had left behind, a certain type of romantic vaudeville Ireland was marketed with great success. The music was rare stuff indeed. At first listen, it can sound like the worst kind of paddywhackery, but even at its most kitsch, there is often extraordinary musicianship.

In among all that toora-loora, there is much to marvel at, and if it doesn't always sound quite right, there's a good reason for it. Many of these first recordings aimed at the Irish music market

were not made by Irish musicians at all. But that's another story altogether.

One of the most successful outfits of the period was The Flanagan Brothers. Mike, Joe and Louis were originally from Waterford, but they had found a new life in Manhattan. Joe played accordion and Mike played banjo—a new departure in Irish music at the time. Louis played banjo, too, but he also played guitar and this was probably the very first time guitar was used in Irish music. The Flanagans came up with a noise that worked in a brand new context and an exuberant Irish American dance music began to shake the ballrooms of New York City. The cultural twist was

Sir éad O'Connor

Boyzone

that their record company, Columbia was in partnership with EMI in Britain. This meant that their records, made under license in England, were suddenly for sale back in Ireland. It was the classic case of bringing it all back home. The music twisted to meet the market and we had Ireland's first pop stars.

And so, somewhere between The Flanagan Brothers and Westlife we have the various chapters in the story of Irish music. But of course there's much more to it than that. Without slipping into that misty world of 'Celtic' marketing it is worth saying that in Ireland, music has long been of particular significance. Indeed, in Ireland

it has been the musicians who have been the actual vessels of the culture itself. It has been largely through music that language, history and myth have survived to this day. It has been entirely through music that we know exactly how Irish people have been feeling for many centuries. As a valued, respected and absolutely vital part of us, it was no accident that Queen Elizabeth I of England once decreed that all the harpers be hanged. It reveals much that in order to subjugate the place, she aimed first at blind men who played the harp.

But the harpers and the music survived, albeit in a ragged state, until the end of the 18th century. In 1790s revolutionary Belfast,

the harpers gathered for one last time. They arrived old, lame, broken and blind from all parts of the country and they brought the music with them. The old Gaelic civilization that they represented was certainly at an end, but the music turned out to be a very hardy part of it. And once Bunting had written down the harpers' music at that Belfast gathering, we were guaranteed it forever. Nowadays The Chieftains play it all over the world. They get Grammys for it, too.

Traditional music also survived in other ways. It was literally the music of the people and in every region of the country, a particular brand of the genre survived as a living thing in the kitchens of rural areas. In the 1960s and 1970s this music re-emerged as a commercial entity as Irish traditional sounds from places like Clare and Donegal began to travel through the recordings of Seán O'Riada, The Chieftains, Planxty, The Bothy Band, Clannad, and others. Today Altan, Sharon Shannon, Martin Hayes and many more keep standards at a breathtaking level, while influencing the even younger musicians who continue to make extraordinary music with endless virtuosity.

Traditional music has also found its way into other places. Horslips came up with a fusion they called Celtic rock. Moving Hearts' attempt at mixed genres took the music into jazzier and funkier territory. Donal Lunny came up with a more global sound as he explored the rhythms

The Cranberries

inherent in the music itself. The Afro-Celt Sound System dig deep into beats and dance grooves. Michael O'Sulleabhain's approach takes much from classical, jazz and chamber music. Enya's distinctive sound owes much to her traditional roots. All of it promotes a very vigorous debate indeed. That, too, is a sign of life and strength.

Of course those legions of pipers and *sean nos* singers have nothing whatsoever to do with Westlife or Boyzone. Attempts are sometimes made to lump everything Irish into one mushy heap, but that's to miss several points. There's nothing distinctly Irish about the music of the boy bands, the rock bands and those odd eccentric gems like The Divine Comedy. Theirs is a music that takes its many influences from without. And yet, while U2 also took their cues from elsewhere, there was nevertheless something intangibly Irish about what they did. Before that, Thin Lizzy also had a uniquely Irish thing

lyrically and musically. Rory Gallagher, a top-notch bluesman, had more than a touch of Irish in his playing style, and Van Morrison is Belfast beyond all telling.

Morrison is by far the most influential Irish act ever. As unique a mixture as Presley in Tupelo, Morrison was a young white kid who had a way with black music. Into the pot, he threw jazz, blues, folk, country, and rhythm and blues and came up with something unique. To attempt to describe him is to invite trouble. I tend to call him a great Irish blues singer and leave words like poet and genius for others to argue about. His collaboration with The Chieftains represented a rare moment in the story of Irish music. Here several musical traditions collided, as they often do, but this time it was with truly exciting results.

But it is U2 who really rule the roost. In the dull and cynical 1980s their album *The Joshua Tree* went platinum in two days, went to Number

Van Morrison

285

The legendary Phil Lynott

one in twenty-two countries and became the first Irish Number One album in the US. In retrospect it all seems very unlikely given what the 1980s were like—a period where such gauche idealism was generally dismissed as naff. They were well out of step and their rash, ecstatic music was not at all in keeping with the mood of the day. But U2 (and Bono in particular) pulled it off. Yes, the Clancy Brothers had done it before, but it was never like this. They were on the cover of *Time* magazine. They became, and remain, the biggest band in the world. And they still live in Dublin, our most mischievous, intelligent and glamorous garage band.

We have taken to congratulating ourselves rather a lot of late. But even on quiet reflection,

we really do have every right to be proud of ourselves when it comes to music. We have an extraordinary tradition of our own that is still yielding yet more amazing music. We have the biggest rock band on the planet. We have Van. We have the spirits of Rory and Phil. And whether you like it or not we have Westlife, The Corrs, and Boyzone. In fact, we have so many musicians that you cannot walk down Grafton Street in Dublin without tripping over one—real or imagined.

Picture the scene. Sinéad O'Connor, Christy Moore, The Boomtown Rats, The Cranberries, The Dubliners, Brian Kennedy, Paul Brady, Therapy? The Undertones, The Virgin Prunes, Ash, and all those mentioned earlier. And then there are those who are eligible to play for

Donal Lunny

Ireland—Dusty Springfield, Morrissey, Elvis Costello, Shane MacGowan, Lonnie Donegan, and many more. It is an impressive roster certainly— good, bad and glorious. And just one more reason for us to bang our bodhran.

Enya

Living Rooms

BY FRANCES POWER

The Waterfall House by Paul Leech

Rejoice. Irish architecture is experiencing, if not a golden moment, at the very least a bronze period. Architect Sam Stephenson, author of the infamous Civic Offices on Dublin's Wood Quay, the Central Bank and Bord na Mona buildings, may bemoan its confused state but, for the first time in many decades, there's a refreshing confidence obvious in modern design.

In terms of residential projects, it first became apparent in the early 1990s in an ambitious urban renewal programme at Temple Bar, in which many of the country's most innovative architects were involved. Since then, the housing boom coupled with the Celtic Tiger has sparked both an increased demand for housing and the funds to attempt something more ambitious architecturally. At the time of writing, Spencer Dock, a 51-acre site in Dublin's Docklands, with proposed conference centre, office and residential development, overseen by Irish emigré architect Kevin Roche, aims to be the most ambitious articulation of urban Ireland yet. Whether it weathers the planning process undiluted has yet to be seen but its scale and confidence would have been unimaginable just a decade ago.

One byproduct is that the paralysing reverence for the glory days of the Georgian period has been shrugged off, so that new residential design can be unashamedly modern without softening touches such as inappropriate period trimmings. Pastiche, or worse, some Frankenstein stitching together of our architectural past, seems to be at an end.

Just take a closer look at Temple Bar. Until the 1990s, a rundown city centre warren of 17th century warehouses, banks, derelict sites and second-hand clothes shops leased by CIE, it was developed by Temple Bar Properties, a semi-state body in 1991 and, designed by a consortium of eight architectural practices known as Group 91, gradually took shape—a shape that for Ireland was radically different. Architectural firms McCullough Mulvin, Derek Tynan, O'Donnell and Tuomey, and Paul Keogh among others all contributed to this showpiece, which incorporated cultural venues—a film centre and archive, gallery spaces and artists' studios—as well as pubs, hotels, restaurants and apartments. In the process they explored the challenge of designing public spaces, even whole streets, for an historic area, sometimes reusing existing buildings, sometimes restoring them, as well as planning several new buildings.

Whatever the criticisms—and the large number of pubs and restaurants acting as a magnet for down-market tourism is just one—it is well to remember that the area could have become a bus station. As a place for young architects to cut their teeth and the more experienced to flex their aesthetic muscle, it has been an unqualified success.

Temple Bar was also crucial in showing the possibilities beyond the three-bedroom semi-detached house, until then the standard form of housing on offer. On completion, each residential development drew huge numbers of potential buyers and a public newly curious about design—and the new lifestyle that some of that design implied.

Most recently, for example, de Blacam and Meagher's Wooden Building in the west end of Temple Bar, a nine-storey tower of apartment buildings clad in iroko and stainless steel showcased multipurpose living spaces, pivoting central doors that doubled as open plan or room dividers, communal roof gardens, shared courtyard areas—all concepts that challenge Irish notions of just how a home should be, re-educating a population more used to associating tower block with economic deprivation and marginalisation than sharp design, while showing that the lessons of other cities have been absorbed—ie, building up may be the best solution to housing in the inner city.

While Temple Bar may have inspired the rash of over-priced and under-designed apartments that have since appeared—in the process fuelling the housing boom as many took advantage of tax breaks to buy property as investments rather than as owner-occupiers—it also gave architects and developers the green light to be more imaginative about design even if modified somewhat to Irish tastes.

In London or New York, for example, warehouses or factories are converted by those willing to live in less desirable addresses in return for acres of cut-price space; in Ireland, with a few pioneering exceptions such as the warehouse entrepreneur Harry Crosbie converted in Dublin's docklands or the old clothing factory sculptor Dorothy Cross turned into her studio-cum-living space, most of what has been marketed as lofts or warehouses is purpose-built by developers and too small in square footage to deserve the name.

But in 1999 The Warehouse, designed by architect Mary Donohue on the perimeters of the oldest part of the city, The Liberties, hit the market. Once home to fashion manufacturers, the development now houses 41 apartments, still bearing the stamp of their origins in original aluminium frame warehouse windows and parquet floors and open-plan interiors, but with luxurious touches such as decks and roof gardens. And most importantly space—the largest boasted over 2,000 square feet, plus balconies and terraces of up to 560 square feet.

For such generosity the developers received the ultimate compliment—buyers in the first phase were all owner-occupiers rather than

The Wooden Building in Temple Bar (above) and The Warehouse in The Liberties (below) epitomise modern urban style

A traditional Irish cottage is flooded with light from French windows

Office and eco-house pavillion by Paul Leech

Stackallen House, a fine example of an early Classical house

investors. But with square footage in the Irish market commanding such a premium, such developments are likely to remain the exception.

At the other end of the market, the mews house has been the focus for many radical design rethinks—perhaps because it is so compact and hence so cost-effective. And with house prices having quadrupled since 1993, fresh approaches to the crisis have been desperately needed. In Rathmines, an area of Dublin where houses routinely go for up to £1 million, young architects Dermot Boyd and Paul Kelly of The Studio came up with a clever solution to the problem of maximising space at minimal cost. On the site of an old flooring manufacturer's shed (purchased for £66,000) they built three self-contained housing units within one oblong box. From the exterior, the block gives little away. But behind the iroko-clad ground floor and the glass-walled second storey, are concealed three identical constructions of refreshingly innovative design. The clean form has the benefit of helping with cost, as construction is very economic (£100,000 a household, in fact).

Each one-bedroom house is roughly 1,000 square feet, about the same as a three-bedroom house, but the architects preferred to keep rooms large rather than squeeze in an extra bedroom or bathroom. What has potential as another bedroom or simply an overflow space on the ground floor is designated for planning purposes as a garage, but that still leaves room for a good-sized bedroom and bathroom at ground level with the entire first floor devoted to an all-purpose living space. Throughout, games are played with light and space, pivoting floor-to-ceiling mirror doors downstairs allow walls to slide away to infinity while on the first floor light is maximized with a roof-window angled to pour light into the house, flooding the living space and stairs. At the rear

of the house, plain and opaque floor-to-ceiling windows alternate to give a mammoth glass screen while at the front this pattern is reversed. The opaque glass gives light a diffused quality, and allows the shadows of an overhanging tree to play across it. All this glass also creates a sense of continuity of space inside and out—the wall-windows at the back seem to invite the communal garden indoors. One of the most striking aspects of the project is the extent to which the various occupants make an impact on the interior of the identical units, showing that contrary to the Irish experience budget housing need not be characterless or uniform.

Similar design elements are found in Louis Lane in Dublin, where architects McCullough Mulvin won an RIAI award for their mews. In a departure from the norm, downstairs contains main and guest bedrooms, bathroom, a music room/study and car port. But upstairs steals the prize—the entire first floor is an open-plan living space so clean and pure it's like being in a light box. Nothing interferes with the impression of simplicity, not even pictures on the wall, while the staircase opening into the middle of the floor introduces no cumbersome banisters or rails. Materials used enhance the effect—a white maple floor blends into white walls and wall-sized windows at each end are of alternating opaque and clear glass, while again light spills in from above via roof windows.

Elsewhere in Dublin, Derek Tynan has created a mews house displaying his architectural signature—simple, clean white lines and right-angled

spaces interlocking. Yet another mews house in Dublin, by Paul Keogh Architects, plays with the notion of an internal courtyard in a novel way.

Forming a central atrium, the courtyard acts as a light well into a three-room deep house, echoed by a second light well on the opposite side of the house where horizontal plaster beams beneath the roof window set up an interesting rhythm of light and shadow.

In the central area, flexible living spaces contain sitting, kitchen and dining spaces marked out by the use of different flooring materials. A kitchen island cleverly shields utilities from view, while other facilities such as washer-dryer and wine storage are tucked into a pantry behind. Double front doors frame a view straight through the house and living space to a Japanese garden at the back, neatly incorporating internal and

The near derelict Lyons Demesne has been restored to its Georgian splendour (left, above and below)

external spaces. Compact and clever, it is thoroughly modernist in approach.

Ironically, this new bravery in design has been accompanied by a growing respect for what is best about our built heritage. Conserving our architectural past was until recently a new concept, but not any more. In a country that has a less than perfect record—think Fitzwilliam Street, and the loss of one of the finest and longest complete Georgian streets in Europe; think Wood Quay, and the fact that government offices were built on a key Viking site; think then of Banker's Georgian on College Street, where all but the facade was demolished to make way for a hotel. However, the tide seems to have turned thanks to the work of a handful of committed individuals and bodies such as the Irish Georgian Society, An Taisce and the Dublin Civic Trust as well as an improved government attitude towards tax breaks for restoration work, allied to welcome legislation on listed buildings that punishes breaches with heavy fines and prison sentences.

Glorious examples of recent restorations spring to mind such as Castletown in County Kildare, probably Ireland's most important house, both architecturally and for its historical links. Credited with introducing the Palladian style to Irish architecture, it spawned many imitations. The man who commissioned it, Sir William Connolly, Speaker of the Irish House of Commons and from 1716 Lord Justice, was determined to

Clean lines and open spaces at Louis Lane (top and above)

foster national pride and envisaged his house as an assertion of all that was best about Ireland. To this end he employed one of the finest architects on the Continent, Florentine Alessandro Galilei, who also designed the Lateran Basilica in Rome, to build what amounted to a national monument. History is confused about the credits on

Castletown, but it seems probable that the central block flanked by colonnades was the work of the Florentine, while much of the interior and the pavilions was designed and carried out by Sir Edward Lovett Pearce, with stuccowork by the Swiss Italian Francini brothers.

By coincidence, a second and very beautiful Castletown is also being restored. Castletown Cox in Kilkenny, built by Michael Cox, Archbishop of Cashel, to the designs of the Italian Davis Duckart (Daviso de Arcourt) in 1767 is under careful restoration by financier George Magan. Again, it has a central block crisp in dressed sandstone and unpolished Kilkenny marble flanked by arcades ending in domed pavilions with pretty cupolas. Inside, stunning rococo plasterwork by the Irish stuccodore Patrick Osborne is being painstakingly restored in the traditional manner, even the lime render being made with goats' hair.

At Charleville in Wicklow, the Rohans have restored both the Regency interior and grounds of this Palladian villa, built in the 1790s to replace an earlier house destroyed by fire. The architect Whitmore Davis appears to have been influenced by Lucan House in Dublin, where the frontage also has Ionic columns standing on the lower storey. Charleville is, however, slightly grander with a columned entrance hall leading to a fabulous staircase hall.

The Naughtons are well known for their patronage of the arts and at Stackallen House in Meath,

Flexible living space at Paul Keogh's mews house

Castletown House in County Kildare is credited with introducing the Palladian style to Irish architecture

an early Classical House, they maintain this reputation with their sensitive restoration work under architect David Sheehan, himself currently restoring a Georgian house in Kilkenny. Here Chanel's prizewinning garden at Chelsea Flower Show, Bosquet de Chanel, was bought and installed complete with other work by garden designer Jim Reynolds.

Finally, Lyons Demesne, a fine Georgian mansion designed by Dublin architect Oliver Grace in 1785 and added to over the next thirty years or so, has recently been restored from near derelict by Tony Ryan's team of 100 craftsmen, and is now open to the public for part of the year. Perhaps one day, some patron of the arts will provide funds to restore Henrietta Street, one of the finest early Georgian streets in Dublin, which is slowly sliding into decay.

Some conservation has been on a less grand scale. One such project is in County Wicklow, designed by architect Arthur Duff of design partnership Duff Tisdall. A perfect example of the vernacular style—single-storey, one room deep, it has been adapted to 21st century expectations with, besides the big pluses of sanitation and heat, bigger windows and more spacious interiors. Rooflights and French windows remove the curse of the Irish cottage—smoke-filled dark and damp rooms. Ceilings have been knocked through to the rafters to add height and space but overall proportions are maintained, while decoration respects the original interiors with soft milky whitewashes and unwaxed pinkish plasters.

The traditional thatched cottage received a conservation boost with grants for maintenance and upgraded listings. A prime example of environmentally appropriate architecture, the thatch varied according to the material available nearby—heather in the west, straw in Wexford, or in County Clare, where the limestone pavings of the Burren are the most abundant material, a roof was likely to be of flagstones. Such harmony with the landscape and the use of environment-friendly materials may once have been the product of necessity, but today many of those involved in eco-housing use the same traditional methods—thatching, flagstones, stonemasonry, lime plaster-work—to serve a different philosophy. Until

recently such projects were usually one-offs by dedicated individuals such as Marcus McCabe of The Centre for Alternative Energy in Monaghan, who runs courses in all aspects of green housing from laying reed beds to sewage to straw bale and stone building, or Mike Keegan in Clare who runs self-build courses in timber houses where the structure—like a big Meccano kit—is simply lifted into place. But since the Green Building (designed by Murray O'Laoire) in Temple Bar broke European records for innovation and, with EU directives coming into effect on carbon taxa-

tion and higher insulation, energy-saving housing looks set to become an increasingly important part of new housing developments. As eco-tects such as Paul Leech of Gaia Associates explore hi-tech approaches such as photovoltaic technology, sunspaces, healthy materials, water-power, it is more than likely these will be absorbed into mainstream design.

Hopeful signs are already beginning to appear. A recently built housing estate incorporated various green concepts—cement blocks padded with aeroboard giving vastly increased insulation

A perfect example of the vernacular style at Arthur Duff's cottage in County Wicklow

Traditional charm by Arthur Duff.

and noise protection; an integrated heating and ventilation system; solar panels fitted into the roof that reduced boiler size to half the normal; filtered air quality that lowers dust levels; a ducting system that runs throughout the house visible only as a central ceiling disc, dispensing with the need for radiators; insulation built into the fabric of the roof that allows attic space to be converted to an extra room. While such houses cost more, long-term energy savings offset this within only a few years, while carbon emissions drop by 85 per cent. Elsewhere, such initiatives seem set to go into large-scale production. Under the EU Thermie Programme, one developer has incorporated timber frames, energy-conserving devices (including solar panels) and flexible layout homes. Timber houses are becoming increasing popular because of their low cost, ease of construction and low environmental impact.

Even in that most traditional of markets then, the housing development, design is on the move—and so is demand, driving up prices and creating a different profile of buyer. In 1999, fifteen detached houses in a traditional-style housing estate sold in four hours, sending shockwaves not just through the housing industry but through Irish society. The reason? Each had an asking price of roughly one million pounds. The buyers were products of the Celtic Tiger—some only in their twenties, mostly in consultancy, the IT industry, finance or medicine, probably with regular

Stylish touches at Louis Lane

incomes of £100,000-plus. It was not just the cost of the houses that was so shocking but the fact that someone with one million pounds to spend would choose to buy not a stately pile in Kildare or Wicklow, but in what was, no matter how well-appointed, a housing estate. Since then, other high-flying developments have come on line. Sadly, their design, like that of less expensive estates, has changed little over the last thirty years, with three-bedroom two-storey semi-detached or detached houses standard. Value is added through trimmings and luxury touches.

Yet in many other countries, the needs of a changing way of living and working are being met through floorplans that the buyers determine themselves. In Ireland, however, until very recently, few developers employed architects; instead, existing plans were re-used to keep costs and time of construction down. But the increase in demand for such developments and the fact that more money is available is already leading to more innovative responses. In Kildare a ten-house development by architect Roisin Murphy shows a fresh approach to design cliches. Comparatively cheap to build, it inspires hope that other developers might be jogged into seeing the possibilities

of breaking the mould. Each single-storey house has five bedrooms, all ensuite, a dining room, living room, den, and hallway (and the hall is as wide as the kitchen to encourage lingering and reading, sitting and chatting); all rooms are grouped around a central glass-roofed courtyard that acts as a lightwell with French windows and doors opening on to kitchen, bedrooms, hallway and even bathrooms. All rooms are double-height with pitched roofs adding both a vernacular touch and unusually generous dimensions. A mezzanine office/bedroom/study runs from the front to the back of the house forming the only upstairs room. Extra light and room comes from a double-height verandah, enclosed on three sides by the den and sitting room. Externally, the houses are thoroughly modern—local black brick, concrete and a wood-cladded frontage, surrounded by an balcony that runs around three sides—but the high-pitched roof and materials draw in vernacular elements.

When radically new design appears in a Kildare housing estate, surely some sort of seismic shift in architectural awareness has occurred. For the punter, such projects demonstrate increased awareness of the built environment, pushing questions about appropriate design, energy-saving building, infrastructure, public amenities and conservation into the public arena. That can only be good. Is Irish architecture in a confused state? Diverse, vibrant, full of talent, not afraid to experiment—but confused? I don't think so.